THE RITUAL MAGIC WO

A carefully conceived twelve month training pr
wishing to take up ceremonial magic.

With best Wishes
from

Dolores Ashcroft Nowicki

THE RITUAL MAGIC WORKBOOK

A Practical Course of Self~Initiation

DOLORES ASHCROFT-NOWICKI

Foreword by J.H. Brennan

THE AQUARIAN PRESS
Wellingborough, Northamptonshire

First published 1986

© DOLORES ASHCROFT-NOWICKI 1986

British Library Cataloguing in Publication Data

Ashcroft-Nowicki, Dolores
   The ritual magic workbook
   1. Magic   2. Ritual
   I. Title
   133.4'3   BF1623.R6

   ISBN 0-85030-467-9

The Aquarian Press is part of the
Thorsons Publishing Group

Printed and bound in Great Britain

Dedication

To Olive Ashcroft — with much love and gratitude for many years of loving friendship and loyalty.

Acknowledgements

More than most, writers need the back-up of other people. They provide encouragement, endless cups of coffee, and a willing ear when you hit the inevitable dry period and nothing you put down on paper looks or reads the way you see it in your head. Without the following friends and relations my life would be a lot harder.

My husband Michael and Sonia Hackwell who took much of the office work off my hands and gave me time to write. Emily Peach and Alan Richardson who listened with untiring ears to my ideas, even the wildest of them, and kept my spirits up when I thought it would never get done. Anne, Laurel, Cathy, Raffi, Jamie, Gordon and Sheila in Sydney who tried out the material, and survived!

Gary Farmer who came up with some beautiful incense recipes and allowed me to use some of them. Mike Herivel, Nick and Chris who keep my Apple II going and always have a smile even when I call them out and the darned thing starts to work the moment they walk into the office!

Last, but never least, to Simon Franklin whose friendship and encouragement spurs me on to try a little harder each time. Thank you.

Contents

Foreword

You are holding in your hands the best practical introduction to the art of magic ever published. Not 'one of the best' or 'arguably the best' or 'possibly the best', but simply the best. It is lucid, down to earth, well structured, accurate and easy to understand. It is a superb tool for the individual who wants to understand what magic is all about not in theory, but in practice.

Dolores Ashcroft-Nowicki, who wrote the book, is an experienced ritual magician and head of a world-wide esoteric fraternity/sorority. In the very earliest lessons she will force you to discuss your motivations for magical study; and she warns, as others have warned before her, that you should not undertake the work laid out in this book if you are depressed; nor should you mix magical training with drugs like mescaline, or lsd, or even pot.

You will want to know why. And here I think I may be able to help you.

When I was even younger than I am today, I drove a horse and cart through those three warnings. I was attracted to magical study without much insight into my real motivations. I began work in a depressed state. And on one curious social occasion during training,

I smoked cannabis. Since there is always considerable entertainment in someone else's misfortune, let me describe what happened. Then let me tell you something you will probably not be able to find elsewhere: the *reason why* it happened.

First, the question of motivation. We all do things for the best possible motives, of course; and nowhere more so than in the esoteric arts. It is relatively easy to discover that the only really acceptable excuse for magical study is embodied in the statement *I desire to know in order to serve.* That was the answer I was prompted to give to the ritual question during my own initiation. I dutifully gave it; and it was a lie.

What actually attracted me to magic was not service but power. Nothing grandiose, of course. I had no burning ambition to rule the world or enslave hordes of beautiful women. (Well, maybe just one or two beautiful women ...) But I was undoubtedly a prey to a disease which is becoming even more prevalent with the increasing complexity of modern society: a feeling of helplessness.

There are many reactions to such a

feeling. Some people embrace political credos. Others get religion. A few (usually male) take to beating their spouses. I turned to magic, which seemed to me to be the ultimate antidote: for what is magic if not a secret system which promises control of damn near everything?

You will be desolate to learn it did not work. Although I spent some nine years in daily Qabalistic training and learned a great deal in the process, I remained Clark Kent: no amount of magical leaps into ritual phone boxes could turn me into Superman.

Because I did not recognize my motivations at the outset (for while my pledge of service was a lie, I did not know that either at the time) I was driven to ignore the warning on depression. I began formal training while at a low ebb, emotionally and mentally. It was the sort of mood swing I had been through before and I thought little of it. Such moods inevitably passed over, usually quite quickly. This one did not. A few months into my initial magical training I had my first full nervous breakdown, which was mercifully brief. A year and a half later, I had my second, which was not. I was soon under psychiatric care, wondering whether to mention magic to my shrink, or whether news of what I had been up to would persuade him to refer me to the funny farm.

In the end, I played down my esoteric involvement and we decided between us that my problem was Oedipal. I now know it was nothing of the sort, but more of that presently.

The problem with arrogance is that it is a quality for which I have a sneaking admiration. Consequently it plays a greater part in my character than it really should. A few years into my training, when the worst of the psychiatric symptoms had died down, I decided I knew enough to make up my own mind about matters like psychedelic substances.

In those prehistoric days, they were, thank God, a great deal more difficult to come by than they are now and since I had no source for mescaline or lsd, I was forced to settle for cannabis. I expected a relaxed and pleasant experience. What I got was a nightmare. I was dragged from my body and hurled in and out of reality in a horrid slow pulse rhythm which, subjectively, went on forever. My spacial perceptions were so distorted I was unable to move unaided. I did not know where I was and my thought patterns were brutally disrupted. Objectively, the experience lasted more than seven hours. *All on a single joint!*

I have no doubt any reader with experience of such things will consider the above description grossly exaggerated or outright fiction. Or, more charitably, that I was smoking something other than cannabis. Pot simply does not affect people this way, as even the most fervent anti-drug campaigner will reluctantly confirm. But that's the way it affected me — and continues to affect me even now. God knows what I would be like on harder drugs: I have never tried them. Nor have I tried pot since. I even stopped taking alcohol.

Experience is a great teacher, but it only teaches you the What, not the Why. Why should esoteric training increase depression to such an extent that it will push you over the edge into neurotic breakdown; Why should it change one's reaction to drugs to such a ludicrous degree? (I am no advocate of drug usage, but I do recognize that the vast majority of pot smokers do not go through what I did.)

The answer to both these questions

lies in the structure of the human body — specifically, the part of the structure which falls under the heading of Esoteric Anatomy.

Interlocked with your purely physical systems, which are superbly well charted by Western medicine, is a further highly complicated system of energy flows which are not terribly well understood in the West, but which have been studied and categorized in the Orient for millenia — especially in India and China. In the former, the study was integrated into Yoga. In the latter, it produced the medical techniques of acupuncture and moxibustion.

I find the details of this energy system quite fascinating and could bore you with them for several hundred pages given the slightest encouragement. But realistically, all you need to know at this point is that:

1. The energy system exists.
2. It is intimately linked with (among other things) the endocrine system.
3. It is capable of manipulation.

Most systems of esoteric training will sooner or later introduce you to breath control, visualization and meditation. All three profoundly affect the energy system.

I want to be clear about this: many occult visualization exercises and most occult breathing exercises are *specifically designed* to influence the energy system. But even those which are not, tend to influence it anyway.

The most common result is simple stimulation. More energy is drawn into the system and consequently more energy flows through it. This is generally quite good news, but not always. I've already mentioned that the energy system is intimately linked with various physical systems. This is the reason why an acupuncture needle in your little finger can influence the function of your heart: the needle is controlling a portion of the energy flow which, in turn, is linked to your internal organs. It is the linkage with the endocrine system which can cause trouble if you are depressed.

Your endocrine system is an interdependent series of tiny factories continually releasing all sorts of chemical messengers into your bloodstream. These messengers tell your heart when to beat, aid your digestion, control your blood pressure and, as any doctor will confirm, profoundly influence your mental and emotional state at any given time.

Endocrine imbalance can lead to depression, a fact well known to the medical profession which habitually uses chemical messengers of its own as treatment. But what is all too often forgotten is that the reverse is also true. A state of depression with purely psychological origins can nonetheless lead to endocrine imbalance.

All this is getting rather technical and I apologise for that. What it really means is that if your glands are upset, you will get depressed; and if you are depressed, your glands will get upset. Whichever of these two very similar states you happen to be in, any blanket stimulation of your glandular system is bad news. It will inevitably make the depression worse; and in some cases it will make it very much worse. In my own case, I ended up with an endocrine system so screwed up that I tilted over into nervous breakdown.

The action of psychedelic drugs (even mild psychedelics like cannabis) on the energy system produces results even more directly. If you study the theory of Hindu Yoga, you will find a strong tradition that at a certain stage on the road to ultimate Enlightenment, the Yogi often develops 'powers' —

interesting psychical abilities like telepathy or trancelike changes of consciousness. Here again the energy system is involved, for as it strengthens with Yoga practice and as the energy flows come to conform more and more with the yogic ideal, so the practitioner's *mind* undergoes a change. For the energy system is linked in *two* directions — to the physical, as we have already seen, and directly to the psychological.

Once you begin occult training, you begin, almost immediately, to change your own energy system. If you then add to the change by ingesting psychedelics, it is remarkably easy to create a temporary situation analogous to blowing a fuse. It's all a little like those medical warnings about not mixing alcohol with certain medications. Either one on its own is okay, but the two together interact in a way that can be downright lethal.

The further you progress with your esoteric training, the greater this problem becomes. Highly trained adepts in the arts tend, you will find, to treat all drugs with considerable caution, including medical staples like aspirin and socially accepted drugs like nicotine and alcohol. It isn't necessarily that they dislike their source; it's just that they can't really handle it any more.

And having gotten all that off my chest, I now feel happier about placing Dolores' book in your anxious hands. Just follow the safety instructions and you'll be fine.

— J.H. Brennan

Introduction

The best and safest way to learn the art of Ritual Magic is to enter a school of good repute and work under the tuition of someone who is a practising magician. From the point of view of the schools involved applicants usually fall into one of three categories:

1. Those who have become addicted to the excruciatingly bad 'occult' videos increasingly offered as the 'real thing', and who think they can become an Adept overnight. They become glamoured by the idea of casting circles, waving magical swords and dashing into disused churches to confound the Forces of Darkness, crucifix in hand, and armed with a few vital sentences from a long lost ritual found by accident in the archives of the British Museum.

2. Those who have hovered about on the edge of the occult for sometime and have decided it is time to 'dip a toe into the water'.

3. Those who are drawn to the Mysteries almost against their will and who find their way by trial and error to the right door.

Seventy per cent of the first group will get tired of the whole thing as soon as they realize that it can take as long as ten years to get halfway to being an Adept, and requires a long, hard and disciplined training. If by any strange chance fate throws a real psychic event their way, it merely hastens their departure. Another ten per cent will leave having acquired some idea of occult terminology and training and on the basis of this will attempt to set up their own Magical Order.

Because the training has not been fully realized on all levels, the Order runs on momentum alone. It has little or no actual contact with the Inner Levels and they will achieve very little. The members will become involved with the outward trappings of ritual, believing that to be the important thing. But any inner contact they may have had to begin with, is lost while they try to decide how many bows should be made to the East, how many circles each officer must make before taking his or her seat, and getting upset when they are not allotted the office they coveted. The entire thing becomes an excuse to dress up, feel important and, above all enter a 'secret' organization. The need to feel that they have something no one else knows about is paramount, but it is a false secrecy. Most Orders have an Outer Court that is more or less public, but their inner levels are held apart. The secrecy that is the hallmark of a false Order is a need to almost, but not quite, let others know what they are missing. If no one has even an inkling of what they are about, much of the 'fun' goes out of the whole affair for them.

A further five per cent, when the first fine careless rapture has worn off, will see opportunities for making money. Then you get the rip offs, the 'you too can become a magician in three months', just 200.00 down and another 50.00 a month. After that a higher grade is offered with a more resounding title, for another 200.00. Unfortunately being part of the occult world does not automatically make you a better person.

That leaves the last fifteen per cent, of these ten per cent *may* see it through against all odds, they will suddenly realize the falsity of their previous assumptions and retrace their steps, this time with a sincere desire to succeed. They will bring to their work understanding and compassion and will invariably become teachers in their turn. The last five per cent will turn to the darker side of the occult, and there *is* a darker side. Drugs, alcohol and perversion will drag them under. Sometimes they can be rescued, there are Lodges whose task it is to look for such people and attempt to redeem them, they are a special breed of occultist with a courage and faith that can and does take them into the corridors of Hell in search of the lost ones.

In the second group the percentage of genuine students will be much higher. Through their reading and research they will already have a good idea of what to expect and the great majority of them will win through the first crucial year. Some will inevitably return to the safer, more comfortable pastime of being an 'armchair occultist'.

The third group will win through against all odds. They are the born magicians who, in past lives have already served their apprenticeship and are now returning to take the higher grades. With each life they aspire higher and higher until the final choice is made, either to go on into other realms and dimensions learning all the time, or to turn back and help those who are still journeying. Such become 'The Masters'.

This book is for the determined ones of the first and second groups, to help them understand what can and cannot be done in ritual magic when working without a personal tutor, or within the protective egregore of a contacted school. As I have said, the best way is to be taught by a personal teacher. Failing that a book written with the pitfalls in mind, one that tries to explain what is needed within oneself to become a magician, and moreover that provides basic bread and butter knowledge with enough ritual jam to make it palatable, is the next best thing. This book will *not* make you an initiate, it will not even make you an expert magician. It *will* keep you from making costly mistakes, and give you a basis upon which you may build further, in time.

Within these pages you will find a complete year's work taking you from the first preparations of yourself as a magician, to real ritual work. Along the way you will learn a little, a very little, from many and varied studies, things that you would undertake in depth if working in ideal conditions. You will learn to work with your hands as well as your mind, with your heart as well as your intuition. If you take each section and work through it carefully there is no reason why, at the end of the year you should not be able to construct, perform and control the effects of simple rituals, control being the most important part!

If you are looking for instant magic, forget it! Work, hard work, is the only thing that will help you to achieve your goal. If you want it badly enough you will do the work. It is as simple as that. You get what you work for.

The training that follows is meant primarily for the solo magician, but I have given adaptations in the rituals for up to five people, that being the ideal number for many reasons, some of which I will explain later. *Do not use the book to try and train a whole group.* Training a large group needs a lot of know-how, a lot more than you can learn in a year. If that fails to sway you remember this, according to an ancient tradition a teacher takes on a part of any Karma incurred by those he or she teaches, and an ill controlled group can incur a *lot* of Karma. Being a teacher in the occult sense has its drawbacks. If two or three of you wish to work together as a group in the future, then each one should work individually through the year of preparation as set down in this book. Then you will start off with a great advantage, three people who *know* what they are doing and what to expect from ritual work.

If you work as a pair or as a threesome, it *must* be a mixed group. A pair *must* be a male and female, in the case of three, one man and two women, or one woman and two men. In this way the vital polarities are kept balanced, this is of great importance in ritual work and in the training that preceeds it.

If you are in poor physical health, do not attempt to start this training until you are well again. If you are suffering from depression, do not start at all, occult work can increase certain types of depressive illness. If you are taking what are referred to as social drugs, i.e. cannabis, lsd, etc., this book is not for you. You need your full wits about you when working magic, and when, as it will, inner level power starts to work through the psyche, you will need to have your full health and strength to cope with it.

There will be a great temptation to start on the rituals right away, and to leave the preparatory work untouched, even unread; that is up to you. You will be the one who will lose by doing so. Some of you will realize this and will proceed as instructed, some will go ahead and make their mistakes and then turn back and start again. Some will ignore any advice I may give, though that will not deter me from giving it anyway. Those who make it through to the end of the year have the makings of a magician in them. They will have touched the indefinable and tasted the excitement of being in control (well almost) of their inner universe; after that life can never be the same.

Learn from the beginning to keep your own counsel, persecution has more subtle guises than the rack and the stake these days. If your tastes run to walking the streets in a flowing cloak and a broad brimmed hat, and wearing a ring the size of a hen's egg, you will find yourself in some predictably bizarre situations. Learn and meditate upon the magician's maxim.

To Dare, To Will, To Know, To Keep Silent.

Couple this with the two attributes that

all true magicians strive to bring to perfection in themselves, Discretion and Discrimination. To imprint these six important rules on your conscious and subconscious minds, your first instruction, before you even turn the next page (is *your* determination strong enough?) get a pen and paper and draw an equal-sided triangle with the apex pointing up. Now superimpose on it another triangle pointing down. You should now have a six pointed star. Write your name in the centre, and in each of the 'points' write one of the six injunctions above. Cut the paper into a suitable shape and use it as a book mark for the next year, replacing it when it wears out. (See figure 1)

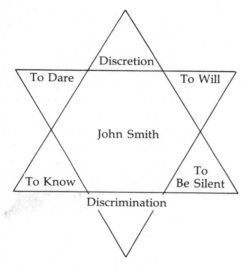

Figure 1

For the next six months, providing you have the determination, and the stamina, you should regard yourself as a novice, one who is applying for entry into a Mystery School on the Inner Planes. If you get past the first six months without giving up (or cheating on the lessons), then you may regard yourself as a neophyte, one who has been accepted for serious training. It is

important that you build this idea into your mind at the conscious and subconscious levels every day until it is accepted as a fact. As there is nothing like throwing you in at the deep end, you can start right now. Read the following instructions two or three times, then put the book aside and create these images in your mind's eye, rather like a day-dream, with as much attention to detail as you can. Don't if you are taking this book seriously, read any further until you have completed the next set of instructions. If you are a verbalizer rather than an imagemaker, keep reading the instructions until they are acceptable to you as fact.

Create an image of yourself, at any age you feel appropriate, dressed in a simple white tunic of thin wool, reaching to the knee for a man, to the ankle for a woman. At the waist is a twisted cord, also white, and you wear simple leather sandals. For the moment you will be known by your own name for you have not yet earned a Magical Name. Get the figure of yourself clear in your mind's eye before going further.

You are one of a group of applicants standing before the steps of an ancient Mystery School. You are waiting to find out if you have been accepted into the Temple as a novice. The building of white stone gleams in the sun and a flight of steps leads up to the impressive entrance. On the top step waits the High Priest of the Temple and beside him the High Priestess. Both wear long cloaks that sweep the ground, blue and gold for the High Priest, black and silver for the High Priestess. As they step forward all talking among the candidates ceases and you crowd forward. The High Priest steps forward with a papyrus scroll in his hand. He begins to read out the names of those who have been accepted as novices. Your name is the last on the list, you have been given a chance to prove your worth, try to use it well.

With the others who have been selected you walk up the steps and with the High Priest and Priestess going before you, the little group enters the cool dim interior of the great temple.

You are in a large circular hall roofed with a dome upheld by many pillars of marble, alternately black and white. The floor is also of white marble but set into it is a labyrinthine pattern laid out in black mosaic. At the very centre of this intricate maze stands the altar, a double cube of black marble, and on it a chalice of blue crystal that gleams in a single shaft of sunlight that lances down from an opening in the dome above.

All those who wish to study the Mysteries must come of their own free will to the Inner Temple. Without this offer of self, freely given and as freely accepted, no further step may be taken. Now is the time to think about this book and what it offers, is it what you really want? Can you offer your best efforts for a whole year knowing that sometimes you will fail as well as succeed? Or do you wish to retrace your steps and offer your place to one of the others still waiting outside? Think about your reasons for being here, are they genuine or are they the result of self glamour fed by the fantasies of an uncontrolled mind? Before you make your offer of service be sure that you understand that this acceptance is for the first six months of your year's training. If you win through you will return here to renew your offer of service for another six months. After that you are free of any obligations except those you seek out for yourself in the future.

First one and then another steps forward and accepts from the High Priestess a black and white twisted cord. This replaces the plain white one at present about your waist, this new cord marks you as a novice. As you wait your turn, two of the candidates refuse and return to the outside world, and two others are accepted in their place. When your turn comes you step forward and accept the cord knowing that for the next six months you have committed yourself to the basic training of a would-be magician.

Now you may return to your own space and time, opening your eyes and looking around you, feeling the chair beneath you and the floor under your feet. Get into the habit of doing this, you must always make quite certain that you are well and truly 'awake' on your own level of being when you return from any inner journey.

You have just experienced your first try at magic. It may have seemed to be no more than a simple day-dream, but understand this right from the beginning. There are three basic ingredients in magic, Desire, Form and Manifestation, you must want something with a real *need/desire* in order to end up with it on this level. That need is first expressed nine times out of ten as an idea in your imagination, to make it clearer, you have to define your imaginings with clarity and precision, only then can your desire manifest on the physical level. All this means that if you cannot imagine clearly and with emotion, you are going to find it hard going to make it as a magician. 'Fantasy is the Ass that carried the Ark', is a saying you will often come across in occult literature. Believe it.

If you were to apply for entry into a modern Mystery School you would almost certainly be expected to answer some form of questionnaire. This book, since it is taking the place of such an entry, is no exception. Put the book down and get yourself a pen and paper, think very carefully about the answers you give to the following questions, make sure they are truthful. The obvious answer is not always the right one. Write down each question on your paper, then underneath, after careful thought, write your answer. Then we will go through the questions again and see how your answers hold up.

Questionnaire

1. Why do you want to work magic?

2. What do you understand by the word *magic*?

3. Always supposing you get through this mini course on the occult arts, have you a goal in mind for the future?

4. There are many Paths in the practice of magic, do you know which would be best for you?

5. Do you think of yourself as a potential magician or as a mystic?

6. What do you think is needed to be a good magician?

7. Do you know what is meant by the Path of the Hearth Fire?

8. Do you know what you are taking on in treading the Path of High Magic?

9. Do you intend to follow this course to the letter, or do you intend to read the exciting bits and leave out the rest?

Every one of these questions can be answered in a dozen different ways, every answer will give away information to the person reading it. Read over your answers and see if there is anything you wish to change, then, put this book away until tomorrow. I know you are anxious to continue, but remember your training started from the moment you opened the book. How can you expect to become a disciplined magician if you cannot exert your will over your own desires? Put the book down and tonight just before you go to sleep think once more about the questions, and about your answers to them. Tomorrow we will go over them again and discuss the implications behind them.

*   *   *

Now you have slept on the questions, we will take a look at each one in turn, remember these are comparatively easy to those you might be asked on entering a Mystery School proper.

1. Why do you want to work magic?

It may be that you have been interested in occult literature for a long time, and feel you would like to know more on a practical level. You will have acquired some basic occult knowledge from your reading and you will at least be familiar with the terminology, if not the actual theory. If you read a lot of fantasy fiction your inner vision will be fairly well developed and that is good, as most magic is concerned with the use of the imagination and the power of the inner eye. You may have had some psychic experiences and feel you need to understand more in order to cope with them. A school would want to know what kind of experience you had and at what age. Strangely not all psychics make good magicians. Once within a school you would be 'closed down' for at least six months while your training took place. This annoys some people who think they are halfway there by reason of their psychism, not so. Basic training for an 'open' psychic can be difficult if not dangerous. So be advised, if you have bought the book because you think it might be fun to do some magic, you are not likely to make it to the end of the first chapter. Actual training in the magical arts can be dull, boring and repetitive with very little in the way of excitement, and very different to what you might see on the screen. If you have been reading seriously for quite a time and feel that you need to extend your knowledge, then this book was written for you.

What do you understand by the word *magic*?

Remember, no magic works like the Blue Fairy's wand in Pinocchio. All magic works along well defined lines of natural force. It is in fact a natural science that as yet we can only handle imperfectly. The ancient world seemed to have a better grasp of it than modern man, but we are able to inquire more deeply into it, and hopefully one day we will have a set of Laws as definable in their predictability as those of physics, and as the laws of physics are pushed back further and further each year, we have a lot of catching up to do.

There are three kinds of magic, High, Low, and Spiritual Alchemy. Don't take too much notice of the words High and Low, they are just terms, not an indication of quality. Low Magic is working with natural but little under-stood forces of Nature, almost anyone can do it, and many do it without knowing anything about magic. Children do it all the time. It is *not* Black Magic. There is no such thing as Black Magic, only the person through whom the power is working makes magic either good or evil. Magical power of itself is neutral. Stop thinking of the word 'black' as compatible with satanic. Good things are also black, rich fertile earth, the night sky, deep space, the inside of a womb carrying a child. The earth hides her loveliest riches in blackness, gold, silver and precious gems are all to be found in darkness.

It is intention that makes anything good or evil, the intention of a human mind. High Magic includes the use of ritual in various forms in order to experience an influx of power that has been coloured or charged by the invoking of a specific archetype, power or God-form. Its object may be to inspire in oneself something connected with that archetype, say courage, inspiration, or love. It may be used to provide a service such as healing to another person, or a thanksgiving to a being of the Higher Levels, there are many reasons for ritual as you will learn in the coming year.

Spiritual Alchemy is the rarified atmosphere of the true Adept. The apex of Cosmic Vision where all that has been learnt, practised, experienced and endured comes together. It is a great and wonderful thing, but only a few in each generation reach such heights, though all may aspire to them. Adepts, with few exceptions, notably those who are specifically trained by the Higher Levels to bring new teachings through, seek neither to be known or sought for. They seek the final transmutation of the self into something unknowable. There is about them a calmness that sets them apart from others. At times another being looks at you from their eyes, then, as swiftly it is gone. All other magic dims beside such power, power all the more potent because it is held lightly and seen for what it is, a transient thing.

Magic works because Nature cannot abide a vacuum, and an intense need for something lacking in your life causes something similar to a vacuum in your personal space. So, it gets filled with what you are asking for via the ritual. The trick is in needing something badly enough. The people who will *never* work magic are those who cannot decide which one of a hundred things they want most, and end up with nothing. Just cause a hole to appear in your personal space, and something will fill it. Simple! Well... it does take time to learn the trick.

Always supposing you get through this mini course on the occult arts, have you a goal in mind for the future?

Do you intend to save the world; look for a school in which to train further; form a group and elect yourself Magus for life; or go over your year's work, take stock and then decide?

Forget about saving the world, you must first save yourself before you can save others. Altruism can be a fine thing but in this kind of work one must aim to clear, polish and train the self on all levels before even thinking about helping others. Without such training you put yourself in the position of trying to rescue a drowning man when you cannot swim yourself. You may have heard the phrase, 'I desire to know in order to serve'. This was and still is used in some forms of initiation ceremony. However before using it one must have a clear understanding of what you will be required to know and to whom the service will be given. The greatest of all questions was that asked in the Castle of the Grail, 'Whom does the Grail Serve?' But as an answer to your question it does at least show willingness.

If you have visions of yourself fighting the Forces of Darkness with sword and wand, think again. Few, very few, of all those who pass through the Pillars of the Temple are fitted to undertake such work. Think instead of learning about yourself, how you think, understand, study, and above all how you *feel*. Aim to make the very best of *yourself* and in that way you will one day be able to see the best in others, and, where it is imprisoned, to free it.

Form a group of like-minded friends by all means, *but for discussion only*, do not take on a job for which you are as yet untrained and untried. Use what you have learned to find the right school or teacher, if you have the talent you will inevitably end up teaching others. If you really want to start a magical group make sure the others go through this book as well, then you will all start on the same footing and it has some chance of stabilizing and not creating havoc in your environment. Remember, magic is not something you can deal with on a hit or miss basis, you are working with powerful latent forces within yourself, look what happened to Dr Jekyll!

There are many Paths in the practice of magic, do you know which would be best for you?

There are many traditions to choose from, Qabalah, Egyptian, Greek, Celtic, Shamanism, and the various traditions of the Craft, sometimes referred to as Wicca, including Gardnerian Craft, Traditional and Family Craft as well as the old and new Pagan religions. Many people choose the Egyptian because it is perhaps the most recognizable, but it is not the easiest. Choosing a Tradition in which to work needs a lot of thought and research, at this early stage all you need to know is that there are choices, but leave them until later.

Part of your year's work will include a text on some of the best known Mystery Religions, with some practical work to help you understand the principles behind them. By now you should be getting an idea of the kind of work that lies ahead of you, and not only the *kind* of work but the *amount* of work.

You will be hearing a good deal about the Western Mystery Tradition (WMT), and it may need some clarification. It is the opinion of many modern occult teachers, myself among them, that if you are of western

descent the best tradition for you (and the WMT includes most of the Mediterranean Mystery Religions) is that belonging to your own hemisphere. This is *not* to decry the eastern philosophies, but they were fashioned for eastern minds and hearts. It does not mean that one is above the other, merely that they work along different lines and see things differently.

Do you think of yourself as a potential magician or as a mystic?

A leading British occultist once said 'All magicians become mystics in the end'. Whilst I balk at the use of the word 'all', I would agree that a large percentage eventually arrive at a point where magic and mysticism blend. The best example can be seen in Ursula Le Guin's trilogy, *The Wizard of Earthsea*. The hero's transition from Mage to Mystic is very finely drawn. Magicians, although they can and do work solo, are most often found within a working group, a mystic, however is almost always found working alone. This fact must play a part in your final choice when the moment of decision is reached, however leave it for now, you cannot possibly make a true decision as yet.

What do you think is needed to be a good magician?

Use the following list as an indication. First and foremost you must have a belief in something even if it is just yourself. You will also need patience, tolerance, understanding, curiosity, and a good memory is vital as you will soon have a head bursting with so many pieces of readily available information it makes the *Encyclopaedia Britannica* look like a paperback. You should have a keen interest in all things around you and good powers of observation. A fertile imagination is basic equipment for a magician. Health and a fair degree of physical strength, the Art of the Mage is not for seven stone weaklings. Good all round general knowledge, common sense, an interest in, and some ability with, handicrafts. A sense of humour is vital, if you can't laugh with your God(s) then leave magic to those who can. A good balance, you will be standing for hours at a time; an extra language is very useful, there are many important books in either French or German that have not been translated. A grasp of mathematics and logic can be important in some areas such as geomancy, astrology, etc. If you enjoy cooking you will do well in alchemy, strange but true. An ear for music is important, a tone deaf Magus can be at a disadvantage in certain areas of occult work. A love of Nature, poetry and art are especially useful when working with elementals. These are a few, there are many more. Read, and keep on reading, but don't take everything as gospel. Always hold in your mind the fact that nothing stays the same forever and change is one of the great patterns of the Universe. Be adaptable, use everything to hand but be prepared to try out new ideas and if they are better, change over. Tradition can be beautiful, but it must be allied to adaptation.

Do you know what is meant by the Path of the Hearth Fire?

This is the name given to ordinary every day life when it is lived as a sacred tradition. Unless you were destined to live alone, then at sometime or another you must conform to this Path and pay its dues. These dues are the work you do every day be it as a doctor, a housewife, a painter or a road sweeper. It should be done to the best of your ability with love and understanding and pride in your work. It can also mean marrying and sharing your life with someone, understanding their highs and lows, their hang-ups and their talents. It means tolerating their faults and acknowledging your own. It is the creation of children and the sharing of their wonder as they grow. Teaching them to see things as they are, but also showing them the other magical mysterious world of enchantment. It is making them aware of their future role as Wardens of the Earth in terms of ecology and the care and maintenance of other forms of life. It is the most important Magical Path you will ever tread, though few are able to see it as such.

If you are in your teens or early twenties read this book through, then, unless you are already on the Path of the Hearth Fire, put it aside until you have made some progress along this most precious of paths. If you ignore this advice remember, the Path will catch up with you, and at some point in your life you will have to put aside the magic and attend to the Hearth. One of the most promising young students the Servants of the Light (SOL) has ever had, started the course at sixteen with the written permission of his mother. His work was brilliant for his age, yet when the time came for university he had within him the courage to set the course aside for a few years, knowing that we would be there when he was ready to return, more mature and with a strong foundation behind him. He will be the better and stronger for showing such strength of purpose.

If you have already set foot on the Path, i.e. you are settled in a job, or you are married, or have a life partner, then make certain of two things:

1. That your partner is not so antagonistic towards your studies that it causes continuous dissension between you.
2. If you are lucky enough to have either an interested partner, or at least one willing to support you in your studies, then thank your God(s) for it and *never* allow the work to possess your time to their exclusion.

Do you know what you are taking on in treading the Path of High Magic?

If, at some future point you do become a fully trained magician, you will not have reached that point without at some time saying to yourself '...if I had known it would be like this I would never have taken it on'. Don't worry, every magician since Moses has said the same thing, and even meant it sometimes. But in some core of your personal being you know darned well you would do the same thing all over again. For the rest of your life no matter what grand title or honour may be bestowed upon you, you will always know yourself to be a beginner. As you reach the top of one level you will be at the bottom of the next. But you will always have something new to take on.

Even at this novice stage expect your life to take on the general aspect of roller coaster. Because you are changing the ideas and habits of a lifetime your own inertia will throw the book at you. Students have been known to change jobs, houses, countries, and partners in the throes of the first year of occult study. The Higher Levels do not believe in taking what is offered without testing it to the limit. The trouble is what *they* define as your limit and what you define as your limit tend to differ, widely. This is not a winter evening class course, it is a whole year of hard work, but the rewards will not only show themselves on the Inner Levels. You will find your everyday life taking a similar turn for the better. The meditations will lower your blood-pressure, alleviate stress and improve your general health. An improvement in the quality of your understanding of people and their problems will show in many ways. When your workmates and neighbours and even your in-laws start asking you for advice and telling you their troubles, then you can be fairly certain that your inner self has begun to shed its light around you.

The hardest lesson to learn is to ride the inevitable brickbats and not be tempted to hit back. This is something that the occult shares with the martial arts. Both make you stronger, in different ways, both train you to achieve inner calmness. A martial art teaches you to fight, then trains you not to do so. The occult art trains you to control your environment, then shows you that control is not needed, all things have their appointed time.

I urge every reader to consider their reasons for taking this course very deeply, especially those coming to the occult for the first time. If you wish to make this study simply one of interest and research, fine, so long as you fully understand that you cannot *work* magic without some kind of training. That training will take time, effort and discipline.

Do you intend to follow this course to the letter, or do you intend to read the exciting bits and leave the rest?

If the first, you are a rarity, good luck. If the second, no comment!

Having done my best to explain and

perhaps to discourage you it is now time to make a decision. Go back and do the pathworking to the Temple again. If you still accept the Temple cord, then I will do my best to help you and to set you on your way.

The First Month

Laying Strong Foundations

Date started ....

Date ended ....

The amount of time and effort put into each month is a matter for you to decide, but remember this, work is reflective, too little effort will show few results. Several hours of hard work once or twice a week and nothing in between will show the same patchiness in your studies. It is better to give small amounts of time spread over the day, each day, with perhaps an extra hour at weekends. This way the continuity of study will soon show results in steady progress.

Preparing Your Temple

When it comes to building a temple or lodge room, to make it effective, keep it simple. It is all too easy to become dazzled by an array of materials and over-elaborate decorations. Keep in mind that you are building a place in which to work, meditate, and contact the more subtle levels of your inner self. A temple does not need to look like a stage set for *Aida* to be fully effective.

This is not something to take up as a hobby, you are laying the foundation stone of the 'Temple Not Made With Hands' that we all carry within us, this is and will always be the *real* temple. As you build the physical temple it will become the reflection of the inner one. If the outer temple is slovenly and untidy, the inner temple will be in a like state. An important rule of all occult work is this: *All work proceeds from within, therefore all work undertaken on the physical level will reflect the state of your inner self at the time.* It is an ideal way in which to keep a check on one's progress.

There is something else you should know, when all the work is done and your temple is finished, you will no longer need it. You will use it and get a great deal of satisfaction and wisdom from its use, but as you progress you will use it less and less for it will internalize within you. This was always the intention. By that time you will have become aware of, and will be using the great Inner Temple available to all who can work at this level. But without the actual building of the physical temple you would never have found the key to its door.

Traditionally a temple is built with all new fittings and equipment. Nowadays this is not always possible, so when circumstances indicate a need for careful spending it is time for tradition to give way to common sense. As long as everything is thoroughly cleaned and freshly painted the all important *Intention* will make it acceptable. If you live in a semi-detached with thin walls, think about using a Floor Cloth (see p.31) instead of a temple. Ritual chanting and strange noises can upset the neighbours, and incense smoke billowing out of the windows could mean a visit from the local fire brigade.

A temple once built should stay that way if at all possible. But if needs must you can at a pinch dismantle it when necessary. However this will mean re-consecrating it each time. If you move house, the temple *must* be de-consecrated, taken down, and the room cleared psychically before you leave. Instructions for this will be given at the end of the book. The temple will also need to be re-consecrated if rebuilt in the new house. The clearing of a room that has been used as a temple or lodge room is very important. Bricks and mortar store power, it is this ability that builds up an 'atmosphere' in old houses and churches. If this power is not released you will leave the incoming tenants with a problem that can range from strange noises and smells to a 'haunted' room with an atmosphere that will render it completely unusable.

Always keep the door to your temple locked, only those who will be using it should be allowed to enter. It is not something to show off to your friends, or to be included in a conducted tour of the house. Watch the children, they can show enterprise at an early age and have been known to charge school friends an entrance fee to look around their parents temple, with embarrassing results for all concerned.

Your temple must be kept spotless at all times. Give it a thorough cleaning before each quarterly ritual, and *never* enter it in a state of anger or filled with resentment, no matter what the cause. Calm down first, then, with a clear idea of what you want to do, or what help is needed you will get a better result and at the same time keep your temple free of any taint.

If you have a choice, the room selected for your temple should be as quiet as possible and preferably with little possibility of being overlooked. Your first task is to empty the room completely and go over the floor with great care, taking out nails, replacing squeaky boards, and smoothing the wood. When this is done get down and scrub... *hard*. Everything must be cleaned thoroughly, walls, ceiling, and paintwork as well as the floor. Inspect the doors and windows and see that they are secure, rattle free and draught proof. Windows should have bolts and the door a good lock and an inside bolt. If the weather permits, work with the windows open to the fresh air for at least part of the time.

Now for the electrical points. You will need a heater in the winter and this must be placed well away from any area where you will be moving about. You might consider a small wall heater set high enough not to interfere with the work. If you intend to work mainly qabalistic magic you will also need a point in the eastern wall where a small light, to be set above the throne of the Magus, can be plugged in. In addition you will need a point for a tape recorder when using music or recording a ritual or both. It is very important that you start a small collection of suitable music for use in the temple. It can help a great deal in the creation of the right mood and atmosphere. In another chapter we will be discussing the basis of such a collection, with some suggestions for titles.

With the preliminary work done it is time to start thinking about paint or wallpaper. I personally prefer paint, it is quicker, easier and there is much more choice of colour. It can also be easily changed when the temple needs renovating. Choose a shade that will blend overall with your intended furnishings and robes. Some of the new tinted whites on the market are ideal. Unless it is a very sunny room go for the warmer shades rather than a cooler tint, then the surrounding paintwork can be done in a deeper matching shade. Aim for a light, warm effect that lifts the spirits when you enter. The ceiling presents you with a choice, you can just paint it white or you can paint it a midnight blue and apply silver stars made from kitchen foil and arrange them in a pattern to match one of the main constellations such as the Plough, Cassiopeia, or Orion, any good astronomy book will give you the basic outline, and the public library will have plenty of them. With the addition of a soft pearl bulb in a white spherical shade this will give the impression that the temple is open to a night sky filled with stars and a full moon. It will take time and effort, but the effect is just short of breathtaking.

Now it is time to think about curtains. Measure each wall (with the exception of the window side) and find the exact centre, then fix a three foot curtain rod at a height to match that of the window. This will enable you to hang a curtain in each quarter that can be changed according to the season. Good choices would be, green for spring, gold for summer, dark red for autumn and perhaps a dark blue for winter. Where the window is concerned, get a good quality net in enough quantity to make it difficult to

see into the room from across the road or garden when the curtains are open. The curtains themselves should be of fairly heavy material and lined. To save expense the quarter curtains can be made in a matching lightweight lining silk. As an alternative you could use panels representing the different traditions such as Egyptian, Greek and Celtic (see Figure 2). Alternatively, you

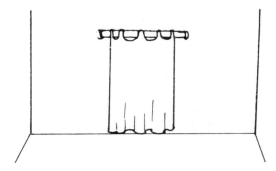

Figure 2

might prefer to use pictures. We will deal more directly with decorations next month. It might also be a useful idea at this time to fix a bracket to the southern wall at a convenient height, this is to hang the thurible (the incense burner) out of harm's way once it has been used to purify the temple.

If you have double glazing that is ideal, if not you might consider making a light wooden frame and filling it with a double layer of heavy duty polythene. Held against the window by wooden pegs this will go a long way to making the room sound proof from the outside, and draught proof as well.

Flooring is very important and unfortunately an area where you cannot afford to skimp on cost. You may be working barefoot during some rites so a plain wooden floor is out. Even if you use varnish or a polyurethane product it will be very cold and uninviting. Carpet if you can afford it is by far the best. Either a plain square that leaves the edges of the room uncovered or wall to wall. To be accurate it should be black and white squared but unless you have a Masonic furnishers near by it will be difficult to obtain, though you can sometimes get a bathroom carpet in coloured squares, alternatively you could try carpet or cork tiles, or a plain one colour carpet. If money is tight use industrial felt or just carpet underlay. Don't use throw rugs, they are slippery and can be extremely dangerous, especially if you are carrying a lighted candle or a sharp ceremonial sword.

Adequate heating is essential and your temple should feel warm and inviting, working in freezing temperatures is neither necessary nor conducive to a good ritual. A night storage heater can be useful, or an electric fire as long as it is fixed to the wall out of harm's way. Remember you will be wearing long robes, and in the summer they will be of light synthetic silk, a material that flares up very easily. *Never* use a gas heater of the portable type in a temple. The slightest brush against them and your robe will catch fire. Whatever kind of heating you use, minimize the risk with a guard. In any case one piece of non occult but essential equipment in any temple is a bucket of sand for just such emergencies. In the hands of the inexperienced a thurible full of burning charcoal and incense can be lethal. Consecrate it if you must but keep the bucket handy!

The temple is now ready for its first magical act, its ritual cleansing. You might like to do this after you have scrubbed the room and before painting, but most people like to do it when the basic work has been done

and the room seems to have some semblance to the temple it will soon become.

From now on, in fact as soon as the flooring is down, do not enter this room wearing your outdoor shoes. Have a pair of soft slippers just inside the door and use them when you are working and change again when you leave. If you have other people working with you get them to do the same, get into the habit now.

Now for the cleansing, first clear the room of all your working tools, paint, brushes, etc, and anything that may be lying around. Now bring in a bowl of water, preferably rainwater or water taken from a running stream and a small quantity of salt. Place them on the floor and kneel beside them. Fold the fingers of your right hand into the blessing position, the first two fingers extended and close together, the others with the thumb folded into the palm of your hand. Now point your fingers at the bowl of water. Fill your mind with the thought of water as man's greatest blessing for without it he cannot live. Take a breath and hold it for a second then intone this blessing prayer:

> *In the name of the one creator/creatrix* (You may change this for any God-name you prefer to use.) *I bless and consecrate this element of water to my use.*

Use your imagination to 'see and feel' a rush of light and heat flow from the top of your head and down your arm, through your fingers and into the water. Do the same with the salt using the same words but substituting the word *salt* for *water*. There are many ways of doing this and you will be taught some of them but for now, at the beginning of your training this is sufficient for your purpose. Tip the salt into the water and gently swirl it round so that it dissolves. Rise to your feet and with the bowl of blessed elements in your hand proceed to cleanse the emerging temple.

Starting in the eastern quarter dip your fingers into the salt water and flick it over the floor saying:

Cleansed and blessed be this quarter of the East where the light is born.
(Move to the South and sprinkle the water as before and repeat:)

Cleansed and blessed be this quarter of the South where honour courage and love are revealed.
(Move to the West and repeat the sprinkling a third time:)

Cleansed and blessed be this quarter of the West where the inner voice of the spirit is heard.
(Move to the North and for the fourth time cleanse with the water:)

Cleansed and blessed be this quarter of the North wherein dwells the spirit of the earth.
(Move to the centre where the altar will stand for most of the time and cast water there saying:)

Cleansed and blessed be this place where the four quarters meet and where the light of this holy place will be lit.
(Now sprinkle the windows and doors saying:)

Cleansed and blessed be these places of entering and departing that nothing of evil shall enter and all that is good shall come forth from this place of peace and harmony.

Now your temple has had its first cleansing, the real consecration will come later, but from this moment this room is a place set apart and blessed and you must treat it as such whenever you enter it. You will find that the atmosphere within the room has changed subtly, and there is a distinct air of the otherworld about it. This feeling will grow and intensify in the coming weeks.

You may not be able to set aside a room purely for use as a temple, and in this case your need is for a temple that can be put down for use, then rolled up and put away. For this you need a Temple Floor Cloth. You will need a large *new* sheet for the base. Bind the edges with a wide gold braid, but leave on one side a space about two feet wide to act as a door. This space will be in the *West*. Now you will need some coloured felt and embroidery silks or wools. Tackle the East first. With some black felt cut out the shape of a pillar about twelve inches (30cm) in length. Use any picture of an ancient pillar as a guide. Do the same in white felt, but outline it with a thin silver braid or silk to make it stand out from the sheet. Set the pillars about two feet (60cm) apart and sew them to the sheet as neatly as you can. If you want to add to the effect you can pad them slightly so that they stand away from the cloth. Now, do the same with the other quarters.

Now cut out a circle of blue felt about 12 inches (30cm) in diameter and sew this between the pillars of the East. Do one in red for the South, one in green for the West and one in gold for the North. Why these colours? Think about it, East is the station of air, so use sky blue, red for fire in the South, the green of the ocean for the West and gold for the cornfields in the North which is the station of the Earth Mother. For the centre of the Temple Floor Cloth make a circle quartered with the four colours (see Figure 3) or you could copy the beautiful Rose

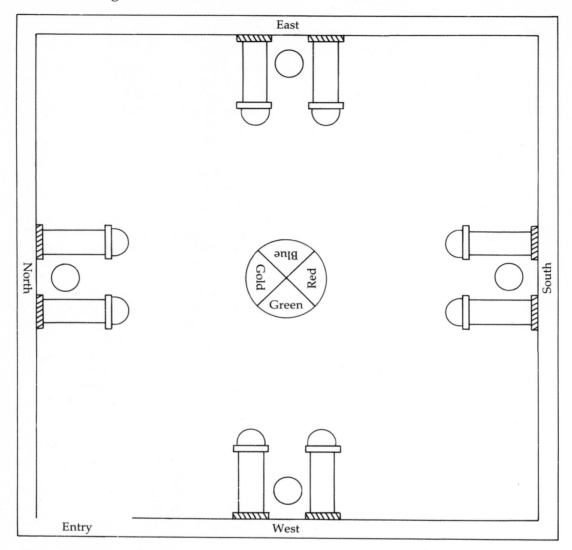

Figure 3 The Temple Floor Cloth

Cross as pictured in the *Golden Dawn*. That however needs real skill with your hands. You now have a basic temple floor plan that can be cleansed and consecrated by the same methods used for the temple room. In addition you will need a linen bag large enough to take the Floor Cloth when it is folded in which to keep it clean and safe. If you line this bag with any kind of silk, real or synthetic, it will also keep it insulated from any undesirable influences.

This Floor Cloth needs only to be unwrapped and spread out for your temple to be ready. However, before it can take on the aura of a temple it has to be used like one. Daily work and meditation must be carried out within its boundaries until it can fill the room with the atmosphere of a true Temple of the Mysteries. This comprises the first month's work on the actual temple, some of it may spill over into the following month, if so don't worry about it, there is no hard and fast rule that says you must do this much in a month, it is merely a guideline.

Now it is time to turn our attention to that other more subtle temple, *you*. You must also be 'built', cleansed and prepared for the work ahead.

Preparation of Self

Self purgation can be as painful as it sounds, nor does it help to tell you that unless it hurts you are not doing it the right way. However if you are serious about this year of work and dedication then some form of clearing out and cleaning up is going to be required.

First, an explanation of what is meant by the term 'self purgation'. When you started to build your temple the first thing you did was to empty it of everything, furniture, curtains, carpets, etc. You scraped off the old paint and scrubbed everything down until it sparkled. It did not seem an odd or unnecessary thing to do, it felt right that the room should be stripped of the old useless things that cluttered it, and that it should be made as fresh and clean as possible. If this is so, how much more important it is that the highest temple of all, *you*, should also be cleared of outworn and dated thoughts and troubles, and made as clean as possible.

All sacred enclosures such as churches, temples, chapels, etc., have a set approach to the sanctum of the Godhead. First there is the place where the ordinary meets the extraordinary, the porch, the entry gate, the peristyle or the physical body. It is the place of meeting, the Horizon of the Human Spirit. From there we pass into the first of the subtle realms, the nave, the

inner court, the hypostyle, the astral body. Then comes the place of separation, in a church it is the screen dividing the main part of the building from the increasingly sacred territory. In the ancient temples it is the narrow passage that leads on towards the place where the God and Goddess dwells, in us it becomes the higher mental body. Finally there is the small empty room, the High Altar, the Veil of the Mysteries, the Adytum, the spiritual spark of a human being.

All these parts of ourselves emanate from that inner divinity that gathers increasingly denser envelopes of matter as it descends earthwards. Once born into a physical body we gather a lot of unwanted things, useless false conceptions gathered during our formative years and after, in the same way that old furniture and unused rooms gather dust. In order to be able to use these parts of ourselves again as they were meant to be used, we must first clean them up and renovate where necessary.

So where do we begin? In the past. Each day as you work in the temple, as you go to work, on the train, waiting for a bus, in the traffic jam, the bath, under the hair dryer or anywhere you find a few mintues to spare, start tracking your life so far. It doesn't have to be precise or even terribly accurate, you may bring back just dim memories but it will be there. Get a pocket notebook, get several, and keep a pen handy at all times especially at your bedside for some things can surface in an early morning dream. Start with what happened to you yesterday and the day before, last week and the week before that, last month and the month before that, and so on. Keep going back and noting down the outstanding memories. Do this throughout the first month and get back as far as you possibly can.

The chances are the clearest images will not be the happiest, this is because we learn important lessons from our unhappy experiences and so we tend to remember them with greater clarity. You will be tempted not to look at them too clearly, but when you hit one of these times stop and look at it more closely. Try to work out what you learnt from that experience and if you have applied the lesson you learnt then. What brought about the incident? Who instigated it? Go through it in your mind with as much detachment as you can. Remember, it cannot hurt you anymore, so try to see it from a distance of time and space and make a new judgement. Note all your findings down.

When you come to the end of the month, read through your notebooks as if you were researching a character from history. Write down the way you see that character noting good and bad points, where they should have acted differently or where they acted well in a given circumstance. Then having weighed up the whole story take a long calm look at that person, who is also yourself. A human being with talents and faults and the ability to learn. What you are now is the sum total of all those joys and griefs. You are no longer tied to the past, so make a fire outside somewhere and burn the notebooks, when nothing remains scatter the ashes to the winds, that part of you has been distilled into what you are *now*, and you will refine it still further in this year of new beginnings. Bless that old 'you' and let it go, you have made it through your trial of self purgation.

You will be hearing a great deal of the word *dedication* in the next year, it means different things to different people. To some it is the dedication to an ideal, to others dedication to money, power or greed. For you the dedication is to yourself for this year, to go deeply into your inner self and to seek out the real person you have been hiding all these years. When you have more experience the word *dedication* will come to mean something much deeper to you. It may be that it will set your feet upon a path from which there will be no turning back, but until then your only dedication is to seek out your inner self.

Real magic is not just a matter of ritual, though ritual can help, nor is it concerned simply with casting spells etc., though again it can help with these things. Real magic is the realization of what you are and what you can become. It is being able to see your potential and knowing you can achieve it, in your everyday world as well as the inner world. Change your perception of yourself and you will start a chain reaction that will sweep through all the levels of your life. So give yourself this one year as a gift and dedicate it to finding the real you.

This will not be easy, the real you has been hidden away for years. It may not want to be brought out into the open. The 'outer' you that has been fronting all these years will most certainly oppose your efforts. It will not want to give up the limelight, it may well succeed in stopping you within a few weeks or even days. Its weapon is one of the most powerful in the world, *inertia*, sometimes called *apathy*. There is a cartoon character called Garfield. Garfield is a cat with very basic aims in life, to eat, sleep, and reign supreme. Anything or anyone that gets between Garfield and these aims gets mauled. The personality can be very much like that! Anything that stops it doing what it wants to do is in for a rough time.

An occult writer famous for his

common sense once wrote, 'it takes about eighty days of consecutive meditation for it to become a habit'. Think about that. My bet is that you are already saying to yourself, 'Well, maybe I could just *read* the book, I don't need to actually *do* it'. Well I'm afraid you will have to do it if you want to find the original self you left lying around somewhere way back. If you don't, you will always wonder if you *could* have done it, and you will never know will you?

Inertia is what makes you turn over in bed on Sunday morning when you promised yourself the night before that you would get up, mow the lawn, wash the car, prune the roses, and take the kids to the Safari Park. Inertia keeps that nearly finished sweater in your workbox when all it needs is one more sleeve. It keeps you looking at a TV programme that bores you stiff when you could turn it off and do something worthwhile. It is the main cause of drop-outs in evening classes every winter because it means getting out of your armchair and catching a bus. The power of inertia is frightening and extends to all walks of life and through all levels of social behaviour. It draws on an unlimited power, *you* and millions like you.

If you turned one tenth of that power towards doing something really constructive and forward thinking you would probably head the firm you currently work for in about five years, at the very least you would have risen considerably higher in the ranks. Yet even now the alarm bell will be ringing in your head. Your inertia beast is stirring restlessly and getting more worried by the minute. It would much rather you went back to reading the evening paper and sleeping through the late night film than think about the mountain of potential power hidden inside you. Digging back into your past and searching for the person you were meant to be is going to happen over your inertia beast's dead body. And *that* is exactly what is needed. That same inertia will dog your footsteps for the whole of this year, I cannot help you, you must help yourself by always being aware of its presence and its power. It will think up the most lucid and convincing of arguments to stop you from doing this work. Inertia keeps the world from going round!

However it *will* weaken as you show determination but the only answer is self-discipline and lots of it. You will hate it, but the rewards will be so great that if you are successful you will never look back, and that goes for both your magical and your non-magical work. Most attempts fail because people set their sights far too high for the first few weeks. Ideally your aims should stretch your ability to cope, but not so much so that inevitably you must fail. Sneak up on your inertia beast.

The first stop is to start a routine that you feel able to keep up with just a little more effort than usual. Break the time needed for your daily disciplines and exercises into small pieces, then with luck the beast will hardly notice… until it is too late. Do just two minutes of relaxing exercises and two more of breathing each morning and at odd times in the day for the next month. And if you think you cannot possibly do enough in four minutes I suggest you sit and look at the minute hand of your watch for four minutes. It is surprising how long it can be. You may as well learn right away that time seems to have a different exchange rate in occult work. Do three or four breathing exercises whenever you have a minute to spare throughout the day. They can be done silently and without anyone being the wiser even jammed together in a rush hour train, or waiting at the supermarket checkout.

That leaves only the meditation period and study time to be found each day. Now traditionally meditations are done in a quiet room sitting in a certain posture. But this book is kicking tradition out of the door in favour of shaping occult training around your everyday life, this is as it should be but rarely is. Your occult life and your everyday life should intermarry, your religion, whatever it is, your beliefs, and the practice of them should *never* become a one day a week affair. They are part of each other and will complement each other, providing you allow them to do so. If you can find the time to do a quiet meditation, fine, but if you are a busy housewife and mother, a student, a nurse or doctor, a harrassed executive of either sex, or working shifts, there are other ways to meditate and get good results.

Meditation can easily be done 'on the hoof', walking the dog is ideal or even a long solitary walk in the early evening. Choose your walk carefully and apply your common sense, you won't get much done if you walk your dog in a much used park. But for those who live within easy distance of a wood, beach or little used common ground this is an easy and pleasant way of meditation, simply fix the mind on your subject and put the rest of you on 'automatic'. Hand washing, ironing, polishing the silver, doing the hoovering, strap hanging on the bus, behind your copy of the *Times* on the 8:15 in the morning and/or on the 5:45 in the evening behind the sports page. Try it listening to your favourite classical music, (no, Mick Jagger is *not* conducive to meditation). You can still put the Sunday paper over your face after the roast, just meditate instead of sleeping. Doctors have found that stroking a cat on your knee is capable of alleviating stress, try it for meditation — I can recommend it. If you are a managing director tell your secretary to hold all calls for ten minutes and put your feet up on the desk, if you are the secretary convert your boss to meditation and do it together! Jogging is another good time, but not the bath, you are inclined to relax too much and slide under the water.

Carry your little notebook with you at all times and jot down the main points of your meditations and write them up later. Change and adaptation is an essential part of occult work and although there will be many 'orthodox' occultists who will object strongly, one of the things that must change is the idea that meditation can only be done effectively in silence, privacy and stillness. This is an ideal, when you can't have it, adapt to what you have.

With regard to how long a meditation should last, there is no set time. However it makes sense to ease into it gently, and just ten minutes a day for the first month is quite enough to spend in meditation. To force yourself into an hour or so right at the start will give your inertia beast real hope for the future. Of course there will be times when you actually feel like spending more time in meditation. Fine, that is the time you will get the most out of it, and as the temple grows you will want to spend more time in it, soon a rapport will grow between you, then once the room is painted you could put in a chair and try doing a meditation there on alternate days.

Meditation subjects for the month

Use each one for two or three days:

1. 'Magic is the Art of Causation'.

2. 'Magic... speaks to the subconscious mind of man through ...symbols and rituals.
3. 'Change is Growth'.
4. 'There is no part of me that is not of the Gods'.
5. 'The subconscious mind ... works through images not words'.
6. 'The Universe is a Living Organism'.
7. 'The Tree of Life'.
8. 'Symbols are a means of communication, a form of shorthand'.
9. 'Astral Magic is meditation materialized to visual imagery'.
10. All things are possible to a trained mind'.

Robes

It is time to think about making your first robe. Nothing elaborate, a simple one with no hood and a plain white cord. According to what time of year you start this course you can choose either wool, cotton or synthetic silk. Do not buy expensive material, you will only use it for a short time. You need only five pieces to make a robe and you will see the pattern in Figure 4. Brown or black is best, no fancy colours. No, black is *not* a symbol of evil, it is the colour of the rich earth where seeds grow to maturity, as you are doing now. Tradition says you should make your own robe, and by hand. You

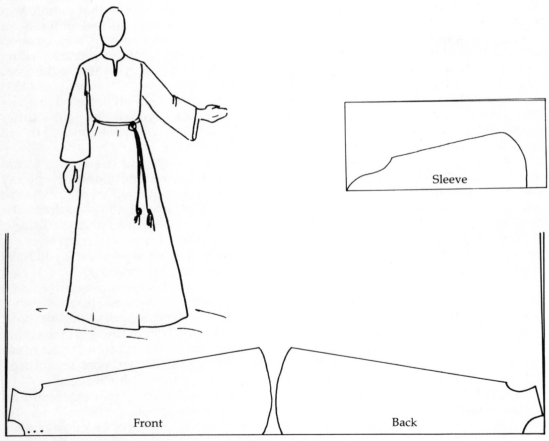

Sleeve

Front

Back

Fold of Material

Figure 4

should at least sew a bit of it, even if it is only the hem. But as there are some people to whom the threading of a needle is one of life's greatest mysteries, seeking help in such cases can be excused.

Reading and Recording

The next thing is to go to your local library and get a reading ticket, get several if you can. If not, persuade a friend or relative to get a ticket and let you use it, you will be doing a lot of reading from now on. If you have the good fortune to live in London then make an effort to obtain a reader's ticket to the British Library. You can find almost every book you could ever want there. You will need the signature of a leading member of your community and it will take a while but it is well worth it.

You must also get into the habit of making daily records. In a Mystery School you would be required to send these to your tutor every month, but even if you never join a school you should keep records of your work, thoughts, and the realizations that stem from your work. It is only because people kept such records that we have any knowledge of the Order of the Golden Dawn, and other ritual groups at all. So keep them each day and don't let anyone but yourself see or handle them. They will make interesting reading in later years, and perhaps provide an inspiration for others when you are no longer here.

These records should note your basic times of exercises, breathing and relaxation, your meditation subject, the duration of the meditation and your realizations on the subject. Keep your entries short and to the point. Allow yourself no more than fourteen lines per day. Get into the habit of extracting just the essential material from your meditation and recording it with accuracy and brevity. Try and make one line do the work of three. This will teach you conciseness of mind, and to arrange your thoughts in a logical pattern. To help you, you will find an example of an entry at the end of this chapter.

You may not know it but you are already building what is called a Magical Personality. This is the 'air' that comes upon a magician when in the temple, it speaks of control, power, and command. You have a long way to go, but you started the seed of your Magical Personality the moment you decided to take this book seriously. You will soon notice that when you enter the temple you feel different in yourself. When you start a meditation or an exercise, or when you are writing your daily report, you feel a different person to the rest of the time. Let this feeling grow slowly, for it is the gradual emergence of the inner magician. We will speak more of this in the next lesson.

Before we go into the exercises and set work for the first month let me say something about your promise and your acceptance of the cord from the High Priestess during the Temple Pathworking. I urge you most strongly not to make such a promise if you have no intention of keeping it. I repeat what I said at the beginning, there is no substitute for a personal teacher and/or a real Mystery School. But this book can take you part of the way, providing you honour the promise you have made to that higher part of yourself you saw as the High Priestess.

In the following pages you will find the exercises, reading studies, text, and illustrations, plus an example of a daily entry to help you begin your records of what I hope will be a year of achievement for both of us.

Relaxation Exercises

Your daily routine must always start with the relaxation exercises. You can do most of these in bed in the few minutes between waking up and getting up. Turn on to your side and curl up into a tight ball and tense your body tightly, hold it for no more than five seconds then let go and flop out straight. Start checking for areas that haven't flopped enough. Shoulders and the back of the neck are prime targets for tense muscles at any time of the day. Concentrate on them and try to loosen them even more. It will take time, after all you have been tensing them up for years. The tiny muscles between the eyes and just over the ears, (the ones that hold your glasses up) are next on your list. Most people who wear glasses brace the muscles just above and behind the ears against the arms. You must teach them to let go. Lastly check fingers, toes and jaws.

Now breathe in, right down into the belly while you count off four seconds, hold it for two seconds then let it out counting four again. Repeat this three times. Now get up and sit on the end of the bed with your feet flat on the floor. Drop your arms and head down between your legs and hang there for a few seconds, then straighten up slowly until you are sitting upright, then let yourself flop right back onto the bed and let go. Do one more breathing exercise, count four in, hold for two, out for four. Now you can get up and have breakfast.

Housewife or outside worker, or both, you will have a coffee break, and you may spend it talking with friends and co-workers; instead try using it to relax the neck and shoulder muscles again. If you do not go out to work make a set time in your day that will allow you a few quiet minutes to yourself. Find a comfortable chair and put it in front of the window and sit down. Breathe as you did this morning, four seconds in, hold for two seconds, then let it out still counting to four. Do this three or four times, and it will make your whole day more relaxed.

Throughout the day, wherever you are, try and relax those shoulder and neck muscles at least three or four times. It is an area very prone to tenseness and is the cause of most headaches. Most of it stems from the use of the wrong type of pillow. The usual shapes are not the best for our neck muscles, we need most support in the hollow where the head slopes into the neck. The old fashioned round bolster was ideal. The Japanese have been using cylindrical wooden neck rests as pillows for centuries. Think of the way people lean back with their hands linked behind the back of the neck, that is the kind of support your neck needs. A small flat pillow with a soft towel rolled into a cylinder and placed in the hollow between neck and head will show you the difference.

If you have the time during the day try this experiment while lying on your bed. In addition to the towel roll under your neck, place one under the small of your back and a third one under your knees. The body will then be fully supported at the three most needed areas, relax into the supports and feel the difference.

If you have an interview, a board meeting, or any event that may be causing you apprehension or stress during the day, just before you go in consciously relax the shoulders, neck, jaw, and those tiny but important muscles between the eyes and behind the ears. Take a few fourfold breaths, then go in there and wow them. Later on in the book we will talk about using magical visualization to aid such times.

Meditation

There are two basic kinds of meditation, all the other kinds spring from one of these. The first is *active*. This means that you take a symbol, a picture, a phrase, or statement and mull it over in your mind to the exclusion of all other thoughts. Look at its basic concept, the way it is phrased, how many ways it can be interpreted. What does it mean to you personally in terms of mental images, abstract meaning, or what knowledge do you already have with which it may be aligned. The aim is to extract everything you can from such a subject and then to record the essence of your thoughts.

The second kind of meditation is *passive*. Here images are allowed to rise in the mind as they will, formulating around a set mantra, symbol or idea. You will use the *active* form of meditation for most of your year of work, this is because you are building a foundation of control over your personality. Later you will be shown the passive way, but after you have established a basis on which to work.

You will find in the first few weeks that other thoughts will intrude as you meditate. Push them aside firmly and bring the mind back to its task. If you are meditating in what is known as the God-form position, that is sitting upright with the hands resting on the knees in the manner of an Egyptian Pharoah, you may find the body getting restless after a few minutes. Interference will range from 'jumpy' legs to an itching nose. Noises you have never bothered about before will annoy and distract you. This is normal

and to be expected, it is the body's way of saying it disapproves of such discipline. Persevere and it will slowly die away.

At the end of your meditation make a quick summary of your thoughts, gathering them together. Now sit up straight and stretch hard, then relax with your usual techniques, do two fourfold breaths and end the session. When doing a meditation whilst walking the dog or in the morning train etc., you may find your surroundings will distract you at first, but you will soon develop the ability to 'switch off'.

Write down your thoughts in note form and extend them later at your leisure. If something pertaining to your meditation comes to mind later in the day, include it in your record under a separate heading marked Further Realizations. Remember to keep the entry short and concise. Head the page with the date, time and place, and note how many times you were distracted from the subject, see Figure 5. Seeing the number decrease over the weeks will give you great satisfaction. If ten minutes is too long for you to meditate at first, cut it down to five minutes, or, cut the ten minutes into two sections of five minutes each. Keep to this for the first two weeks, then gradually increase the time until you are up to the full ten minutes by the end of the first month. Take it at a pace you can keep up with just a little more effort than usual.

For the first week concentrate on slipping into a routine of relaxing and breathing exercises first thing in the morning and at odd times during the day, plus five minutes minimum meditation on one of the set subjects. Try to do a little on the temple each day or evening even if only half an hour or so, that is your main task this month, along with the cutting and fitting of

Day

	Monday	Tuesday	Wednesday	Thursday	Friday	Saturday	Sunday
1							
2							
3							
4							
5							
6							
7							
8							
9							
10							
11							
12							
13							
14							
15							
16							
17							
18							
19							
20							
21							
22							
23							
24							
25							
26							
27							
28							
29							
30							
Total							

Distractions (vertical axis label)

Figure 5 Distraction graph

your robe. If the work on the temple spills over into the next month, do not worry, do what you can.

This month's required reading consists of two books, *Magic, Its Ritual, Power and Purpose* by W.E. Butler, and *An Introduction to the Mystical Qabalah*, by Alan Richardson. Both are published by the Aquarian Press and though inexpensive to buy, will lay a firm foundation for your understanding of the world of magic.

Read the W.E. Butler book a few pages at a time either in bed or just before retiring, then think over what you have read before you go to sleep.

You may find the terminology somewhat dated, it is thirty years since it was first published, but the author was undoubtedly one of the finest teachers of the occult in the last fifty years.

An Introduction to the Mystical Qabalah, is by contrast a book designed purely to instruct, and this it does admirably in easy to understand language. Since the Qabalah is the mainstay of the Western Mysteries it is important that you read this book thoroughly and make yourself familiar with the mandala of the Tree of Life. We will go into this in more detail next

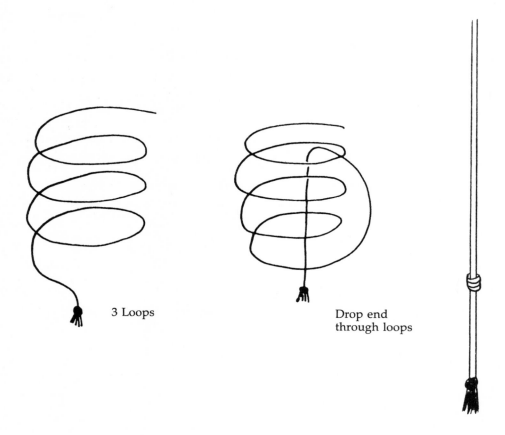

3 Loops

Drop end
through loops

Figure 6

month, but until then keep reading the book and drawing the Tree of Life as described until you are able to do so from memory. It may be small compared with some magical tomes but it is packed with common sense teaching and will be a mainstay during your year of training. Do not start the course without first obtaining these two books.

This has been a long chapter but many things needed to be explained in depth, it is important for your future progress that you start with the right basics. Each month I will give you the titles of the books needed for the following month so you will have them ready to hand. When you have finished this month's work and *not before*, buy yourself two lengths of cord, one black and one white, long enough to go round your waist twice and hang down in front of your knees. Twist the two colours into one cord. You have worked hard this month and you can celebrate by tying the first knot in your waist cord, it is a special kind of knot and instructions on how to tie it are given in Figure 6. Your last task is to read over the questionnaire and your answers and see if your viewpoint on them has changed. Re-examine your aims in taking this course and record your findings.

Example of Record Entry

Friday 25th January, 1986
Walking dog on the Beach.
7:30 pm.
Subject: 'The Universe is a living organism.'

Realizations: As I understand the words 'living organism', it means something that lives and thinks and recreates itself and interacts with other forms of life. Could this mean that the Universe as an organism is what we would call *'God'*? Living beings are composed of other living organisms, i.e. cells. Are, we, and indeed all forms of life, cells in a much vaster living being. If so we are all part and parcel of each other and everything that lives, including any aliens we may meet 'out there'. (Distraction, remembered scenes from film *ET*, also feeling of pleasure that my dog and I were part of each other, not so happy about being part of my boss!) Aware of sea birds and in a strange way of the sea itself being part of me, and me a part of them.

Saturday 26th January, 1986
Bedroom
10:30 am.
Subject: as the 25th.

Realizations: Have been thinking about this belonging to everything everywhere. It could have a lot of disadvantages! Realized that if one accepts this view, you have to take the good with the not so good. It means I am even a part of certain activities undertaken by other people with which I personally disagree, like vivisection. (Distraction, children outside.) This means I must bear part of any blame there may be attached to such activity. This is getting deeper than I like... If I am part of all things I am also part of and therefore in part responsible for the things other people do... But it includes the good things as well. Had an image of a bee in a hive, an individual within a wholeness.

Further Realizations:

This subject keeps linking in with my life in general. I don't always find it comfortable, it makes me think about things I'd rather not think about!

Take note of the fact that associated

symbols and images are beginning to rise, i.e. the bee and the scenes from a film, this means that the meditation is beginning to affect the subconscious mind already.

Reading List

Ashcroft-Nowicki, Dolores, *Building a Temple* (Aquariana Publications, BCM-OPAL, London WC1N 3XX)

Brennan, J.H., *Experimental Magic* (Aquarian Press, 1976)

Butler, W.E., *Magic, Its Ritual, Power and Purpose* (Aquarian Press, 1982)

Butler, W.E., *The Magician, His Training and Work* (Aquarian Press, 1982)

Fortune, Dion, *The Mystical Qabalah* (Benn, 1935)

Richardson, Alan, *An Introduction to the Mystical Qabalah* (Aquarian Press, 1981)

Wang, Robert, *The Secret Temple* (Weisers, 1981)

The Second Month

The Four Cornerstones — Sight, Sound, Scent, Touch

Date started ....   Date ended ....

In this second month your meditations should be coming along well and reasonably free of distractions though there will always be a few to contend with from time to time. But keep your 'distraction graph' going for another month, or even two if you feel you need the incentive. Remember, in the absence of a personal tutor *you* must keep an eye on your progress. The success of a book such as this relies heavily upon your integrity in keeping to the schedule and your determination to make it through to the end of the year.

The Pillars

By now the temple should be spick and span, newly painted or papered, and hopefully with the curtains up and the floor covering down, so we are ready for the next step. Whether your final choice of tradition is Qabalah, Greek, Egyptian or whatever, you will need two pillars in your temple, one black, and one white or silver. There is a great deal of symbolism attached to these pillars and all of it may be used with any tradition you may come across now or in the future.

They represent the two great archetypal forces of *form* and *force, male* and *female, positive* and *negative, spirit* and *matter, construction* and *destruction,* but *never* think of them in terms of *good* and *evil.* If you have read the *Introduction to the Mystical Qabalah,* as required, you will also know that they represent the two side-pillars of the Tree of Life and as such you will be working with them a great deal. They are also the Gateway to the Inner and Higher levels and as such they guard the way to knowledge. All problems can be reduced to one or other of these two power points, to stand between them at initiation is to stand between the worlds. To work between them, as in the office of the East, is a great responsibility, and not to be taken lightly.

The pillars themselves are fairly simple to make and there are two ways of approaching the task (see Figure 7). You either buy two lengths of plastic drain pipe from a DIY shop or ask a local furniture shop to let you have two of the heavy duty cardboard cylinders around which carpets are rolled. I prefer the latter as they are bigger (get them about 6-inches (15cm) in diameter

Figure 7

Figure 8

and cut them to no more than 6 feet (2m) in height) and being heavier are more stable when placed in position. For each pillar you will need two squares of wood, one about 14 inches (35cm) square and the other 11 inches (28cm) square, and 2½ to 3 inches (6–8cm) deep.

Get a local carpenter to cut holes in them to fit the pillars, then with impact adhesive stick the squares together and fit the pillars down into the holes. If necessary add some more adhesive round the base of the pillar so that it remains firm and snug. This gives you a base of two steps to each pillar (see Figure 8). An alternative method is to

get two square shaped boxes (as strongly made as possible) or two tins. Gone are the days of large biscuit tins, but a good substitute can be found in very large sized paint tins. This gives a round base instead of square but that does not matter. Place the pillar into the box or tin and fill with sand or in the case of tins you might try quick drying cement (see Figure 9). Since the pillars are sometimes used in the other quarters make sure they are not top heavy and are easily moved.

The capitals or tops of the pillars will need two more squares of wood, about 10 inches (25cm) square. Plywood or chipboard will do. These are fixed to the top of the pillar with a good coating of adhesive. On top of this, glue a circle of cardboard (a slice taken from the rest of the cardboard roll is ideal). For the sphere that traditionally crowns the Pillars of the Pylon Gate, use two childrens' playballs painted to match. These are glued to the cardboard ring which will hold them firmly to the top of the chapter.

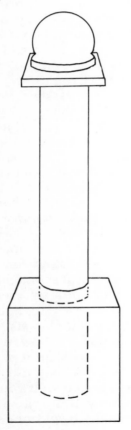

Figure 9

All that remains to be done is the painting. Use a gloss paint for the black pillar and either an aluminium paint or a spray canister for the silver. When you place the pillars in position put the black pillar on your left as you face into the room, and the silver pillar on your right as you face into the room. This is done so that all influences enter the temple from the inner and higher levels. In this position the pillars attract things into the sacred space. There is a time when the pillars are reversed, you will learn about this at a later stage of your training.

The Altar

There are three shapes an altar can take, the double cube, which is the one you will be using, and is known as the 'Altar of Sacrifice', the rectangular or 'Altar of Communion', and the circular 'Round Table of Companionship'.

The altar of the double cube is traditionally 'navel height to a six foot man', but you may have to adjust this to suit your own comfort. It is no use sticking to tradition if you happen to stand five foot six, or six foot five. Unless you are a good amateur carpenter have your altar made professionally. It should be in the form of a cupboard with a shelf inside to take such things as candles, altar cloths, incenses, wicks for the lamps, and a file with your rituals, etc. (see Figure 10). The door should close

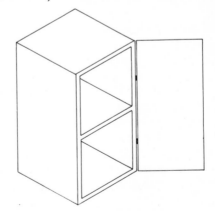

Figure 10 The Altar of Sacrifice

firmly and be provided with a catch or small bolt (black). When finished, paint it black outside and white within and place it in the centre of your temple.

With the placing of pillars and altar, the atmosphere in the room, which has been growing steadily, will take on a much deeper and more subtle quality. It has ceased to be a 'room', it is now a 'temple in waiting'. As each item is added the mood will increase and absorb the new piece into itself. This is why you do not need to consecrate each piece separately, the atmosphere will seep into it on all levels. Something for you to remember and understand is that *all* things have subtle levels not just living things. Every chair, table and lamp has its counterpart on the astral and spiritual levels. As the level gets higher the shape changes and eventually can be seen by those who have the sight as the shimmering energy pattern that is the original thought-form of the designer.

When you finally consecrate your temple, the blessing and intention bestowed upon it will cover and penetrate all things within that space both living and inanimate.

You now have pillars and altar, time to look for chairs. First of all try the local markets and second-hand shops. Look out for those with a high elegant back and arm rests. If necessary start with one for the East, and make do with ordinary chairs until you can pick up the kind you want. Clean them thoroughly and whilst doing so bless all those who have owned them before and the craftsman who made them. This helps to dispel any unwanted attachments from former owners. Re-varnish if needed, polish them until they gleam then put them in place. If you are aiming to work in a group at some time in the future, look for small tables to stand beside each chair. They will hold candles, lamps, rituals, instruments and things like spectacles

and water glasses. The latter are a good idea, as the combined effect of incense and candles can dry the throat and cause interruptions in the form of coughing bouts. While we are thinking of candles and lamps, now is the time to get in that bucket of sand in case of fire!

You should have finished your robe by now so you can start making the altar cloths. You will need a large square of black silk, again the kind used to line coats will do if you cannot run to pure silk. It should cover the altar top with a drape of around 12 inches (30cm) all round. At each corner sew a black silk tassle. These can be bought in furnishing stores, if you cannot find black, get white and dye them, you want them as large as possible. On top of the black cloth you will need a white linen cloth that can be either plain or edged with lace if you prefer. A large size man's handkerchief with a small neat edge makes a good cloth. Try to have at least two cloths so you always have one clean.

Start looking around for a bowl of blue glass, ideally it should have a stem and be the size of a small soup bowl. You are most likely to find them in antique shops and markets. This is for the altar light, fill the bowl with oil and float a lighted wick on top, or, if you find oil too messy, use a child's nightlight in the bowl. If you do, make sure to use only those with a foil cup as this protects the bowl from cracking.

A word or two about the altar light. No ritual should ever be attempted unless this light gleams upon your altar. It is the same for almost every tradition and there is a good reason for it. It represents your contact with the Higher Levels, you may call them the Great White Brotherhood, the Lords of the Bright Face, the Gods, the Archangels or whatever. On a deeper

East

West

Figure 11 The Quarter Banners of East and West

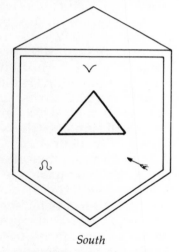

South

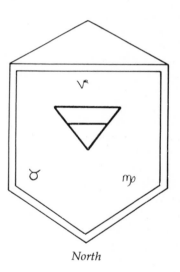

North

Figure 12 The Quarter Banners of North and South

level it connects all within the temple with the Lord of the present Aeon, it is at once a protection and a beacon on the Inner Levels that states where your adherence lies; with the Forces of Light. The bowl is blue because it symbolizes the Great Mother who carries the Lord of the Aeon. Precise names do not matter here, it is the great and unknowable principle behind those names that lie at the core of every faith.

If you have a fairly large room you may have enough space for a small single wardrobe in which to hang your robes. If this is not possible try to have one on a landing or tucked away in another room. It is essential to keep robes away from contact with other clothes, the influences and residue from the outside world can stick to the sensitized robes and can enter the temple with them. This applies also to the slippers you use in temple work.

These should be placed neatly inside the door of the temple and never used outside it. If you are tied for space you might consider a small curtain fitted across one of the corners. This blends in quite well and with small coat hooks will take at least four robes.

The Quarter Banners

Decorations should be kept to the minimum for effect. One piece to each wall is quite sufficient. Always make and use them in sets and do not mix the traditions or you will get a confused ritual as the Forces try to amalgamate the different symbolism. The easiest to begin with are the quarter banners (see Figures 11 and 12). They are made from a good quality satin in the appropriate colour for the quarter, i.e. blue or gold for the East, red or crimson for the South, sea green or deep blue for the West, and corn gold or the Qabalistic colours of Malkuth for the North.

Cut out a pentagon/shield shape, adjusting the size to your own needs, but leaving 1½ inches (4cm) all round to turn under as a hem. Tack up the hem, then cut out a matching shape, but ½ inch (1cm) less all round, in one of the new iron-on interlinings. This can be bought by length at any material counter, ask for a coat weight. Lightly pin the interlining to the back of the banner taking care that you cover the turned-in hem to within 1 inch (3cm) of the edge. Now simply iron it on and remove the tacking thread.

If you want to go further you may edge each banner with a contrasting ribbon and finish off with a ready-made fringe on the two lower edges. Fix a cord to the top edge, or even sew a painted coat hanger into the top edge and you can hang it up neatly. The symbols applied to the banner are your own choice. You can copy those designed for the Golden Dawn. You can use the triangles of the four quarters with their astrological symbols as in the illustration, or you can use Egyptian or Greek symbols as you wish. Cut them out of heavy felt and tack them lightly to the banner, then you can change them as you wish.

You can of course make the banners much longer, and using the technique of felt applique, copy figures of mythology and their symbols. You can let your creative talents run free on this one, but keep it to the one piece of decoration for each wall otherwise it will begin to look like an art exhibition rather than a temple.

One final word about decorations, many shops nowadays use polystyrene shapes as windows decorations, and you would be surprised how many 'occult' type symbols turn up in shop windows, Tutankhamun heads and Greek figures among them. Often a shop can be persuaded to part with them for a small sum once the window is redressed. Try your local DIY or home decoration shop, they often have polystyrene tiles that imitate the ceiling moulds in stately homes. Some of these are very appropriate, such as a sunburst, or a classical moulding. Hand-painted they can be used with great advantage in a temple, either as quarter decorations, or on the ceiling itself.

Using Incense

Next month will see the completion of your temple and now is the time to start increasing the atmosphere with the use of incense. Smell is the most evocative of all our senses and later on we will be exploring its use as a means of contacting the Inner Levels, but for now we will concentrate on the use of smell to build a feeling of 'being apart and sacred' in the temple. First of all what do you intend using as an incense burner? The cheapest and one of the safest is a small clay plant pot with a pot saucer under it. Fill it with one third earth and one third fine sand (aquarium sand from the pet shop is fine). On top of this you may safely place your charcoal and incense. The clay saucer will enable you to carry it without getting burnt, and there is virtually no danger of it toppling over. A thurible is a special burner for incense and has three long chains with which the container is swung from side to side. It takes an expert to use it with safety, if you have been an altar boy in your youth, then go ahead, if not stick to the clay pot!

Charcoal can be bought already impregnated with material making it easier to light, otherwise you have to mess around with methylated spirit and that adds to any danger there might be. Better safe than sorry where burning charcoal is concerned. Fancy burners on slender stems may look elegant but one swipe of a sleeve and your consecrated bucket of sand will be needed.

A bundle of long wax tapers are a useful thing to have in your altar cupboard, use them to light quarter candles, charcoal (with matches you need at least 3 or 4 to get them well alight) and of course your centre light, which is always the first one to be lit, and all others are ignited from this centre point of light.

To begin with all you will need is a store of three or four basic incenses that are ready made by a reputable firm. A list of addresses is provided on page 251. You can of course get and use a good quality church incense from most branches of the S.P.C.K. They may also sell you wax church candles in various sizes and lengths as well as sanctuary oil, wicks, and charcoal. However they may refuse you unless you prove that you represent a genuine church or chapel.

All suppliers have a comprehensive list of ready made incenses. From this choose a Solar and a Lunar incense, one specifically for meditation, and an ancient one still in use after thousands of years called 'Kyphi'. These give you a fairly wide range of uses, and you can add to them slowly. Your inner self will soon become accustomed to certain incenses and will automatically slip into the right frame of mind when it is smelt. Throughout history incense has been used in connection with ritual and worship, and without it temple work feels flat and uninspired.

There is no doubt that when sitting quietly in a softly lit temple, watching the incense smoke spiralling upwards and smelling the age old perfumes something stirs within. It has been proven that smell is an aid to memory, and perhaps sitting thus within a sacred enclosure the mind can reach back into its own far off past and return with fragments of knowledge long since forgotten.

You will find that there is an incense for every day of the week, every month, every planet and zodiac sign. So much in fact that you will soon forgo buying and will get the urge to make your own incense. It is easier than you think, though the most effective and the most ancient need sound herbal knowledge and great skill to blend correctly. Still there is no reason why you should not be able to put together a sweet smelling and practical incense for your own use.

All herbs and aromatics are aligned with one or other of the planets. Once you understand this you can blend one with another using resins and gums to bind them. If you are really going into this you will need a pestle and mortar to grind up the raw materials and some small airtight jars in which to keep them. The table of planetary incenses can vary from tradition to tradition, but a good basic one would be:

Sun: Mastic, Frankincense, Ambergris, Saffron, Laurel, Orange rind, Storax.
Moon: Myrtle, Camphor (both solid and oil), Benzoin, Jasmine, Tuberose.
Mercury: Lavender, Cinnamon, Cloves, Galbanum, Mace, Storax. Hawthorne.
Venus: Rose and Rose oil, Lignium Aloes, Musk, Sandalwood, Saffron, Violet.
Mars: Tobacco, Lignium, Aloes, Hellebore, Rowan oil, Dragons Blood, Benzoin.
Jupiter: Nutmeg, Ash, Gum Benjamin, Sage, Basil, Agrimony, Henbane, Cedar.
Saturn: Cumin, Mandrake, Pine, Rue, Yew, Sandalwood, Myrrh, Black Poppy.
Neptune: Camphor, Red Storax, Opoponax, Elm, Willow, Heliotrope.
Uranus: Patchouli, Clover, Hyacinth, Red Storax.
Pluto: Holly, Origanum, Eucalyptus.

The simplest of incenses for a ritual concerning knowledge, communication or mind in any form would be a mixture of lavender and pine resin gathered straight from the tree and ground together with a little oil of lavender. You can have a lot of fun if you simply forget about which scent goes with which planet and just mix handfuls of sweet smelling herbs together with a little essential oil added. Garden herbs and culinary herbs can all be pressed into use.

There are some excellent, inexpensive books on the subject of herbs and incenses as well as the more comprehensive and of course more expensive ones. I have given you a list at the end of this chapter as well as one for suppliers both of ready-made incenses and the raw materials, see p.251.

Your library will be able to come up with a copy of *Culpepper's Herbal* which will tell you the planetary influence for almost every herb you can name, and more than a few you never knew existed. It is an area of knowledge that repays study and has a wide variety of information easily available.

Music

As with incense, music is an important adjunct to your temple work and will enhance your ritual work considerably if time is spent on a little research and a careful selection is made. Of course you may not like the type of music most useful to you. Your personal choice may run to traditional jazz or Heavy Metal. To use the vernacular, 'Tough', because there is no way you are going to be able to use either in the temple, not if you want it to remain on its contacts anyway.

Music is capable of effects at least as strange and certainly as uplifting as incense, but, you must also understand that just as there are some scents that call up the darker forces, so there are certain types of music, and even certain combinations of notes, that can tear apart the fragile fabric of magical work. Therefore you must choose your temple music with care.

There are obvious pieces of music such as Holst's Planet Suite which gives a complete range for all the planets, but you will need other kinds as well. Get yourself a filing case, or a *Dalex Expanding Wallet* which is a cardboard file with pockets for each letter of the alphabet. Make and keep an index of your occult books with a card for each one containing title, author, publisher and date of publication. Do the same for your music but head the card with the type of ritual or meditation for which you intend to use the cassette, for example:

GREEK
Manos Hadijadakis
15 Hesperinoi

CELTIC
Bob Stewart
Journey to the Underworld

CRAFT
M. Oldfield
Celebration

This will make it easier for you to choose without going through each one. Because music is so personal, I can only give you a sample of the kind of thing I use in my own temple and you will find a small list at the end of the chapter. If you look around the record shops you will find an amazing amount of usable material. I have come across Egyptian harp music, Greek temple hymns (a little odd sounding to our modern ears but very evocative), traditional Jewish music and things like Alan Stivell's Celtic harp music. All or any of this is just the thing with which to build up a small but adequate collection.

Music has been one of the sacred arts since ancient times and has been used for healing, education, meditation, and all forms of Inner Level work. As you will learn in the next chapter, it is intimately concerned with colour for both are basically rates of vibration. The Old Testament is full of references to the use of music as a form of worship, one of the most evocative images being that of David dancing before the Ark. The early church also used music to great effect culminating in the beautiful Plainsong and Gregorian Chants. Though primarily Christian, these chants can be used in many different rituals and traditions simply because they are specially designed to lift the consciousness onto another level.

All music is composed of three elements or threads that combine to create special vibrations that act and react on the ear, the consciousness, and the soul. These three elements can be classed as rhythm, melody and harmony. Harmony is the basic ingredient of music. A musician friend has described harmony as the receptacle or Grail of music, with rhythm as the vital essence or energy poured into the harmonic form. Melody organizes these two basics into the finished product. Music will, indeed must, be an integral part of your temple work, and at the end of the chapter I have given book titles that will help you to understand its importance.

This completes the second month of temple preparation and we can now turn to this month's preparation of self.

Preparation of Self

'Does the magician believe in many gods?' asks W.E. Butler in his book *Magic, Its Ritual Power and Purpose*. He goes on to answer himself in this way. 'Yes, but his views on their nature are not quite what may be expected from him'. Like his contemporary, friend and tutor Colonel C.R.F. Seymour,

Butler believed that there is no real difference between spirit and matter. That God, gods, and man as well as everything else in the universe were part and parcel of each other. The gods therefore were extensions of that mystery we call the Creator or Creatrix, the Sons of God spoken of in the Bible, beings made perfect in previous manifestations of the universe and thus standing in relation to mankind as a kind of elder brother. Mankind is another, less perfect extension, with some way to go before it attains the same status, *but* with one great advantage, man has knowledge of life in a physical body.

This may not seem to be an advantage when you are out of work, or facing a difficult exam, or the baby wakes up and cries just when you thought you had got it to sleep, but it will be, one day! As Butler says in his book 'See (yourself) not as a stranger in the universe, not even as a separate being apart from it, but as part of that living diversity in unity, and say.....I am a Child of Earth, but my Race is from the Starry Heavens.' This is not just a fanciful thought, the sooner you realize that you are as much a part of the Pole Star as you are of your family, that the only difference between you and the gods is one of experience on their part, and the use of a body on yours, the sooner you will be able to work with and through both the gods and the universal laws.

By now you should have a fair idea of the Tree of Life mandala. So if instead of drawing the sephiroth as spheres you substituted ten differently shaped containers in different colours and imagined them being filled from above the topmost glass you would have a pretty good idea of how the same influence/spirit/God-form fills each

and every container from the most spiritual (Kether) to the most physical (Malkuth) without changing the basic

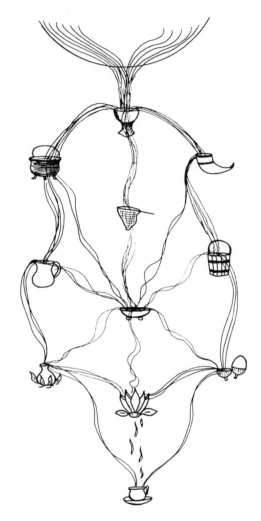

Figure 13 The Tree of Life

essence (see Figure 13). All that changes is the shape and colour of the form holding the essence. You are one kind of form, a God, or an Inner Level being is another kind of form, but they contain the very same essence of life. Kether may be a chalice of the thinnest and finest crystal, and Malkuth may be an old chipped toothmug, but the 'champagne' tastes just the same.

What you are working towards in this year of self study is the realization of your own place in the universe, an important if very small part. 'Know Thyself' said the ancients, but it is not so easy. Knowing yourself means not lying to yourself about yourself. It means learning to love yourself as you are with all your faults, it does *not* mean doing nothing about those faults.

Draw the Tree of Life on a piece of paper and start at the top. Think over what you have read about Kether in the *Introduction to the Mystical Qabalah*. Leaving out all the highly spiritual symbols we see that Kether is the highest sphere (not the holiest...they are all holy). We will take it therefore as symbolizing the best in ourselves. What do you consider to be the best thing about yourself? Take your time and think about it. When you have an answer write it down within the sphere of Kether. Now go on to Chockmah, this is the wisdom aspect of the Tree. Look at yourself honestly, think back and find a time in your life when you said or did something that was wise. Write it down in the sphere, and move on to Binah. Binah symbolizes understanding, so you have to ferret out some time in your life when you were truly understanding, we are not talking about sympathy or pity, but *understanding*. When you have found it, write it down. Work your way through the Tree like this until you have a Tree picture of yourself. Now draw another Tree in the same way and note all the times when you were the opposite of each sephiroth, again you must be very honest.

When you have worked your way through the two Trees, use them as meditation subjects working with the positive Kether on one day and the negative Kether the next, and so on down the Trees. This will occupy twenty days out of your month, but it will also give you a valuable insight into yourself. Remember to keep your daily records.

Meditation

Your ability to meditate should by now be getting much easier to handle and with less and less interruptions on your graph. There are at least seven levels to meditation, ranging from a light reverie to a deep trance that is next door to coma. A highly trained magician will be able to achieve a fourth level without too much trouble; fifth and sixth are the province of the mediator, something quite different to meditation.

The light day-dream is very much a first level, you are using, or should be using, a second level in your daily meditations. This is a level at which you can gain much useful information, but from which you can be fairly easily awakened. If you were aroused by a sudden loud noise or some kind of emergency the worst that would happen is a feeling similar to a 'falling' dream when you wake with a start. At the third level the same kind of thing might cause a rapid heartbeat, some rise in blood-pressure, or sometimes a sudden drop, and very probably a bad headache later on. At the fourth level, which is approaching a light trance, the results might cause a fainting fit, cold hands and feet, and some disorientation, or even a slight loss of memory for a few hours.

From this you will see that if you are attempting a deeper level of meditation you must ensure as far as possible that you will not be disturbed. You will rouse quite naturally from the session after your usual ten minutes or so. Your mind and body have become used to this stretch of time and will keep to it unless trained to take longer. When working on the deeper levels you will be using the temple and locking the door, and even using a 'Do Not Disturb' notice if need be. Ordinary household noises, phones and voices will not touch you.

Make sure your back is well supported, a small footstool is a good idea so that the knees are slightly higher than the hips, this is a position often seen in Egyptian heiroglyphics (see Figure 14). Start your meditation

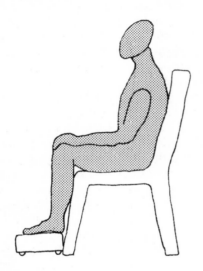

Figure 14 Meditation Position

as you always do, but make doubly certain that you are fully relaxed. Before you begin, build in the idea that your temple, or wherever you are meditating, contains a winding staircase that leads up through the ceiling to another room just like it. Concentrate on your subject and follow the meditation through for a few minutes, then, in your imagination, get up, leaving your physical body sitting quietly and walk to the staircase. Climb steadily getting the feel of going round as you climb until you move right up

into the replica of the room you have just left.

Go over to where your chair is waiting and sit down in it, allow yourself to sink into another, but deeper level of meditation. For the first few times you will find yourself flipping back into your room downstairs. When this happens just climb the stairs again and repeat your actions. Try to keep the third level going for a few minutes (increasing this gradually until you can do at least five minutes), then stand up and go down the stairs into the first and physical room. Then allow yourself to come out of it making sure that you earth yourself well, feeling the chair beneath you and the floor under your feet. Have a glass of milk or something to drink and a plain biscuit beside you as this helps you to settle into the physical quicker than anything else.

Third level meditation is not something to do every day, but only when you feel you need to go deeper into a subject. Not more than once a week until you have been doing it for at least six months. Then try twice a week, but if you start to get a reaction, headaches or any disorientation no matter how slight, leave it alone for a month then go back to just once a week. You may be one of those people who have a natural barrier at the second level and it is unwise to force an entry in such circumstances.

Creative Visualization

By using your imagination to climb the staircase you are entering a new phase in your training, that of creative visualization. You may already possess a good 'inner eye' but it will still need to be trained to create detail and to replicate sound, taste, touch and smell on the inner levels. If you do not have a fairly good imagination you will have to put in some hard work for almost eighty per cent of magic depends upon this talent.

Everyone without exception has the equivalent of a T.V. screen inside their head. It is on to this screen we flash pictures from our memory bank when needed. This is how we recognize people, things and places, even how some of us read books. If, as you read these pages you make them into a series of pictures inside your head then you are already using one of the basic cornerstones of magic, your imagination. Man is the only animal with this faculty, and because of it we have art, sculpture, literature and music. But it goes even further. There is nothing around you at this moment that is not the product of someone's imaginative idea. Everything you see comes from a thought, an idea, a vision in someone's mind. Later on that idea becomes a drawing, a plan, or a blueprint. From there it progresses to the prototype, and finally it comes fully fledged into the material world.

You may not want to believe it but everytime this happens, even with something as mundane as a new design for a vacuum cleaner, it follows an age old magical rule, Idea/Pattern/Object, in occult terms, Desire/Emotion/Manifestation. The trick in magic is to concentrate to the exclusion of all else on the desired objective, to fill your mind with a charged emotion, and to make your inner picture as detailed as you can. This is not as easy as it sounds. It takes time and patience and without a trained imagination it is almost impossible.

So how do you begin to train the inner eye? First things first, before you can build a correct and detailed picture in your inner eye you have to know what things look like on the outer level. So your first task is to observe and to retain what you observe. Much of this training will also involve memory so you can cheer yourself up with the thought that you are doing two things at once.

One of the fun ways to train your observational powers is to play what occultists call 'Kim's Game', after the Kipling character. In the book the young Kim is shown a tray of some dozen or so objects, he is given two minutes in which to commit them to memory. Then the tray is covered and the objects have to be named. As you grow more skilled you will be able to say how many are of the same colour, the same shape or type. When this is achieved start using a picture, preferably of a group of people. When the picture is covered try to remember who was standing where, who were wearing hats or were bare-headed, what the person in the left hand corner was holding, was it in the right or left hand?

You can get the whole family in on this, you will be doing them a favour as well as yourself. After all why should you be the only one in training! As you do your shopping, or walking the dog, going to work or even in your office block, look about you and try to find things you have not noticed before. Especially try looking *up*, you will be amazed at the interesting and unusual things ten feet above your head. Give yourself a target of ten new things every day for a month, but, do *not* write them down, recall them in situ in as much detail as you possibly can.

If you are in a town or city new to you take some time out to walk around and notice outstanding landmarks, *but in sequence*. If you do it this way I guarantee you will never get lost in a strange city again. Your mind will automatically come up with a map of those same landmarks even after years away from the place. After a while this observation of surroundings becomes second nature and you will be able to recall not only places but the people you were with and the conversations you held.

At night before you sleep you can take the same route and see in detail everything you saw in the physical. This is one of the ways in which your magical training will benefit your everyday life. When you meet someone new, note the surroundings as well, and in your mind's eye write their name on some convenient but conspicuous place. Later you will be able to recall the place and your subconscious mind will put up the picture of the person complete with name.

Children think in pictures until they go to school, then eighty per cent of the time their imagination is 'educated' out of them. The subconscious mind of man is like a child, it too thinks, learns and works through the medium of pictures. It is a part of us that evolved long before words and writing became our foremost means of communication, but the subconscious has never forgotten the old way, which is why ancient heiroglyphics arouse such interest and emotion in some people. The picture writing stirs something deep within them. Although it is old this part of our mind is very powerful, it is the magician part of us and once allowed to practice its old skills will soon regain its expertise.

When a child leans to talk, it 'pictures' the action or object with the word. Watch a two year old concentrating on a new toy that he has been told is a donkey. To him the picture of that sound has four legs, long furry ears and feels soft and silky. Show him a picture of a horse and he will probably say 'donkey', the picture in his mind comes up with four legs, long ears, and a soft coat. He now learns by associating a new word with a similar picture that a horse is larger, a different colour, etc. By linking picture and word together a child can learn a language very quickly.

When we as adults learn a new language we tend to forget, unless there is a marked aptitude for learning, to make the association between word and object, this makes it very hard going. The old biblical phrase 'ye must become as little children' can take on a whole new meaning in occult training.

Think back for a moment to what I have said about incense and how it evokes memories from your past. Can you see how it all fits together? The evocative power of scent, the highly trained inner eye, the unfolding of memories going further and further back (as you did during your first month's training). One day you will pass an invisible barrier deep in your mind and find yourself in an age and maybe a country strange to you, yet at the same time familiar. This is the beginning of far memory, and the experience of lives lived long ago.

A good magician stores useful images in the same way a good farmer stores hay for the winter. In the early stages of training, relaxation and meditation help to clear the mental attics of unwanted clutter. Once neat and tidy, they can then be used to hold new and potentially useful magical images against a time when they will be needed.

The use of creative imagery to enrich your life on all levels is part of your heritage as a Star Child. But it has been brought into ridicule and decried as 'fantasy and day-dreaming' because man is afraid of its power over him. Yet it has a way of seeping through and making itself felt, as in the hugely popular Fantasy Role Playing Games, and the Dungeons and Dragons industry.

Poets, bards, and wandering troubadours were held in high esteem in the middle ages because of their store of tales, songs, and epic poems, but most of all because in their telling of these things they were able to cause pictures to rise in the minds of their listeners. They were transported into the realms of fantasy by the use of voice and word. Such men could, and did, sway the minds of kings and emperors, and some changed the course of history. When they spoke, the draughty halls were silent, their listeners transported to battlefields and strange lands.

Listen to any good storyteller today, there is always one in your office, or frequenting your local pub or bar, and see how their way of telling a tale evokes clear and detailed images in the minds of those listening. This is the secret of the successful comedian, he is someone whose way of telling a joke makes you laugh not at him, but at the image he has created in your mind.

As I have told you before, everything has an opposite, this creative imagery has a dark side, for anyone who learns to project the images in his mind with force and emotion can sway the masses. Look at history and see the power of men like Hitler and Churchill, so different in motive, yet both wielding the same kind of power. Any charismatic leader has learned this technique, or uses it unconsciously. But it starts within the mind's eye.

What do we mean when we use the word visualization. Many people think quite wrongly that to visualize means to project an actual image in front of them. Not so. Let me use analogy to show you what is meant by visualization. Put the book down for a

moment and lean back in your chair, no doubt you have a photograph album in your house with pictures of your parents, relatives, or friends. Perhaps you have a favourite photo, if so recall it to mind. If you can, speak out loud and describe the photo in detail, who is in it, where it was taken, what they were wearing, etc. What you are doing is visualizing. You are 'looking' at that picture with an internal part of your mind that acts like a screen.

Let's try again. Imagine that you have been stopped outside your house by a stranger and asked for directions to the nearest post office. Again if possible speak the directions out loud. You will find as you do so that pictures of the various streets and landmarks you are using as guidelines are appearing on your mental screen. You can train your visual techniques at odd moments during the day in the same way (I hope) that you are still doing the odd relaxation exercises and interim meditations. By making it into a game that can be played on railway stations, in airports, and anywhere that involves waiting a while, you can train without taking time away from other things, and without it ever becoming a boring discipline, something that kills most people's initial enthusiasm for occult training after a few weeks. I have given you some extra visualization exercises in the monthly summary at the end of the chapter.

The Temple Ring

Let us return to the subject of the Magical Personality about which we spoke in the first chapter. By now you will be spending quite a bit of time in the temple and no doubt you will have noticed that when you enter it you feel a very different person, and of course you are, your task is to consolidate this Temple Personality and to make sure that it manifests only when you allow it to do so. Therefore it is time to buy or, if you have the skill to make, your Temple Ring.

Gold is of course the best, but expensive, silver slightly less so, but a magical ring must have a stone, and a genuine one, this will put the price up even more. If you can afford it, fine, if not then look for an old one. Maybe an elderly relative has one to give or even sell to you, if not, a second-hand one can be bought and ritually cleansed of its former influences.

To clean a ring, or indeed anything small like jewellery one of the best ways is to place it in clear running water overnight. A mountain stream is ideal if there is one fairly near. Place the ring inside a tin in which you have made several holes top and bottom, then tie the tin firmly to a heavy stone so that it will not get washed away. If possible it is a good idea to camp overnight near the stream then you can meditate on the ring and use your visualization techniques to 'see' it being freed of all former influences. Alternatively, you can tie the ring securely to a fishing line and anchor the line to a tree or stone, this way the ring floats freely in the running water.

If this method of cleaning is not practical then you can try another way. Remember how you blessed salt and water for the ritual cleansing of your temple room? You can use the same method to clean your ring. When the elements have been blessed, tip the salt into the water in the same way as before (use only a minute amount of salt as it can corrode) and suspend the ring in the mixture for at least seven hours.

Now you can consecrate it to your own use, your second real piece of ritual work. Prepare yourself by reading Appendix C and work on the Middle Pillar exercise until you know it by heart. On your altar place the centre light, a bowl of water, a small saucer of salt, some incense, and a fan made from the feathers of wild birds collected by yourself from wood, common or beach. Put on your robe and your slippers and sit in meditation for a few minutes with the ring on the altar as a focal point. Think of its stone as being porous, waiting to be filled with your Magical Personality. See it as being totally empty, clean and fresh.

Now perform the Middle Pillar exercise until you can feel the spheres lighting up inside you. Then continue into the circulation of force until you can feel yourself surrounded by an egg-shaped aura of power. Hold this as steady as you can and imagine a beam of brilliant white light coming from between your eyes and entering the ring on the altar. This beam carries from your Higher Self the gift of 'Search for Perfection'. Now feel a second beam of light coming from your throat, it is a pale lavender colour and carries your desire for 'Knowledge in order to Serve', it too enters and fills the ring. From the heart centre comes a brilliant golden light aiming for the ring and filling it with 'Desire for Harmony Within the Self'. From the genitals comes a ray of deep indigo. It rests upon the ring imbuing it with 'The Understanding of Creative Power'. Finally from your feet comes a banded ray of russet red, olive green and black, it fills the ring with 'Strength, Endurance, Discretion, and Discrimination.

Now go to the altar and bless the water and salt, (the charcoal block should already be lit) sprinkle on enough incense to give a small amount of smoke (but not enough to choke you!). Pick up your ring and hold it over the water, sprinkle it with a few drops and repeat:

With the element of Water, symbol of Understanding and Faith I consecrate this ring to my use.

(Do the same with the salt and repeat:)

With the element of Earth, symbol of Spiritual Growth I consecrate this ring to my use.

(Now pass the ring through the incense smoke and say:)

With the element of Fire, symbol of Service, Honour, and Loyalty I consecrate this ring to my use.

(Finally, wave the fan of feathers over the ring and say:)

With the element of Air, symbol of the Creative Words of Power I consecrate this ring to my use, oh ye mighty ones of the Inner Realms take note of my promise made this day. I shall strive with all my strength to wear this ring with grace, truth, and full understanding of my responsibilites, so mote it be this day.

(Now place the ring on your finger [the right forefinger] and let the stored powers and blessings flow through you. Sit again in meditation for a while and think on what you have just done. Then clear away your things from the altar, leave the light burning for a while longer to 'feed' the atmosphere, and record your working in your diary. Make a silk bag with a drawstring in which to keep your ring, do *not* wear it for show, it is a working ring. It is put on last of all your ritual apparel and completes the build-up of the assumption of the Magical Personality.)

From now on when you are working in the temple practise the Banishing and Invoking ritual given in the Appendix D. Read the ritual carefully and work on it until you can do it from memory. Also begin to build up the Astral Temple by means of pathworking. To do this you place your chair just in front of the door and sit in a meditation posture, take two or three fourfold breaths and relax body and mind. Then start to build in your mind the picture of a door, make it distinctive, old and heavy, with ornate hinges and lock. Take a few days to get this door just right, until you can recall it instantly. Now open it and stand on the threshold looking into your Astral Temple. Keep to your position in the doorway for a few days and gradually build in your imagination the temple of your dreams. Keep it fairly simple, it can be Greek or Egyptian or qabalistic, it can mirror your physical temple or not, but build it day by day, little by little. Do this until you can move about in it as easily as in the physical one. Furnish it with all that you think you need, spend time on visualizing each item as clearly as possible. Always remember to close the door firmly when you leave.

Meditation Subjects for the Month

'All magical work begins within and is projected outwards.'
'The Tree is a diagram of *forces* not things.'
'The subconscious mind is the Magical Agent...the conscious mind controls and directs.'
(These subjects are taken from W.E. Butler's book, take note of his remarks about the use of phantasy and symbols)
'To the magician, mind and matter are a continuity.'

'Magic has not died, merely increased in complexity.'

Now you have worked through your second month no doubt you are wondering at the heavy workload. Be assured....it gets harder!

Reading List

Culpepper's Herbal (Foulsham, 1952)

Maple, E., *The Magic of Perfume* (Aquarian Press, 1976)

Miller, Richard Alan, *The Magical and Ritual Use of Herbs* (Destiny Books, 1985)

Miller, Richard Alan, *The Magical and Ritual Use of Aphrodisiacs* (Destiny Books, 1985)

Stebbing, Lionel, *Music Therapy* (New Knowledge Books)

Sturzaker, J., *Aromatics in Ritual and Therapeutics* (Metatron Publications)

Tame, David *The Secret Power of Music* (Turnstone Press, 1984)

Vinci, Leo, *Incense* (Aquarian Press, 1980)

Recommended Music

Call of Camelot, Norman Miller (Summit Lighthouse, Box A, Malibu, Calif 90 28 5)

Lamer, Debussy

Pelleas Melisand, Debussy

Fantasia on Greensleeves, Vaughan Williams

On Wenlock Edge, Vaughan Williams

'Morning', 'The Death of Aase', 'Anetra's Dance', *Peer Gynt Suite*, Grieg

New World Symphony, Dvorak

Ammadawn, Mike Oldfield

Hymn of Jesus, Holst

Findlandia, Sibelius

Second Symphony, Sibelius

Heaven and Hell, Vangelis

Summer Song, Delius

Hebridean Overture, Mendelssohn

Parcival, Wagner

Zarathustra, Strauss

The Third Month

Guardians and Gateways

Date started ....   **Date ended** ....

You now enter the third and final month of preparatory work. Because of necessity the work has had to be condensed, you must bear in mind that in this book the normal four years work has been crammed into twelve short months. However you are now well on the way and this month should see the room almost completed, and after next month's work of consolidation you will be ready for the consecration of your temple.

Finishing Touches

The main temple work this month will be the making of the quarter candlesticks, but before we start on them let's think about some of the incidentals, the final touches to your temple. Not all rituals require the officers to stand throughout, but sitting can be just as uncomfortable if the chair is hard. Cushions for the quarter chairs with removable covers are a good idea. A fire-resistant foam filling for the basic cushion is better than kapok. You might also think about looking for some small footstools as well. If sitting in meditation for long periods it helps if the feet are at least two to 3 inches

(5–8cm) off the floor. Cover both cushions and footstools in the quarter colours.

A candle snuffer on a pole is a useful idea. Church furnishers stock them with a holder for a lighting taper on one side and the snuffer on the other. Otherwise a junk shop/jumble sale/ antique shop may be able to come up with an old snuffer that only needs a polish.

If you intend to work along qabalistic lines exclusively you may like to include in your altar furnishings the Ashlars. A pair of stones, usually of marble though they can be of any stone that will take a polish, the Ashlars symbolize the unregenerated soul of man, i.e. the rough unpolished stone, and the perfected soul of man, the polished and lewised (topped with a ring for lifting) stone. A local stone mason can do this for you, but it will be expensive, a masonic furnishers may be able to provide them a little cheaper. However, unless you intend keeping to the one tradition they are not strictly necessary.

A small glass vase for the holding of a single flower is useful. A ritual can be enhanced by a single rose or any flower on the altar. A small flat plate on which bread can be placed, a glass jug to hold wine for the chalice. Remember to keep matches inside the altar cupboard for lighting the centre light. The used matches can be placed on the hot charcoal so that nothing is left lying around. You will need two small jars for salt and water, on an altar they represent Earth and Spirit. I sometimes use sea shells for this, but also have some small heavy glass salt holders of the old fashioned kind, they don't tip up and take little room.

You can often find in sales or antique shops a carved wooden book rest, they are very useful on the altar for holding rituals etc., leaving you with both hands free. Most of them fold flat for storage. You should also have a Bible, and perhaps some of the other holy books of the world stored in the altar cupboard. When not using the temple it is a good idea to keep a bowl of fresh flowers on the altar, they do not have to be expensive, in fact wild flowers are best of all, but the scent and the life force exuded from them helps to build and keep the temple atmosphere going.

The Quarter Candlesticks

If you are not short of money you can buy some really lovely examples. Usually they stand about 4½–5 feet (1.5m) high and have a slightly concave top with a brass spike on which the candle is stuck. But you can make them with a little time and effort and very little money.

If you read my booklet, *Building a Temple* you will see at that time I advised using only three lights in the Temple, explaining that the North was kept dark as it was the place of the Planetary Being, who was held to be behind mankind in evolution. Now

one of the things I want you to remember is that everyone grows wiser, and at some time or other they change their minds and their ideas. I am no exception and since I wrote those words way back in 1974 I have gained a lot more experience and hopefully have grown more in knowledge and wisdom. One of the things I learned is that there is more need for light in the northern quarter than in any other, for it is there that we need to see more clearly the ravages mankind perpetrates on the Earth Mother.

With this in mind you will need *four* candlesticks and not three. Now you can have these hung upon the walls, or you can have them free-standing. If you decide upon the wall lights you will need four wire plant pot holders of the kind obtainable in seed merchants, (see Figure 15). They usually have a

Figure 15 The Quarter Candles

small plastic base on which you can stand the candle but be sure to soften the candle on the bottom and stick it firmly to the plastic base. This is the

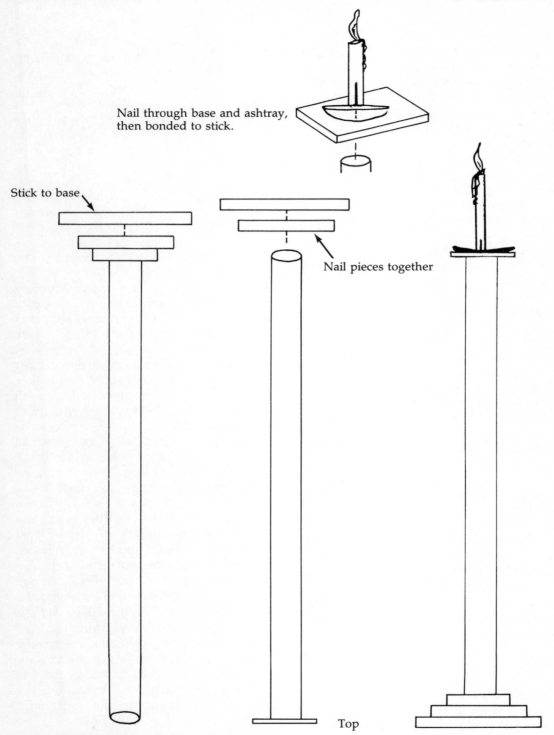

Nail through base and ashtray, then bonded to stick.

Stick to base

Nail pieces together

Top

Figure 16 Candlesticks for the Quarters

quickest and easiest way to cope with your quarter lights problem. But the lighting of a temple can be made into a beautiful and very meaningful part of your future rituals, so with a bit more time and trouble you can make four candlesticks as shown in Figure 16.

You will need four broom handles cut to 30 inches (75cm) in length. For each base you need three squares of wood 8, 6, and 4 inches (20, 15, 10cm) square respectively. See that both ends of the broom handles are flat and smooth, then nail the smallest pieces of wood to the bottom of the candlesticks. Now fix the 6 inch (15cm) squares to the first one with a good strong adhesive, and when it's firmly in place do the same with the 8 inch (20cm) squares. You now have the bases ready. For the tops you will need four metal ashtrays all the same kind and with a fairly deep tray, this will catch the melting wax and save it from dripping down on to the carpet. Candles can melt quite quickly so the deeper the ashtray the better it will be for the flooring.

Now you have two choices open to you. 1. Cut the bottoms off four plastic bottles, (allow about 3 inches (8cm)), hammer a nail through the ashtrays to make a hole, then putting the plastic 'cup' on top of the ashtray fix both to the base with a 2 inch (5cm) screw. 2. Hammer a 2 inch (5cm) nail through the ashtrays so that the nail points *upwards*, then fix them to the base with a good impact adhesive. The candle can then be pressed onto the nail which will hold it steady.

To finish off, get some lengths of wooden or plastic beading, enough to make four strips down each of the candlesticks and stick on firmly. Spray or paint the whole thing with gold or silver paint. The finished product will provide an elegant addition to your temple.

The Magical Implements

If you have done a fair amount of reading along occult lines you will no doubt have heard about the magical implements sometimes called quite wrongly, weapons. The word weapon implies the use of these things to cause harm, they are in fact simply symbolic extensions of the magician himself in the spiritual sense. You can work perfectly well without any of them, indeed you should practice working without them, since any magician worth his consecrated salt should be capable of working stark naked in the middle of a desert with his mind as the only magical tool available.

In the days of the great Mystery Schools the temple apprentices made their own tools with care and attention to detail. Once made they were treasured for a lifetime and sometimes passed on to a favoured student, a gift that was highly esteemed. At other times they were destroyed at the death of their maker. Something you must think about in the next few weeks is what is to be done with your magical tools, books, robes, etc. if anything should happen to you. Too often such consecrated things are left lying around or, even worse, sold off to a second-hand dealer. In this way they come into the hands of those least fitted to have them and can even cause trouble of a serious nature if steps are not taken to prevent this. If such things are handed on deliberately to someone qualified to hold them, all is well, if not, you, the late owner must take the blame for any trouble caused. Arrange with either a lawyer, or a trusted friend to remove all such tools etc. as soon as possible and either destroy them or arrange for them to be otherwise disposed of. You can of course be buried in your robe and have your magical tools with you, there is no law to stop you doing this.

Since medieval times there have been certain traditional ways to obtain the magical instruments. The Cup is best received as a gift; the Sword should be won if it is impossible for you to forge it yourself; the Rod must be cut and made; the Pantacle, if made of wood, must be cut and fashioned by your own hand, if metal, it should be incised with symbols by its owner. If you should choose to have a Horn rather than a Pantacle, it must be found in the wild i.e., where the animal has died or otherwise dropped a horn, or you must take it from the animal yourself.

The Rod or Wand

Let us look at each one in more detail starting with the best known the Rod. Every child is weaned on magic wands as used by a variety of fairy godmothers and evil witches, and while on the subject let me state here and now that ninety per cent of witches are anything but evil. Most are in fact very kind, gentle, hard-working people who have been sadly maligned over the centuries. There are some who rely on publicity for their kicks and who deserve all they get, but in the main witches are mostly healers and dedicated conservationists whose worship is anything but evil, much of their symbology can also be found in Christianity if you care to look.

Before you start looking for a suitable ash or thorn let's look at the history of the Rod or Wand. For thousands of years gods, kings, priests and emperors have been depicted carrying a symbol of their power in the form of a straight staff. Sometimes it is topped by a totemic animal, bird, or an abstract symbol that shows the type of power being used by the bearer. By compar-

ing such symbols in ancient wall or tomb paintings it is possible to decipher which priest is portraying which god.

It is not enough to have or make a Wand or Rod, you must be able to see and understand beyond the form and material used to the archetypal symbol at the very root of that shape. Archetypes are not always in the form of a being. Each pure form or shape has its root in an archaic, and symbolic form from which all other concepts of that shape evolve.

An animal will work better with someone it likes and trusts, so too will a magical implement if it becomes a part of you. All of them must be made because of a basic desire or need for them that wells up inside you, in this way they emerge from the Supernal Archetypes of Form and Force. These you will know from your study of the Qabalah, are Binah and Chockmah, and the symbol of Chockmah is the Rod, the prime example of the symbol.

Think of all the other forms of the Rod of Power. A king's sceptre, a Field Marshall's baton, and those carried by major-domos and drum majors (and majorettes). Mace bearers' and master sergeants, Aaron's Rod and the Rods of Moses and Aesculapius, the Caduceus of Hermes, the war clubs of Polynesian chiefs, and the shillelaghs of the Irish warlords, the ancient weapons used to dispatch the outgoing 'oak kings'. The Crook and the Flail of the Pharoahs, the bishop's crozier, the witch's broom and the shepherd's crook, the ox goad, the lightning conductor, and the baton of an orchestral conductor. The star-tipped wand of the fairy queen and a billiard cue in the hands of a master. All are Rods, emblems of power and force carried through from the higher levels to the physical. All, to a greater or

Date	Letter	Druidic Letter	Tree
Dec.24–Jan.20	B	Beth	Birch
Jan.21–Feb.17	L	Luis	Rowan
Feb.18–Mar.17	N	Nion	Ash
Mar.18–Apr.14	F	Fear	Alder
Apr.15–May 12	S	Saille	Willow
May 13–June 9	H	Uath	Hawthorn
June 10–July 7	D	Duir	Oak
July 8–Aug.4	T	Tinne	Holly
Aug.5–Sept.1	C	Coll	Hazel
Sept.2–Sept.29	M	Muin	Vine
Sept.30–Oct.27	G	Gort	Ivy
Oct.28–Nov.24	NG	Ngetal	Reed
Nov.25–Dec.23	R	Ruis	Elder

lesser extent are magic wands.

Most saints, hermits and prophets are shown with a staff or some kind. The Egyptians held a feast day called the 'Nativity of the Sun's Stick', they believed that as the year grew older and the days shorter the sun needed a stick to help him along, keeping this in mind who has not seen an old woman shaking a stick at a mischievous youngster, an archetypal symbol of the witch. Then there are the Dod-Men or Ley-Men who laid out the ancient tracks using two staves as measuring tools, and left their images cut into the green turf of England; standing stones; totem poles and miraculous staffs that flower when thrust into the ground, and chalk images like the unashamedly phallic giant of Cerne Abbas, bringing us full circle to Chockmah whose symbol is the Rod, the arrow, the lingam and the erect male penis.

In ritual the purpose of the Rod is to extend the will, to add strength to the desire or wish of the magician. At source it is like a pointing finger, the finger of accusation, the finger crooked to bring someone to you, the finger shaken to punish, the child told 'don't point, it's rude'. The finger of scorn is still potent. The laser beam of modern technology is a perfect example of a magic wand that can both destroy and heal.

In the days of the Golden Dawn, one was expected to make several Wands, but you can make one do the work of many. The best woods for a Wand are Oak, Ash, Rowan, and Hawthorn. Or you can choose according to your birth month by means of the Tree Calendar at the top of this page.

If you would like to know more about this ancient alphabet you will find it all described in a book called *The White Goddess* by Robert Graves. It is published by Faber and contains a great deal of esoteric knowledge. It will be a useful reference book for you in the future.

When you have located a wood containing the type of tree you want there are some rules to obey. First and foremost *ask the tree's permission to cut a branch*. Give it time to make its preparations, choose your branch carefully, as straight as possible and not too long, anything between 2 and 3 feet (60–90cm) is enough. Then run your hand along the branch letting it rest lightly over the place where it joins the main trunk. After a while you may be able to feel it grow cooler about 2 inches (5cm) from the join. This is the place to cut, the tree has withdrawn its

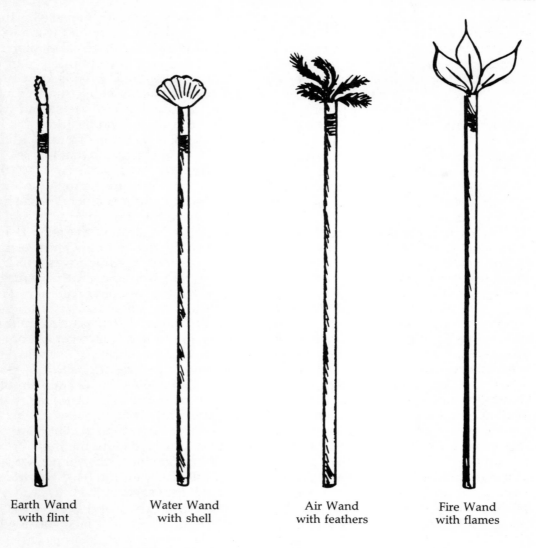

Earth Wand
with flint

Water Wand
with shell

Air Wand
with feathers

Fire Wand
with flames

Figure 17   The Wand or Rod

life-force from that area, though leaving a little in the piece you have chosen so that it wll be 'livewood'. Cut with a very sharp knife as quickly as possible, *do not ever break the branch off*. Cut on a waxing moon so your wand will grow in power, and leave a silver coin among the roots of the tree. Before you leave, cut off the surplus leaves etc. and bury them at the root of the

tree so that all will return to it in time. While waiting for the tree to adjust tell it what you want the wood for, it has a right to know. If you feel daft talking to a tree remember there is a point in the universal life-force where you and the tree are one. You are cutting off a piece of yourself!

Now dry out the wood, this will take time as it must be done slowly, no sticking it in the oven! An airing cupboard will do, or a dry airy shed. Once dry cut away any small knots and with coarse sand paper start to smooth it down. Progress to finer grades of paper until it feels silky smooth to the hand. Now with a very sharp knife and a steady hand make a thin cut about 1½ inches (4cm) deep in the top of the wand, it must be as thin as possible so it will grip anything placed in it.

Using either a clear or darker toned varnish give your wand several coats allowing it to dry thoroughly before adding each successive coat. Give a final polish with beeswax and a rub with a silk cloth and you will have a beautiful wand.

Now take a piece of piano wire and magnetize it by stroking it with a magnet (remember to stroke it the same way all the time) then bind it around the wand 3 inches (8cm) below the top. This wand can be used for all your temple work and with any element simply by inserting different symbols into the top. For Earth use a thin sliver of flint or slate, for Water use a piece of flat shell or any shell pierced with a wire ring that can be slipped through the cut. For Fire cut out three flame shapes from red/yellow felt and staple them together. For Air use a small bunch of feathers picked up from a wood or common. (See Figure 17) From such simple things you can make a very effective wand. Using your own ingenuity you can make and use many other symbols from any tradition.

The Cup

The Cup has so many meanings it needs a book to itself, but its primary function is to contain and form. To primitive man the first Cup was a woman. Within her, new life was shaped in some miraculous way that was magical to early man. It was a very long time before he realized that he played any part in conception. Out of this ignorance grew what is known as the 'Sacred Relationship'. A man could never be sure that his wife's child was his, on the other hand he knew that he and his sister had come from the same mother, so he reasoned that his sister's son was his true kin. And so the nephew became in many cases the successor to a king or chief. We see this acted out in the story of Anubis, son of Osiris and Nephthys, the child being accepted by Isis, wife of Osiris, as her own. Like Moses, Anubis was set adrift on the river Nile and drawn from the water by the adoptive mother. Lot, nephew of Abraham, is another example of the status of the nephew. Abraham risked a war to get Lot out of trouble, not because of family loyalty but because he was the heir.

That is one meaning of the Cup, the fertility of the female. Another is the Cauldron or container of wisdom. In *The White Goddess* you can read the story of Ceridwen and the transformation of Gwion Bach, the simple peasant boy, into Taliesin, the Bard and Mage, through the magic of the Cauldron. All Grails, Cauldrons and Cups have a similar function, they feed those who find them with their heart's desire. If that desire is wisdom then it is given, if the desire is power, then that too is given, though not always in the way one would wish. In this ability to apparently make wishes come true the Cup shares a place with Aladdin's Lamp.

If the Wand was the first magical instrument, the Cup was the one that early man revered most. It held the promise of rebirth into Godhood, unity with knowledge and power added. Even today the church communion promises at-one-ment with the Godhead. This practice of eating the body and drinking the blood of the sacrificed God-King is not new, it was known and practised in one form or another in most of the Mystery Religions. Jesus adapted an already ancient rite to his own use, thereby linking the old and the new together. By this act he intimated that the old ways were still valid and not to be despised.

The Cup is then above all a container, that which is invoked by the Wand is contained within the Cup, they form a pair, a polarity. In another sense they symbolize the creative act with the Wand as the phallus and the Cup as the womb. According to the ancient Law of 'As above, so below' the interaction between the two symbols brings into manifestation that which is desired by the magician.

The emphasis is on the desire or need for the object or event being invoked. Just as desire on the physical level can bring about a new being, so it is held in magic that the Wand and the Cup create what is desired by magical arts. Without desire the magician can do nothing, though that desire is on a very high level of consciousness.

Sometimes locations can act as Cups of Power; Silbury Hill is one, its rounded shape suggesting both the female breast and the upturned Cup. Some countries because of their special vibrations act like racial cauldrons, containing within their soil and their races special bloodlines that throw up great men and women when times dictate a need for them.

We compared the Wand with the modern laser beam, we can compare the Cup with the Early warning radar installations and atomic reactors which can hold both life and death within their 'wombs'.

Once you have your Cup you must fill it. Place it on your altar and use it as a meditation symbol for several days. Try to 'see' it from the inside, from its own highest levels, fill it with yourself almost in the sense of sacrifice, fill it with memories both bitter and sweet, for the Cup of Cups contains both honey and myrhh. When you feel your Cup is full, pour in a little wine and drink it down. With this symbolic act you accept all that is within your Cup, all that the future holds for you, all that the past has made of you. Truth they say is found at the bottom of a well, it may well be found at the bottom of a Chalice. It has been said that 'the all important thing is the empty inner', there must be a space into which knowledge and grace can be poured. It is up to you to make that space within yourself, unless you do there will be 'no room at the inn' for the light to enter. Lastly, whatever you receive from the Cup, let it flow outwards to others, then more will enter to keep it filled.

The Sword

Next to the Rod, the Sword is probably the best known of the magical instruments — unfortunately it is also the most misunderstood and misused. Its main purpose is to defend, rarely if ever to attack, certainly not to carve up anything that may come your way on the Inner Levels. As the Wand is to Air, so the Sword is to Fire, it is an expression of the magician's energy on the Inner Levels, and as such it should be conserved.

There are many uses for a Sword and later you may find you need more than one, but for the present one will be enough. They are part of initiation ceremonies where the Sword is held to be part of the equipment of the Officer of the West. In a working group, the temple guardian, who is responsible for guarding the door against physical plane intruders (there is an Inner Level guardian to take care of other kinds), would also carry a Sword of Office. There would also be a Sword for general temple use, but the Sword we are concerned with now is the personal Sword.

Like the Rod and the Cup, the Sword has a long tradition behind it, the sword that drove Adam and Eve from the Garden of Eden being perhaps the first example of a magical weapon. Myths and legends are full of the exploits of heroes and their swords and you would do well to add them to your researches. Nearly all the great swords have been dignified with a name that described their power and purpose. The Answerer was the weapon of Manannan the Mighty who gave his name to the Isle of Man, Durandel belonged to Roland the greatest of Charlemagne's Paladins. Four swords are used at the coronation of a British monarch, the Sword of State, the Sword of Mercy, named Curtana, the Sword of Spiritual Power and its twin the Sword of Temporal Power. Set at the four corners of the canopy they are the protectors of the Kingdom.

A sword is worn by all Solar Gods and Heroes, and the higher degrees of Knighthood. In the West it has a straight phallic shape, in the East however it takes on a curved female shape as their mythos looks on the woman as a threatening figure and this is reflected in the shape of the weapons. In some respects it is a counterpart of the Distaff, a true female symbol, both, you will remember from the story of Sleeping Beauty, can inflict a wound.

Excalibur is perhaps the best known sword. In its earliest version it is called Excaliburn, or Excaliban meaning 'out of earth'. It was only loaned to Arthur by the Lady of the Lake, and had to be returned to her at his death. We could say that once Arthur was dead the inner plane energy that was available to him through Excalibur was no longer needed.

There is an ancient belief that a sword once drawn must be blooded before being sheathed again or it will lose its power and sharpness. This lays emphasis on the part played in sword symbolism by the scabbard which is 'female' as it is a container, and reveals the meaning behind the action of a knight laying his sword between himself and any lady with whom he might be travelling when they rested at night.

Arthur lost the scabbard of Excalibur to Morgan le Fay, a tragedy, for while it was in his possession he would never have lost any blood no matter how deep the wound. This again points to the feminine aspect of the scabbard, and tells us that had Arthur been more in touch with his Anima or female side, he might have won that last battle.

To the modern magician his magical Sword is a reservoir of strength and energy he may draw on at will. Because it is almost impossible for anyone except a trained blacksmith to make a sword nowadays, you will probably end up buying a sword either from a Masonic Furnishers or from one of the occult suppliers on the list supplied at the end of this book. But, you have to earn it. In the days of Chivalry, a knight spent a vigil in a church or chapel on the eve of his entry into the Order of Knighthood. The night was spent on his knees praying that he might prove worthy of the sword that lay upon the altar in front of him. Can you do less to earn your sword?

You will unfortunately find very few vicars willing to let you lay a sword on the altar of the local church, still less allow you to spend the night there. But churches are not the only sacred ground. A circle of standing stones will do just as well and there are many in the wilder places of Britain where you would be undisturbed. If you do not live in Britain, then search for any kind of sacred site and provided it has not been used for evil purposes you can hold your vigil there. If you really cannot find a place, or circumstances will not allow you to follow these instructions, then as a last resort use your temple as a place for your vigil, but you will have to wait until it has been consecrated. Then you can spend the night before the altar on which lies your sword.

Give your sword a name and choose that name carefully, in fact this can be made part of the vigil, to meditate upon a suitable choice. Once chosen keep the name secret. An ex-student of mine many years ago named his sword 'Spirit Ripper', when I pointed out the fact that the word spirit could also be taken to mean the Holy Spirit, he replied that he assumed spirits were bright enough to know the difference! Don't count on it. In magic learn to *specify*. Power is neither good nor evil, it is mindless, taking its direction from the one who is (we hope) in charge. It will take you at your word every time, which may not be the way to survive as a magician. You will find an interesting chapter on swords in *Oriental Magic* by Idries Shah. Any books on chivalry will give details of the Knight's Vigil.

The Pantacle

The Pantacle is an Earth symbol, and the least known of all the magical implements. It can be made of wood or metal and it is the only one that grows and changes with the magician himself. It takes the form of a disc inscribed on both sides with symbols of personal value to the magician. On one side is depicted his idea in symbolic form of the Godhead in whatever tradition he is working, these symbols are the result of much meditation and deep thinking. On the other side through the same form of mental discipline he must evolve a symbol depicting himself in relation to that Godhead.

Just as the universe and the Godhead changes and adapts to new growth, so those symbols will change over a period of time. You start with an idea of the Creator and yourself in juxtaposition as you see it now...but that will change as you grow in understanding and wisdom. Then you will need to make a new Pantacle with new symbols. The Pantacle is very similar to the Wheel of Fortune in the Tarot pack, the wheel of life, birth and death. Each new disc will show evidence of your growth.

No two people have the same pattern of change. For some the symbols will last longer than others, the time is not a criterion of success or failure, time is a misnomer for it indicates only the spacing between the rings in the personal spiral of attainment. For the rare few the disc may never have to be changed, for in a flash of insight they have a moment of complete knowingness, but they will still have to grow into what they have seen.

In seeking your symbol you should tax your mind to its utmost, take your time, a Pantacle can be used in the temple without its symbols for a while. When finally ready, you should meditate on those symbols at least once a week. As each Pantacle becomes redundant it must be buried deep in the earth. If wooden, seek out a tree of the same wood so it can return to its native element. This return journey will take with it a great blessing for the earth, all that the wood has absorbed during its time in the temple will now be absorbed into the Earth Being.

Basically your Pantacle is a circular piece of wood about 6 inches (15cm) across. Alternatively, it can be made of metal such as copper or tin. Use the same Druidic tree calendar to help you choose the wood. It is fairly easy to make, but if you have no skill in woodwork you can ask a carpenter to make you a plain circle of wood with which to start. The edges should be sanded either by hand or electric sander until it is smooth and rounded. Now do the rest of the wood so the whole thing is satin smooth to the touch. Start on a New Moon and let your mind dwell on the Earth symbols while you work.

When you have your symbols you can either paint them on then varnish the whole thing or you can draw it on with a new type of pen that writes in gold or silver ink. You may prefer to draw the design lightly in pencil, then with a thin sharp chisel cut a line around the design. This cut is then filled in with a thick fuse wire which is hammered in to outline the symbols, producing an inlay effect.

This magical tool is a link between you and the Earth, in some rituals it can represent you as an earth being, in others it will stand for the Earth herself. (See Figure 18.)

You may choose to use a Horn instead of a Pantacle, in this case it must be cleaned thoroughly and disinfected with a non-toxic sterilizing solution. The edge must be banded with a metal which may have to be done professionally. It should also

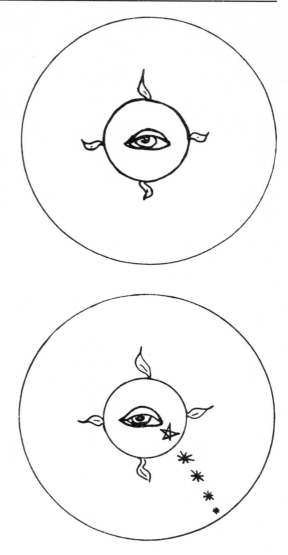

Figure 18 The Pantacle

have a ring around it with two small legs so that it stands upright (see Figure 19). The horn should be filled with corn, seed, grapes, or bread.

Dedicating Your Temple

Your temple, when it is consecrated, must be dedicated to some aspect of the Godhead. It can be offered simply to 'the Light', or you may choose a

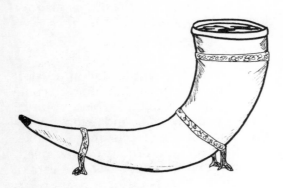

Figure 19 The Horn

great teacher of the past, Melchisedek, Enoch, Hermes, Orpheus, Jesus of Nazareth, Isis, Athene, Ceridwen, Serapis, Anubis, Narada, Joseph of Aramathea, the list can go on. A lot will depend on what is to be your basic working tradition. You still have a little time before the consecration so think on this very deeply. The Qabalah makes a good base simply because it adapts to all other traditions and encompasses them without losing itself, or them, in the process.

Select two or three and look into their principles, and read up on their god(s) and ideals. Meditate on what you find and record it, then read it over and make a choice.

Besides a temple deity you will also need a temple guardian. Again there is quite a choice: dragons (small), dogs (large), lions, griffins, wyverns, unicorns, eagles, wolves, bears. Any kind of animal real or imaginary providing it can look fierce. A small fluffy rabbit is not going to strike fear into an intruder!

Find a good illustration of the chosen beast and using your creative imagination build it up, and see it standing just inside the door of the temple on guard. Give it a name, and at the same time choose a simple password and link the two in your mind. Make up a little pathworking in which you and the guardian have a friendly relationship, but an intruder, on any level, will be challenged and routed. Never program your guardian to cause serious harm, just to halt, and as a last resort to badly frighten anyone trying to enter illegally.

Never forget to include your guardian in your closing blessing prayer, using the words, *May you be blessed to the amount that you are able to receive.* In a Mystery School you would be taught how to ensoul such a guardian ritually. But even without the ensouling process you can have a dependable and very determined astral 'bouncer'. From now on use your password whenever you enter the temple, say it quietly under your breath, or just think of it. You can use a symbol instead of a password, it is equally effective.

A password can link you with the guardian when you are thousands of miles away. In fact once you get used to the idea, you can work astrally in your temple in London, Manchester or New York, while you are sun-bathing in Majorca or the Bahamas, or you can bring the temple to you. Either way you can have your temple and work in it.

Preparation of Self

Your meditations this month will be taken up with your choice of tradition and the temple deity, your magical weapons, and the symbols for your Pantacle. With that lot you have no room for any extras. You will continue with your early morning relaxing, stretching and breathing exercises, and the odd relaxing exercise during the day. The meditations can be done either in the temple, or mulled over during a walk or any work that can be performed safely on 'mental automatic' as you have done in the preceding months. Books to look for are *The Symbolic Weapons of Ritual Magic* by A. Highfield, *Symbolism* by J.C. Cooper, and *Magic for the Aquarian Age* by M. Green. All of them will explain further the work you are presently undertaking, and will expand on it in a way impossible in just one book.

The Four Quarters

This month we will explore the four quarters of the temple and prepare for the time when they are ritually opened. We will look at their symbols, god-forms, the qualities needed in those who stand as officers, and their inner landscapes.

No one quarter is above another, all are equal in rank and in power, but the fact that the Magus sits in the East tends to add a little more lustre to that area. The role of the Magus is to control the ritual as well as the quarter itself, he directs the power coming into the temple and is ultimately responsible for whatever happens, good or bad.

In temperament, the Magus should be unflappable, physically fit and not given to panic when things do not go as planned, something on which you can confidently rely in ritual magic! The golden rule for any would-be Magus can be summed up thus: if you can work the mistake into the ritual by ad libbing, go ahead, if you can't halt the ritual, if you are not too far into it, go back to the beginning and start again. If this is impossible, simply close the temple down using extra care in closing the quarters and leave the ritual until another time. If something funny happens, have your laugh and go on from there, laughter in a temple is a lovely thing, it is not just for solemn faces and dignified rites, it is also for love and laughter and music.

The East

Because the East is the station of Air it is a forgone conclusion that at some time things will fall off tables, you will forget your words, and even unwittingly start a row! Air is unpredictable, one famous lady occultist, now dead, was reputed to have boxed the ears of her fellow officer during a Rite of Air, so you have a precedent! Opening this quarter needs a steady hand and a lot of self confidence. I must confess to being less than happy when required to sit in the East, but then I am a Gemini and know what it would let me in for.

Symbols for the East include fans, birds, feathers, wind instruments, hunting horns especially, but think before you blow them, horns are calling symbols and who or what answers that call can be heart stopping. Something that you must realize as you work on through the year is that your psychic centres are beginning to open, slowly but surely. You must be prepared to start seeing and noticing things that are not always seen by other people. That can come as a shock, and many eager would-be magicians give up there and then, unable to cope with 'The Sight'.

The East is the Gate of the Sun at Dawn, and all dawn symbols, as well as those of Air, apply here. All aspects of the Wand or Rod including the staff of the hermit, the djed of Osiris, the lance, the pointing finger are used here. Its colours are sky blue, ivory, rose, amber, pale gold, turquoise, and white. Its astrological signs are Aquarius, Libra and Gemini.

God-forms for the East might include Osiris, Kephra, Aurora, Apollo, Orpheus, Hermes, Mercury, Prometheus, Quetzalcoatl, Frey, and Iduna. You can also use the 'enlighteners', the great teachers of the past, Merlin, Narada, Serapis, Jesus of Nazareth, Imhotep, Kham-ua-set, Bhudda and so on. When building a foursome of God-forms make sure they are all from the same tradition, don't mix them. For example if you are working along Arthurian lines, starting from the East and working clockwise you could have Merlin, Arthur, Nimue, and Guenevere, but you couldn't put Isis or Hermes in with the same group.

We have already established that the Officer of the East is also the Magus. Traditionally it is a man and before I get accused of being sexist let me add that there are reasons. In the occult you had better forget about ultra-feminism, everything is balanced in sexual polarity with male and female working together each in the place for which they are most suited.

A woman brings power into the temple, she is strongest on the Inner Levels and in deeper touch with the fluid world of the astral. A man is best at directing that power once it has been passed to him. He is at his strongest on the physical plane. This alternates up the planes. There have been and are, good female Magi, but in general it is best for a male to take the East.

A Magus has the task of holding things together in a temple, he sets the pace of the ritual and its intention. He mediates the quality of communication in all its aspects, and the dissemination of knowledge is his province. Dignity of bearing and calmness of mind are among the attributes to cultivate. He is also responsible for the behaviour in the temple about which more later.

The Inner Levels of the East

Beyond the Pillars of the East, and indeed beyond all the Gates of the Quarters, there are on the Inner Levels, the landscapes of the mind appertaining to that quarter. It takes many years to know them well, but you can make a start now. Place your chair just before the pillars facing into the East, begin by relaxing and taking two or three fourfold breaths. Build up in your imagination the figure of Hermes as you think of him. Try for as much detail as possible. Behind him in the East see a pair of tall gates that are opening slowly. Hermes holds out his hand and you get up and walk towards him. Here in this place you may trust with safety, although not yet consecrated it has been cleansed and you will come to no harm. With Hermes go through the Gate of the East.

This is *your* Country of the Eastern Gate, I cannot tell you what you will see or find, or what you will learn there. You must look carefully, listen and try to remember all that you see, hear, and do. If you have done your reading and your research, your mind will have access to a great deal of symbology already. If you see something you do not understand search out its meaning when you return. Your guide will tell you when it is time to come back. Walk through the gates and take your place in the chair, see the Gates closing with Hermes behind them. Let your mind adjust slowly to the everyday world, and be sure to have something to eat and drink to help you close down. Record your journey as soon as possible, this is one time when you are not held down to a required number of lines, write as fully as you like.

The South

The station of the South is the Gate of the Noonday Sun, its officer has the task of mediating the powers of love, honour, and courage to those in the temple. The symbols are strength, the sword, the dagger, the shield, the chariot, bow and arrows, the torch, hammer and anvil, the double headed axe, the winged disk, the Eye of Horus, the lyre, and many more. The gods include Mars, Helios as the Sun God at noon, hawk-headed Ra, Ares, Sekmet, Horus Athene, Brigid, Bran, Vulcan, and Hephasteus. Heroes and teachers are Arthur, Hercules, Llew, Gawain, Aesculapius, and Cheiron. That will do to start with. Colours are all the reds, oranges, and golds. The astrological signs are Aries, Leo and Sagittarius.

The Officer of the South should be loyal and courageous, it can be either a man or a woman but they should not be easily scared or upset, they must exude calmness and dignity. With the temple guardian, he is responsible for the safety of those within the sacred enclosure.

The Inner Levels of the South

Place your chair before the Southern Gate. When you have done the relaxing and breathing build up the figure of Apollo using as a pattern any picture or statue you may have. The Gates open and the golden figure holds out its hand, you rise and move towards the South and enter the landscape of the Southern Gate.

Explore with the Sun god and try to store all that you see and hear. When it is time for you to return, Apollo will bring you back. Settle into your chair and see the Gates closing with the figure behind them. When they are finally closed, allow your mind to return to the physical level. Record your impressions as usual. Do not attempt to do all these journeys in one day, take one quarter each week and make the journey no more than three times within that week. You will not see the same things each time so be sure to keep as accurate a record as you can.

The West

The station of the West is the Gate of the Setting Sun and the point of contact between the temple and the Inner Levels. The officer should be a woman, with some psychic power if possible. Her task in the temple is to mediate the influence of the Inner Levels, to become a point of communication using the polarity of the East and West to achieve this. The West is the point where, if it is destined, the acutal temple *contact* will be made. This is not the contact of communication but the actual acceptance of a group for training by an inner plane Master. It does not happen to every group, though most groups will make a smaller contact with one of the angelic or minor Adepti sooner or later, usually later. You may ask how you will know when such a contact is made, and I would have to say I really cannot explain how... you will just know. There is no mistaking the difference in the quality of work that will be done, or the difference in the people doing that work.

All the fluid and containing female symbols are those of the West. Water, cups, cauldrons, shells, caves, oceans, lakes, scabbards, the moon, the womb, seeds, etc. The dark jewel colours of indigo, royal blue, silver, dark wine red, purple, lavender, and grey. The god-forms that can be used are Isis, Nephthys, Thoth, Sin, Artemis, Selene, Hecate, Diana, Arianrhod,

Ishtar and Astarte, Neptune and Poseidon. You can call on the help of Oannes, Dagon, Ea, Hypatia, the Virgin. The astrological signs are Scorpio, Cancer and Pisces.

The Officer of the West is the Seer of the temple and as such she must be honest and truthful with herself and with others, of all levels. Of all the Gates this is the one through which the power of the temple will enter. There must be great strength of purpose here.

The Inner Levels of the West

Place your chair before the West and when you have worked through the exercises, build up the Gates, seeing behind them a night sky full of stars. They open to reveal the Moon Goddess Artemis. She wears a short hunting kilt of white and silver and leather sandals. She carries a bow and on her back a quiver full of arrows. Beside her two great wolfhounds wait patiently. She holds out her hand and beckons you to rise. Follow her through the Gate of the West and explore its regions. When you return take leave of the Goddess and when you are fully back on this level record what you have seen.

The North

The last Gate is that of the Earth, sometimes called the Gate of the Midnight Sun. The officer should be a woman with an affinity with the earth and growing things. Here the emphasis is on growth both actual and spiritual, on benevolence and understanding of the needs of all life on Earth. It is an important Gate because of the crisis mankind faces if he continues to rape the Earth as he has been doing for the last century. A great deal can be done in this quarter with the right officer.

The colours are all the ambers, leaf greens, russet reds and earth browns. The symbols are those of the Earth goddesses, cornucopia, basket, sickle, flail, plough, horn, seed, furrow, spindle, corn dolly, bread, wheatsheaf, corn, and scythe. Gods including, Pluto, Ge, Rhea, Geb, Ceridwen, Isis, Demeter, Kore, Persephone, Ceres, Hades, Rhiannon, and Changing Woman of the American Indian. The astrological signs are Virgo, Capricorn, and Taurus.

This is also the station where the Planetary Being as an intelligence in Her own right may be contacted, helped, and listened to.

The Inner Levels of the North

Place your chair before the Northern Gate and build the portals as before. The gates open to reveal Persephone crowned with flowers and carrying a basket of fruit. Take her hand and follow her into the Garden of the North. Learn all you can, for it will help the Earth Mother. When you return record your findings as always.

More about the Quarters

Since this book leans mainly towards the Qabalistic, you should learn about the Chaioth Ha Kadesh, the Four Holy Creatures, depicted in religious art as the Man, the Lion, the Eagle and the Bull. All are winged and usually shown with haloes. They equate with the four Evangelists thus: Matthew with the Man, Mark with the Lion, John with the Eagle, and Luke with the Bull. Quarterwise, you work with the man in the East, the Lion, in the South, the Eagle in the West, and the Bull in the North.

On the Tree of Life the Four Holy Creatures are placed on Daath, the invisible sphere that symbolizes knowledge distilled from the Wisdom of Chockmah and the Understanding of Binah. You will find them in the Bible in the Vision of Ezekiel and they make very powerful meditation symbols, in fact they are Gateways to the Quarters on a higher level than you would reach using God-forms. If you have been reading your books as you should you will know by now that there are four levels to the Tree of Life. They are Assiah the Earthly level, Yetsirah the Creative level, Briah the Mental level, and Atziluth the Spiritual level. By placing one of the Holy Creatures in each quarter as a guardian, rather than using a God-form, you can open that Gate onto one of the Four levels of the Tree.

Or, you can use Archangels as Quarter Guards: Raphael in the East, Michael in the South, Gabriel in the West, and Uriel in the North. This will give you yet another quarterly 'land-scape' to explore. The gods will take you into a mythic, creative landscape, the Archangels will show you a more spiritual aspect, the Holy Creatures will show you the highest mental realms.

Your Inner Temple

Last month you started to work on the astral counterpart to your physical temple, now you can take this a step further. On the Inner Levels your temple would look very strange to your eyes, it has four levels, one on top of the other, each one on a higher level than the one below. Thus the physical temple you are building exists in Assiah, the level of matter. The one you started to build last month (remember you had to mount a stairway to reach it?) was the temple in Yetsirah, above that reached by yet another stairway is your temple's counterpart in Briah, but you will have difficulty in staying there for more than a few minutes because of the mental pressure. As you progress you will be able to stay longer, after many years you will be able to actually work in it. Above that again is the primal spiritual temple where all is pure light. It corresponds to Atziluth.

So as you build your temple you are in fact building a great shining tower, but it does not end there. Beyond each quarter also lies a temple, the temples of the East, South, West and North, and they also have four levels. At this point stop and go back to the questionnaire and re-read questions six and eight and your answers. Do you still think magic can be learned in a few weeks?

Lastly, make a final re-examination of your aims and ideals in this work. You have done well. But there is more hard work ahead of you. This book is limited in the amount it can teach you simply because of size. I have barely hinted at subjects that need a whole month to themselves, and encouraged you to read selected books that will tell you more. Examine your will to succeed, and if you are still determined to go on, put the second knot on your girdle.

Reading List

Cooper, J.C., *Symbolism* (Aquarian Press, 1982)

Graves, Robert, *The White Goddess* (Faber, 1952)

Green, Marian, *Experiments in Aquarian Magic* (Aquarian Press, 1985)

Green, Marian, *Magic for the Aquarian Age* (Aquarian Press, 1983)

Highfield, Andrew, *The Symbolic Weapons of Ritual Magic* (Aquarian Press, 1983)

Larousse Encyclopaedia of Mythology (Hamlyn, 1963)

Shah, Idries, *Oriental Magic* (Paladin, 1973)

The Fourth Month

Sealing the Temple

Date started ....   **Date ended** ....

With the fourth month you come to the end of your preparatory work. From now on it is a case of practice makes perfect, and the acquiring of knowledge, facts, and experience. Much of the future will depend on how faithfully you have done the work of the last few months. You have been building a foundation and any structure you raise on that foundation will only be as strong as the work that has gone into it. If you have serious doubts, then my advice is to go back to Chapter One and start again — at least where the preparation of self is concerned.

Setting up the Seals

There is more than a chance that you will be behind in the work on the temple, so this month will give you extra time to finish up. In the meantime you can go ahead with at least some of the pre-ritual work that has to be done but does not require a fully consecrated temple in which to work. The first of these tasks is setting up the Seals.

Your temple at the moment is vulnerable, it is open although the ritual cleansing that you performed will give a certain amount of protection until the full consecration takes place. But now that you have begun to actually use the Gates as crossing points between the worlds it is time to set the Seals so that you may use them to move in and out, but other less desirable Inner Level beings cannot gain access to this level through them. This is not to say that everything on the 'other side' is evil. But some of them can be mischievous and disruptive.

Because the Qabalistic magic is universal and encompasses within its Mandala, (the Tree of Life) all the symbology of other traditions, we will use a basic Qabalistic Seal but with a twist to it that will enable you to align all four quarters to whatever tradition you wish to use.

Think of your temple as a walled citadel with four great Gates as points of entry. At the points between the Gates stand four tall towers. These towers will be the focus of the second Seals. Next month the final Seals will be placed above and below, then your temple will be made safe and impregnable.

There are some preparations to be

made and things to gather for the Sealings. For each quarter you will need four small containers, the smallest glass tubes with stoppers you can get are ideal. If not, small pill or even perfume bottles well washed. But the quantities you are dealing with are so minute, the smaller the container the better. Now you will need about a tablespoon of coarse salt crystals, about the same of sulphur (from a chemist), some water, sea water is best, if not, from a river or stream, not from a tap. Lastly you will need some mercury. All you need to do is buy a thermometer and crack the tube to obtain the quicksilver within. Do this over a container or you will never 'catch' it. You now need four small silk bags with drawstring tops, a piece of white cartridge paper, some felt tip pens, and four drawing pins.

Sew the bags, and make a phial of salt, water, sulphur and mercury for each Quarter. Then cut four, five-pointed stars out of the cartridge paper. Colour each of the five points in a different shade — gold, blue, green, violet, red. Paint the middle part, two with gold and two with silver. With a pen write on the gold point of the eastern star the name Zeus, on the blue point write Osiris, on the green write Merlin, on the violet write Raphael, and on the red write Odin. Now prepare your altar. Place the four stars with the silk bags on top of them at the four quarters of the altar. Lay four sets of phials on each bag, and light the altar light. The first Seal will be set on the eastern gate.

Take the star for the eastern quarter and pin it to the wall below the banner, or, if you have a long banner or curtain, pin it to the banner. (Always relocate it *behind* the banner after the ritual has been completed.) Place it with the golden point uppermost. This is the only time when the God-forms of different traditions can be invoked together without causing havoc. Remember that all the gods are one God and all the goddesses are one goddess and they all emanate from the Primal Conception.

Sealing the Eastern Gate

Build in your mind's eye the great Gate of the East, let the eastern wall of the temple melt away, and see a Greek temple of white marble before you. Hold it as steady as you can, now see coming towards you the figure of Zeus, the Greek sky god and ruler of Olympus. He is much taller than a man, golden of skin with eyes of brilliant blue, his hair and beard are the colour of honey. He appears to be in the prime of life. He wears a robe of blue and white and carries in his hand a golden lightning bolt. At the Gateway he stops and waits. You now start the invocation:

Great Zeus, ruler of Heaven and Earth, King of Olympus, son of Chronus, giver of justice and protection to mankind, hear me. Look upon this Gate of the East with favour, and grant us your divine protection, seal this Gate with your lightning bolt that all within may be safe.

(Zeus raises his arm and strikes the ground with the lightning bolt. It disappears into the earth leaving a flat white paving stone set into the threshold of the Gateway. When working with the Greek mysteries the Gate of the Gate is now sealed against unwanted influences. Make your thanks.)

My thanks for this favour great Zeus. May there be peace and harmony between us. Be welcome in this place.

(The figure smiles, then turns and moves away into the dawn landscape.)

(Turn the star so that the blue point is now uppermost. When you step back, see with the inner sight a great throne of red sandstone and seated upon it the Egyptian god Osiris. His skin is of a reddish hue, his hair black beneath the crown of white linen. He wears a simple white kilt and plain sandals and around his neck a pectoral of seven layers of gold and jewels. He holds the Crook and the Flail, symbols of his authority. You make the invocation.)

Osiris, Lord of the World Unseen, and of life reborn, father of the sun hawk and the jackal, hear me, grant to this place and those within your protection against all evil. Seal the Gate of the East in the name of the mysteries of Egypt that we may work in peace and harmony.

(Osiris rises from his throne and strikes the ground with the flail, a sound like a great chord struck upon a harp hits the ear and there appears another flat white stone, the second seal of the East. In the name of the Egyptian mysteries make your thanks.)

My thanks for your favour Lord of Amenti. May there be peace and harmony between us. Be welcome in this place.

(The figure inclines its head and there is a swirling of sand that hides all from view, when it clears the figure has gone.)

(Turn the star with the green point upward now, and this time when you return to your place, you build up in the Gateway the green hill of Glastonbury Tor. Coming down from its grassy summit is a figure dressed in a dark green robe and carrying a staff topped with a carved dragon. Merlin the Archmage of the Blessed Isles comes to add the seal of the Celtic mysteries. You begin the invocation:)

Merlin, priest of ancient Atlantis, keeper of the Great Seal of the Pendragon, hereditary Mage of Grammarye, hear and grant our request. Place upon this Gateway the Seal of the Pendragon that all may be made safe, and the Work go forward in safety.

(Merlin raises his staff on high and brings it down hard on the earth beside the other two Seals. The sound of a deep toned gong is heard and there appears the third Seal on the Eastern Gate. Make your thanks.)

All honour to thee Mage of Britain, and gratitude for this favour, may there be peace between us. Be welcome in this place.

(Merlin salutes with upraised staff, then turns and climbs the Tor, fading into the distance.)

(Turn the star with the violet point upmost. Now the Gateway shows a shimmering haze of amber and rose. It parts like a curtain and standing before you is Raphael, Archangel of the East. He holds a spear of light in his right hand and the scent of wild flowers fills the temple. Speak:)

Raphael, healing angel of the East, regent of the Element of Air and guardian of the Lance of Longinus, place your Seal upon this Gateway that it may prove a bastion of safety for those who work within.

(Raphael turns the spear and thrusts

it into the ground, A trumpet call rings out and the fourth stone seal appears. Give thanks.)

Be forever blessed Raphael angel of the Presence. Our thanks to thee for this favour. Let there be peace between us. You are welcome in this place.

(Raphael lifts the Lance in farewell and fades from our sight.)

(Turn the star till the red point is topmost. The Gateway shows a shimmering rainbow bridge. Riding over it on a great grey horse comes the Godking of the Norsemen, Odin. His horse is named Sleipnir and has eight legs. In his hand, Odin carries a magnificent sword and with this he salutes. Make your request:)

Odin, god of the one eye that sees all things, Lord of Valhalla, all father. Set your Seal upon this Gate that it be made safe against the strongest foe.

(Odin plunges his sword into the ground and gives a mighty warcry that echoes through your head. The final Seal comes into being. Give thanks:)

Mighty hero of Ragnarok, thy Seal is set and accepted. Let there be peace between us. Be welcome here.

(Odin lifts his sword and wheels the great horse and rides over the rainbow bridge.)

Your seals are now set in five of the great traditions, Greek, Egyptian, Celtic, Judaic/Christian, and Norse. Now place the phials in the bag and tie it tightly, place it against the wall and tape if firmly there. Step back facing the East and say;

I invoke the protection of the Four Elements for the Eastern Gate. Let

Earth, Water, Fire and Air combine to form the Shield of the East So mote it be.

The East is now sealed.

Sealing the Southern Gate

Wait a few days, then begin the Seals for the South. Write on the golden point the name Hephasteus, on the blue point Sekmet, on the green Bran, on the violet Michael, and on the red Thor.

(Pin the star as before, with the golden point upwards. Face the South and build up the figure of Hephasteus the armourer of Olympus, son of Zeus and Hera. Behind him glows the fire of the forge and in his hand is a mighty hammer. Request the Seal.)

Great son of Zeus, mighty in thy power, set the Seal upon the Gate of the South that it be made fast against all comers.

(Hephasteus lifts the hammer and brings it down hard, a sharp crack is heard, and beneath the hammer a white stone shines, the first seal is set. Give your thanks.)

My thanks for this great Hephasteus. Peace be between us. Be welcome here always.

(The Smith waves farewell and disappears into the smoke of the forge.)

Turn the star to the blue point and return to face the South. A hot dry desert grows upon the inner eye, and from the dunes comes the slender figure of a woman, lion-headed Sekmet. Request her Seal.

Sekmet of the Lion's Head, avenger of Ra, mighty in thy strength, make fast this place against mine enemies I pray thee.

(The Goddess gives a mighty roar, then bends down and with a claw scores a deep line in the sand, under it a white stone gleams. The seal is yours, give thanks.)

For this favour thanks are given. Peace be between thee and me. Be welcome in this place.

(A golden paw is raised in farewell and the goddess returns to the desert.)
Turn the star to the green point and take your place. Beyond the Gate you see a mighty figure, taller than a mountain pine, with golden hair and beard, it is Bran the Mighty hero of heroes. Ask for the Seal.)

Bran of the Golden Head, King of the Islands of the Blessed, Grant us thy Seal of safety upon this place that our Work may be undisturbed.

(Bran gives a great laugh and the enormous hand reaches down to place a white stone alongside the others, the seal is set. Give thanks.)

The gift is accepted with love and thanks. Peace be between us. Be welcome here great Bran.

(Turn the star to the violet point, and take your place. Out of a glowing red sun comes the figure of a young man dressed in golden armour. He bears a sword of living flame. Michael the warrior Archangel comes.)

Michael, angel guardian of the Southern Gate, who stands before the throne of the Mighty One, give the Angelic Seal to this place that we may work in peace and harmony.

(The sword flames along the ground, the Seal emerges and a chord of music swells from behind Michael like a mighty organ. Give thanks.)

For this our thanks, be blessed among your peers. Peace be between us. Be welcome here.

(The sword is lifted in salute and the figure returns into the sun.)

(Turn the point of the star to red, then take your place. From fire lit halls comes the giant god Thor. From his wrist hangs his magical hammer Moljnir. He stands at the Southern Gate looking down on the temple.)

Mighty Thor, God of Thunder, striker of the ice giants, grant us thy protection son of Odin, that our work may prosper.

(The hammer is swung in a blinding arc of light and the sound of it is like the howl of northern winds. The fifth stone emerges and the seal is set. Thor growls like a great bear and accepts the thanks.)

May your strength never fail mighty Thor. Peace be between us. Be welcome here.

(The Southern Seals are now set, put the phials for the South in the bag and place it by the wall and invoke the four Elements.)

I invoke the protection of the four elements for the Southern Gate let Earth, Water, Fire, and Air combine to make the shield of the South. So mote it be.

This completes the Southern Seals.

Sealing the Western Gate

After a few days commence the sealing of the Western Gate by writing the names on the Star. On the golden point write Artemis, on the blue write Isis, on the green write Arianrhod, on the violet Gabriel, and on the red,

Freya. Place the star, golden point up, then take your place facing the Western Gate. Build up the scene of a night sky with a Full Moon, from behind the clouds comes Artemis the Huntress ready to give her Seal.

Artemis, night's slender daughter, ruler of the starlit forest of the night, grant thy Seal and protect us with the arrows of the Moon.

(The silver goddess shoots an arrow into the ground before the Gate and the first stone is placed. She shoots another that makes a singing sound as it carries her away. We send our thanks winging after her.)

Our thanks to thee sweet goddess. Peace reign between us. Be welcome here.

(Turn the star to the blue point. This time from the starry blackness comes a vision of loveliness that outshines all else. Isis in all her beauty comes to the Western Gate. Make your request.)

Silver footed Isis, daughter of Nuit, ruler of the tides of life grant us thy Seal that we may rest under thy hand in safety.

(The goddess takes a hair from her head and draws it across the Gate. It makes the sound of wind harps, and the Seal appears in response to the sound. She smiles and blesses the temple before her.)

Great one, mother of all living, be one with us. Be welcome here.

(The goddess returns to the starry sky and the star is turned to the green point. Now the scene is that of a moonlit shore where stands a silver castle. From its door there comes a young woman dressed in green and silver. Arianrhod, lady of the Moon approaches.)

Silver wheel in the night sky, daughter of beauty and joy, halt thy night's journey and grant to us thy Seal.

(Arianrhod takes a star from her sleeve and places it on the earth where it becomes the third Seal. Behind her we hear the sound of the conch shell horn calling her back into the castle.)

Our thanks sweet lady for thy help. Peace be between us. Be welcome here.

(Now the violet point. The scene beyond the Gate shows a waterfall, it has a sound like singing voices. From within the fall comes a tall figure wrapped in a cloak of indigo blue. Great dark eyes look upon us. The cloak is thrown back and we see not a cloak but great violet wings that stretch across the sky. Gabriel waits for our request.)

Gabriel of the Annunciation, bringer of joy to mankind, voice of the one beyond all gods, grant to this place thy Seal that we may work in peace and love.

(A single glossy feather floats down and becomes the fourth Seal and our thanks follow the Archangel back within the waterfall.)

To thee our thanks. Be blessed among thy peers. Peace lie between us. Thou art welcome here.

(Turn the star to the final point, and build up the figure of a woman dressed in red and crowned with flowers, she carries in her hand a horn filled with wine. This is Freya the Beautiful giver of love and joy.)

Goddess of love and joy draw near and grant this request, that you will grant your Seal upon this place and make it one of joy and song.

(Freya tips the wine from the horn and it washes the earth from the final stone. Then singing, she returns to the mountains she loves.)

Lady of joy receive our thanks. Peace be between us. Be welcome here.

(Now the Seals of the West are set in place. Put the phials into the bag and put it in the West and invoke the four quarters as before.)

I invoke the protection of the four elements for the Western Gate. Let Earth, Water, Fire, and Air combine to form the shield of the West. So mote it be.

Sealing the Northern Gate

The Seals of the West being completed, wait a few days and then seal the North in the same way. On the golden point write the name Demeter, on the blue point, Anubis, on the green Ceridwen, on the violet write Uriel, and on the red, Baldur.

(Place the star as before with the golden point uppermost then sit facing the North. Build up a mountain-side covered in flowers, feel a warm breeze blowing in your face. Coming down the mountain path is a woman of mature beauty, her arms are full of flowers and the full, nodding heads of yellow corn. Invoke the Seal.)

Goddess of the Cornfields, lady of the harvest, graceful Demeter of Olympus, grant the favour asked of you, set thy Seal upon this Gate that we may work in safety.

(The Goddess throws down an ear of corn and it becomes the first stone Seal of the North. A bird flutters down to perch on her hand, singing with a full heart.)

Lady of the wheatsheaves we thank thee for this gift. Peace be between us. Be welcome in this place.

(Turn the star to the blue point and return to your seat. The Gate shows an ancient temple of red stone. On a simple throne sits the figure of a man with the head of a jackal. Anubis son of Osiris waits. In his hand he holds a golden ankh. Ask for the Seal.)

Anubis, guardian of the great mother, lord of the two worlds, place thy Seal upon this temple that we may serve and worship without fear.

(The god rises and comes to the Gate and lays the ankh down at his feet, it melts into the second Seal of the North. Then he returns to his throne.)

Lord of light and darkness, conductor of souls, for this gift many thanks. Peace be between us. Be welcome always.

(Now it is the turn of the green point. When you are seated again build up an ancient stone circle on a grassy slope. From between the stones comes a woman of the Celts bearing a small cauldron in her hands. Ask for the Seal.)

Ceridwen, Earth goddess, keeper of the sacred cauldron and giver of wisdom, place the third Seal at the Gate of the North if it please you.

(The goddess tips the cauldron and the wine of wisdom flows over the gateway washing the earth away from the third Seal, then she returns to the stone circle.)

Our love and thanks Ceridwen of the Hills. Peace be between us. Thou art welcome here.

(Now it is the turn of the violet point. The scene shows a rocky point above a green and fertile country. Looking out over the fields and woods is a tall dark figure in a cloak of deep green. Uriel the Archangel of the planet Earth turns to us.)

Uriel, Angel of Terra, giver of bread to the hungry, comforter of the wounded animal, sharer of Earth's tears, place thy Seal upon this place that we may work with thee in tranquillity.

(The Archangel takes a ring from his finger and places it by the other Seals. It becomes a white stone sealing the angelic tradition of the North. We offer thanks.)

For the grace and favour our thanks. Peace be between us. Be welcome here.

(Now the last point, and we see a young man in a dark red tunic, his fair hair is bound with a silver band and he holds a branch of mistletoe in his hand. Baldur the beautiful waits to place the last Seal.)

Baldur beloved son of Odin, grant to us the final Seal of the North that this temple may be enclosed in love safety and power.

(The young God places the branch by the other stones and it becomes the final Seal.)

All is now sealed against evil. To thee Baldur our thanks. Peace be between us. Thou art welcome in this place.

(Place the phials in the North as before and invoke the Elements.)

I invoke the protection of the four Elements for the Northern Gate. Let Earth, Water, Fire, and Air combine to form the shield of the North. So mote it be.

Now your temple is sealed on the first level, the second level sealing can be carried out during the last week of this month's work and will consist of the invocations to the Four Holy Creatures. The third and final sealing will be done during the consecration of the temple. You have done well, this work was of necessity, magic of quite a high level. Place the third knot in your girdle.

If you are worried about your ability to build up images there is a very helpful book that will show you exactly how to go about it. Written by Andrew Highfield its title is *The Book of Celestial Images*, published by the Aquarian Press. This will describe the angelic and God-form images that are used in ritual magic, and will be a valuable reference book for your future work.

Making the Robe

Much of this month's temple work is preparation for the final consecration next month. You are now a third of the way through your year's course and have coped with quite a lot of ritual work already. For some light relief let's turn to the making of your robe, the real one that you will wear for the consecration and for all future ritual work.

Colour plays a big part in magic so choose carefully. Black or white are perennial favourites and are always a good safe choice. However you might like to consider some other colours. A deep violet worn with a silver or gold cord offers an alternative. Violet reflects the influence of both Yesod and Daath on the Tree of Life, both are concerned with knowledge and creativity. Blue is also a good choice but it should be a deep jewel shade, perhaps worn with a white or lavender cord. If you are particularly involved with the Nature aspect of magic then a green robe with a deep yellow or amber cord will harmonize your Ray colour with your surroundings. Take your time in choosing a colour, you must feel happy in it.

Weight of cloth will depend on how well heated your temple will be. Thin wool, silk, linen, or cotton are all suitable, but not polyester for some reason it tends to negate the use of power in a temple — perhaps due to its tendency to build up static electricity. Later on you will probably have two or three different robes and then you can vary colour and weight. It is also a good idea to make a heavy ankle length cloak with a hood for outdoor work. With this you will also need a pair of good quality black training shoes. For indoor temple work a pair of thin travelling slippers, the kind that fold up flat in a case, are ideal.

The cord should be of good quality with a fairly heavy tassle at each end. If you can afford just the one robe, then you might like to ring the changes with different coloured tabards (see Figure 20). These can be made in the four colours of the quarters and used accordingly.

Some magicians wear a Lamen, this is a symbol worn about the neck and resting on the breast. It can be made of metal, precious or otherwise, or drawn on heavy card and coloured in, or even made with felts. The multicoloured Rose Cross used by the Golden Dawn is quite easily made in coloured felts sewn or glued to a backing of buckram or interlining. Against the darker shade of the robe it stands out very well. Making it will be an excellent lesson on the Hebrew alphabet and elemental symbols.

Meditating on the Archangels and Four Holy Creatures

On the days between the Sealing of the Quarters, you will meditate on the Archangels of those Quarters, and the Four Holy Creatures assigned to them. When working with the angelic beings, sit with your chair backed on to the

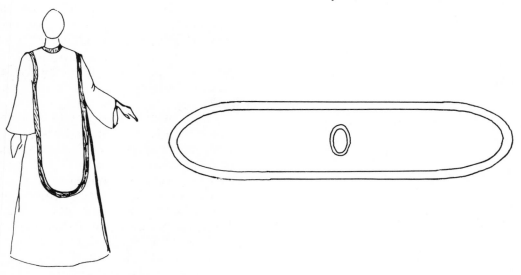

Figure 20 The Tabard

Quarter looking towards the altar. When meditating on the Holy Creatures place your chair with its back to the altar and look into the Quarter.

Start with the East. Build up the figure of Raphael standing behind you. Work on it until you can 'feel' the presence breathing down the back of your neck. When you have it steady, start the meditation. Go over in your mind all that you know about Raphael. (It goes without saying that a little homework beforehand helps the meditation along. Ask your library to get you a copy of *A Dictionary of Angels* by Gustave Davidson. This is a delightful compendium containing the names and attributes of every angel ever mentioned in any book, an angelic *tour de force*.)

Do the same with Michael in the South, Gabriel in the West, and Uriel in the North. Incidently, according to Davidson, Uriel is the tallest angel in heaven, he can stand with his feet on the earth and still sing his Hosannas in the presence of God! He is also the angel with the sharpest sight and is reputed to be able to see anything or anyone anywhere from the steps of the Throne of Heaven.

A few years ago I wrote a book called *The Shining Paths*. It is a collection of pathworkings for the Tree of Life. In it you will find a description of all the angels of the Tree, plus instructions for getting closer to them on a one-to-one basis. It also describes the temples of the Tree in detail. You can use the 'Experience of Tiphereth' for the East and Raphael, the 'Experience of Hod' for the South and Michael, the 'Experience of Yesod' for the West and Gabriel, and the 'Experience of Malkuth' for the North. This can be done instead of the meditation, or as part of the meditation.

When meditating on the Four Holy Creatures, first look for pictures of an Eagle, Ox, Lion and Man, in the case of the latter a picture of either St John the Baptist, or St John the Divine is a good choice, but if your prefer to make your own choice do so. Using your creative eye, build up in each Quarter a circular window with the appropriate creature within it, as described in *The Shining Paths*. Fix the image firmly, then change the figure from a painted one into a real one. This will take a while to accomplish but persevere. Once you can get this changeover, you can then hold an internal conversation with the Holy Creature of the Quarter. The feedback obtained in this form of meditation can be of great value to your future progress. You can try this technique with the Archangels as well.

The Ritual of the Second Seals

When you have completed the meditations on the Four Quarters, you can begin the Ritual of the Second Sealing. Set your altar with the Light and your magical implements, if you do not have all of them, improvise with a wine glass, a paper knife, a pantacle cut out of paper, and a twig of oak or ash. Alternatively you can use the four Aces of a pack of Tarot cards. One of magic's many maxims states, 'INTENTION is everything'.

Take up the Rod and approach the East, bow slightly and raise the rod above your head, then with it trace the Banishing Pentagram as given on page 247.

Winged creature of the East, guardian of the higher portals of the dawn, Seal this sacred place against all evil and open it to the highest concept of wisdom.

(Place the rod across the Eastern Gate and leave it there, step back, bow, then turn and collect the

Sword and approach the South. Raise the Sword above your head, then make the Banishing Pentagram as before.

Winged creature of the South, guardian of the higher portals of the noonday Sun, Seal this sacred place against all evil and open it to the highest concept of service.

Place the Sword across the Southern Gate and leave it there. Take the Cup and approach the West. Lift the Cup, then make the same Pentagram as before.)

Winged creature of the West, guardian of the higher portals of the setting Sun, Seal this place against all evil and open it to the highest concept of Understanding.

(Leave the Cup in the West and go to the North with the Pantacle. Lift it up, then make the Banishing Pentagram.)

Winged creature of the North, guardian of the higher portals of the midnight Sun, Seal this place against all evil and open it to the highest concept of Compassion.

(Leave the Pantacle in the North and return to the altar. Lift the Light and salute the four Quarters with it. Leave the Light burning for a few hours, and the implements where they are all night. This ends the Second Sealing of the Temple.)

Self Work

Choosing a Magical Name

Amongst Qabalists this tends to be a phrase rather than an actual name, the Golden Dawn magicians provide a good example of such names. Usually the phrase is one of aspiration, 'For the Greater God', 'I will Serve', etc. This is alright as far as it goes, but there is a tendency for it to become a little overdone. For you, working alone, or at best with two or three friends, a proper name is better. Such a name can be drawn from legend, mythology, scriptures, any sacred text, or simply a name that you like personally. Once chosen you give it to no one, not even your nearest and dearest. To give the name to another person, especially another magician, is a mark of the highest trust, for you can be summoned by it, even against your will. Use just the first letter, and become Frater, or Soror X. This name is used in all temple work. When doing solo ritual work you can use your name to summon, invoke, or command. But first it has to have weight...this only comes by the quality of your work. In the everyday world a name earns recognition by a person's ability, talent or position. A magical name is no different.

Take your time and look into the meaning of the name you are thinking of taking. Meditate on it, mull it over, try it for size. You will probably need to change it after a year or so, one grows out of magical names sometimes. If you are wise you will *not* use a name that has already been linked with another magician, a good example of what not to use would be 'Perdurabo' one of Aleister Crowley's pseudonyms.

Take some time to be by yourself during this month, soon it will be time for the consecration and afterwards both you and the temple will be committed to the service of the Inner Plane Adepti. They have strict ideas about how those entering their service should conduct themselves. Your life will soon be changing in many ways, not all of them expected. A magician's life is never dull; hectic, busy, eventful, but never dull.

The Threefold Law of Ritual

Magic and ritual are often confused, but they are not at all the same thing. Magic involves being able to alter or influence the existing status quo through a shift in personal consciousness. Ritual is a means by which man may contact energies and forces that are otherwise beyond his comprehension. They can of course be combined, but in their natural state they are two very different aspects of occult science.

By following the instructions of this book you are learning to apply your natural but hitherto unused mental powers in a magical way. You do not need a ritual or a temple to do this, you can work magic in the middle of Waterloo station in the rush hour, no one would be any the wiser. No movement is necessary, no invocations, no Quarter images, nothing except a trained and disciplined mind.

But mankind has a built-in barrier about what can be achieved through his own mental capacity, so when there is a need to go further than this barrier allows, he enlists the aid of the 'Gods'. This is done through the use of ritual. Ninety per cent of the time the Gods so invoked are aspects of the magician's own higher and far more capable self. This is not to decry their efforts, what they are doing is sliding under the mental barrier by tricking their conscious mind into believing that something, or someone, else is doing the work, i.e. the 'Gods'.

Does this mean that these Gods do not exist? Far from it, they most certainly do exist but in forms and dimensions that we cannot comprehend. Just keep in mind that all the Gods are emanations of a Primal Creative Energy Pattern that is sometimes simply called, God. But what that Primal Energy is, or looks like, or how it behaves, we simply do not know, nor can we ever know at this stage of man's evolution.

Over countless thousands of years man has used his imagination to create 'forms' to account for his fears, joys, hopes, and troubles. It was thus that the Gods came into being, drawn from the Primal Unmanifested God by mankind's overwhelming emotional need for something nearer to his own form, something that he could give a name to, could identify with, and to which he could offer his worship (and blame for his own waywardness). Because these forms emanated from the Primal God they contained enough raw energy, undiluted by a physical body, to wield great power. Man fed this power by his worship, thus creating a circuit of force. And because man fed in both good and evil from his own make-up, the Gods also became differentiated into good and evil forces over the centuries.

A rare few of mankind evolved faster than others, and over long periods of time have attained what we call Adepthood, or Mastership. Such Masters, like the Gods, can be contacted through ritual. If progress is maintained and the magician strives to perfect himself on all levels there comes a time during a ritual when one of these Higher Beings makes a personal contact with him, working with and through him. It is a melding process, brief in time, but eternal in effect. This is the *true* meaning of the occult term, 'Assumption of the God-form'.

You will understand from this explanation that ritual is far from being the magical version of charades that some deem it to be. There are three categories of ritual, and you will no doubt be trying all of them. There are rituals for improving oneself mentally, spiritually, and physically. Rituals for obtaining things, and rituals for causing effects. There is one other form, and I will explain that last of all.

Rituals for obtaining things are the most popular, with those for causing effects running a close second. Self-improvement rituals come a poor third, mainly because they take a long time to manifest on this level and they take a lot of hard work. It also requires a lot of self knowledge to admit that you *need* improving. Although you have been thrown in at the deep end as regards ritual, you must understand that it is an art and requires years of work to perfect.

It also requires a general knowledge of encyclopaedian proportions involving some very unlikely sources. Learn to store away odd bits of information about anything at all. But even with this you will need to apply the threefold Law of Ritual; Method, Motive and Meaning. Let's take Motive first.

Motive

A ritual must have a motive or it becomes meaningless. Motive means simply, 'why are you doing this ritual'? Ideally it is because something good will come out of it, but magicians are human and very often the reason is less than altruistic. Let us link Motive to the three catagories of ritual and see how they can shed light on each other.

Self-improvement: What kind of improvement are you looking for? A better memory, more will power, control of a bad habit, or a bad temper, help with an exam or an important job interview? This type of ritual takes in everything from an aid to further study, to a cure for biting your nails. But what we need to know is *why*? For this you need to be painfully honest

with yourself, a good subject for a ritual of this type anyway. Is it so that you can chalk up one more ritual than a fellow magician, so you can boast, even to yourself, how good a magician you are, or do you honestly think you need this ritual? And will it *be* an improvement? It might help you, but will it make you harder to live with, or will it cause a gap between you and your family?

What about your motives in a ritual for obtaining things? A rare book for instance. Do you really need it, or do you want it on your shelves as a talking point? A bigger house or car, again, is it really necessary, or are you saying, 'look what I have, and I got it by ritual'? When you call something to you by ritual means, it has to come from somewhere, it *does not appear out of nothing*. It will therefore leave a gap somewhere that must be filled. Someone might have just the thing you are looking for, and might hold it dear, a book, a painting, a piece of period furniture, a house in a particular location, all these may be owned already, loved, and treasured by someone else. For you to obtain it, circumstances must arise that will force them into giving them up. It may be an heirloom passed from generation to generation and you come along and ritually 'steal' it.

Like all power, ritual is neither good nor evil of itself, but takes colour from those who perform it. The motive adds the plus or minus even when it is done in good faith. The only way to avoid causing pain and distress is to state clearly in the ritual the intention that the object should come to you without causing hurt or hinderance to another person.

If the ritual is done to obtain the affections of another person you are treading on dangerous ground. Ethics in the magical arts are of great importance and never more so than in ritual. That person may have been intended for someone else, if you override fragile destiny with your ritual, and it can be done, you stand a chance of interfering with history. Children that should have been born, that have been planned for hundreds of years may not see the light, and vice versa. It can cause a situation whereby you, or another person, may not be in the right place at the right time to aid or prevent an important event.

What about causing effect on the environment. A simple ritual to ensure a sunny day on your birthday may mean the sunshine that would have enabled a farmer to cut his hay or gather in the wheat is diverted and the resulting 'hole' filled in with rain that could cause financial ruin.

Wishing and cursing rituals come under this heading and you should be fully aware of the consequences of such a thing. A curse thrown ritually in a moment of high emotion can last for centuries causing great harm to innocent people as yet unborn. It can also have the effect of holding the thrower of such a curse within the astral orbit of the planet for the same length of time. Motives for any ritual must be examined well before going ahead. Sometimes there is a case for not doing the ritual at all and letting events happen as they were intended to happen. If you read Ursula Le Guin's beautiful triology *The Wizard of Earthsea* you will see how the hero Ged, finds this out as a final truth. There is no need for causing effects via ritual when there is no *outstanding* need for them. The real fact is this, ritual is rarely needed anyway!

Method

If you are committed to one tradition you will almost certainly have set rituals for certain purposes and will choose that which is closest to your needs, or adapt it to your ritual purpose. You will probably have a set opening and closing but the important 'intention' of the ritual will have been carefully screened and the correct incenses, robes, and colours chosen to enhance the effect. If the motive is self-improvement the intention area of the ritual must be balanced between the positivity of calling on the God or Archangel concerned with what you are seeking, and the passivity that will allow the result of the ritual to penetrate your levels of being starting with the highest and earthing itself in the physical. When you seek the improvement of a skill or ability, or anything to be used on the physical level, you *must* start at the highest point first and saturate each level in turn with the power you are invoking. You cannot absorb it only on the physical/astral levels and expect it to last.

When a ritual is designed for effects, seven times out of ten you will at some point be dealing with the elemental world. Here you *must always* work with the Elemental Kings first, and then work down to the sylphs, salamanders, etc. By doing so you safeguard the ritual and yourself. Method and Motive when dealing with elementals must be watertight. Murphy's Law of 'if anything *can* go wrong, it will', was probably thought up by a failed elemental magician! Once this world of water sprites and fire spirits *et al*, come to accept you, a lot of natural energy and ability will be yours, but you have to earn it the hard way, and always use it with caution. Like fairy gold the gifts of the elemental world can be short lived.

When working a ritual to obtain something on the physical level your methods must provide an opening for it to *reach* you on the physical level. You are mistaken if you think it will appear with no further effort on your part. The ritual is just the first step in a chain of events. The first rule is to sit down and write out in minute detail what it is you require. And I *mean* minute detail, otherwise you can be in deep trouble. If you want a couple of goldfish in a bowl, specify, *live* goldfish, two of, complete with bowl, *and* water in the bowl please. *That* specific. It is also a good idea to put a time limit on the arrival of the object. I know a lady who asked for a coat as her old one was threadbare. Within twenty-four hours she had half a dozen and they kept coming. The trouble was they were all old and outworn coats, she had not specified a *new* coat.

Ritual sets the energy in motion, you must provide openings for its arrival. Perhaps you want a particular book now out of print, or a piece of ritual jewellery with a certain semiprecious stone. Once the ritual has been performed, start looking, look in jumble sales, auction sales, second-hand shops, Oxfam, street markets, anywhere you think you might have a chance of picking up your object. Place an advert in your local paper, you would be surprised what that can bring.

If you need money, buy a lottery ticket, or a premium bond, that may seem silly spending out money when you need it coming in, but like attracts like and you are opening a gate for the money to come to you. You may come into a small legacy, or someone may ask you to do them a service and will pay you the required amount. Very often when requesting money you will find it needs to be earned, a fact which may disappoint many new magicians, but one you must get used to, you get nothing free... even in magic.

I repeat do not close doors — raffle tickets, competitions, beauty contests, try anything and your money will come in. If by any chance you need something quickly and there is no time or possibility for a ritual, there is something else you can try. You might put an advert in the *Inner Plane Gazette*. Sounds daft? Maybe. Childish? Yes, but children are the world's best magicians. It is simply a means of concentrating your creative visualization techniques. See in your mind's eye the front page of a tabloid clearly marked the *Inner Plane Gazette*. Take a few minutes to build up the image as clearly as you can. See your hand turning the pages to the one you need, 'Wants'. Now see your 'ad' among the others, read it to yourself making sure that it specifies exactly what you want, add the time limit, 'within seven days' or whatever, and your name and address. Now do it again but instead of reading words, see pictures of yourself with the object you need in your hand or on the ground in front of you. You are looking happy, and you are standing in front of your present house. This fixes the image on the astral levels. It works according to your ability to 'see'.

This can also be used in reverse, remember there is no real time on the Inner Levels, so you can have a copy of the *Inner Level Gazette*, or the *Daily Astral* several days ahead... you may even get a glimpse of some forthcoming event one day! All this may seem silly, but it is not always the spectacular rituals that get the best results. The kind of magic you have just learnt about dates back in an unbroken line to the cave paintings of primitive man. You want a new car or a gold watch, he wanted bison for food and clothing, he got what he wanted by painting pictures on the walls of a cave, you can get it by painting pictures on your mental screen.

Meaning

The last part of the Threefold Law is meaning. All rituals have meanings on many levels and it is part of your training once the ritual is finshed to go over it in your memory to seek out and align those meanings. Plus of course you must keep a record of each and every ritual — how it was done, what the intention was, how it went and the results over the next twenty-eight days. Often you will find that the obvious meaning gives way to another below the surface, much deeper and richer in scope. All this happens in the days and weeks after a a successful ritual. Again it depends on the Threefold Law. Self-improvement may bring you the knowledge that what you asked for was not what you needed. Then the ritual will self adjust to bring you the right thing at the right time, because you placed yourself in the way of self-improvement. Causing effect via ritual can give you a great deal of insight into inner meanings, because those effects tend to go on and on.

Now I must mention one last type of ritual, the best and the purest of all. This is the ritual that is offered simply as praise or worship of whatever deity you serve. They are expressions of love and trust and joy. They share without demanding, offer without expectation of reward. Such were the first rituals man ever worked, whatever else you may do along magical lines, do not neglect these things, they will in the end give you the greatest of gifts, peace of mind and contentment with what the gods offer.

Behaviour in Lodge

Behaviour in Lodge, is a term that in a Mystery School holds much meaning. Just because you are undergoing a much shortened version of training does not mean that the finer points of ritual work can be dismissed. It does not matter if you are, at present, the only one working in your temple, or if you are working with friends, your main concern at all times should be the spiritual cleanliness of your sacred place. This means that your work, your attitude, your behaviour within these walls must be dignifed, honourable and without ulterior motive.

Move quietly and with grace, the voice should be firm, but not strident (we will go into the use of voice more deeply later on), if you make a gesture it should be decisive, not half-hearted. Do not chatter about trivialities once you have entered, all should have been arranged beforehand. Do not make remarks about your fellow officers, watch and learn. If you are angered, do not enter the temple until you have calmed down. Make this place one of utter peace so that if one day you need its strength and help it will be ready to fill you with its peace.

Be courteous in your dealings with the beings of other dimensions, good manners count for as much on other levels of existence as they do on your own. Never forget to offer thanks to those who have worked with you unseen. This includes the temple guardian and the overall aspect of deity or the teacher who presides over your temple. Keep the temple clean, keep your robes and any other vestments clean and sweet. Never enter in your outdoor shoes, clean the silver, linen and glass regularly. Bathe before a ritual. Try to keep flowers in your temple at all times, preferably growing in a small pot rather than cut. Clean the chalice immediately after the ritual if you use it for wine. Don't throw any wine or wafer away just anywhere. Pour leftover wine onto the garden, give the bread or wafer to the birds, it has all been blessed and the Earth and the birds will share in that blessing.

As you come up to the consecration slow down a little and spend some time in the temple, just sitting, not meditating but letting your mind fill and be filled with the wonder of it all. As you sew your robe think about the years ahead of you and the work you will be doing, the vibrations will be sewn into the fabric as you work. Go over your records for the year so far, see how you have changed and improved, look at your everyday life and see if that has changed at all. Finally, seek out a sacred place within reasonable distance to you. It might be a stone circle, or an old Roman fort, a well, a standing stone or menhir, a hill topped with a ring of trees, or just one very old oak tree. It could be the Lady chapel of a pre-reformation church. Make it a little pilgrimage. Walk at least part of the way, enough to make you tired but not exhausted. Take a small offering with you, flowers for the Lady chapel, a silver coin for the stone circle or standing stones, a wreath of ivy and wild flowers for the oak tree, or light a small fire on the site of the fort (taking care that you comply with the laws on the lighting of fires.)

Call on your temple deity, and the guardian, invite them to be with you in this place, link all three of you with the Earth Mother as a living entity. Offer Her a place in your temple, that she may have a voice there. As a token of your new oneness with the planetary being, cut off a lock of your hair and bury it. Then take a spoonful of earth with you when you go, and place it under the carpet by the door of the temple. This will bring the whole Earth Force into your temple and make those within constantly aware of that presence.

Robing Prayers

Robing prayers are not often used in the temple these days, but they provide a link with the past and are nice to use if you so wish. Each item has its own prayer, and although you will not be using all the ritual wear, it is a good idea to have them for future reference.

The Inner Robe

This is always white, made of thin silk and loosely cut. It symbolises the Higher Self. You could keep a set of white underwear for temple use and this could take the place of the inner robe.

In purity of heart and simplicity of spirit I take this(these) garment(s) upon myself. As they enclose me so may my own Higher Self enclose my physical self and both become one during this rite.

The Outer Robe

This is the robe you are now making and which you will use in your temple. It can be in any colour and is worn with a girdle of the same or contrasting colour.

Thus is my Higher Self concealed, hidden away from prying eyes, as this robe encloses and conceals the sacred part of me. So too does the temple enclose and conceal the adytum, thus the temple and the outer robe are one.

The Cloak

The cloak is the protection of that which it hides. It is synonymous with the male aspect, covering the sacred female aspect of the inner and outer robes.

Be this my protection against all that may come upon me. I shall cast my cloak about the defenceless ones to give them warmth and succour.

The Girdle

The girdle is a female symbol as it encloses or contains. It represents the sacred zone bound about with spiritual protection.

I cast about me this sacred circle that nothing evil may enter the temple of my body. With this girdle I bind evil to its own domain. With this girdle I help the weary to climb the mountain of attainment. This is my zodiac, my belt of stars, symbol of my priesthood.

The Slippers

The slippers symbolize understanding, they carry the initiate over the rainbow bridge and between the worlds. With these upon annointed feet, the priest crosses the Abyss.

The gods have annointed my feet with oil and they shall be shod with understanding. Thus I will traverse the bridge between the worlds. The silver slippers of the Moon and the golden slippers of the Sun are mine, I shall walk in light with joy, and in darkness without fear.

The Headdress

This represents the spiritual crown of Kether, the first point of manifestation. Understandable because it is usually the first part of the body to be born. At the moment of birth a child is crowned by the pelvic girdle. If you could see this from the right perspective, you would see the child crowned as if with antler horns. Just one of many reasons for the Horned Lord of the Craft to be seen as the giver of fertility.

The head of the priest and the head of the king shall be covered, so saith the old laws. This is the point of entry of the spirit at birth and its departure at death. Concealed and protected, the sacred head is not defiled.

The Ring

We have already spoken of the Magical Ring and its symbolism. It is put on last of all and at that time the full Magical Personality is assumed.

Now do I call upon .... (Magical name) to come forth and take the place alloted. This symbol of my power I place in the service of ....(temple deity).

Learn these prayers, those that you wish to use, by heart and use them regularly.

Choosing Music for the Consecration

You should now choose some music for your consecration ceremony, if you are working with the Qabalah, then select a tape of Gregorian chant. This played very softly will add dimension to the smallest temple, If you would like something along more pagan lines I suggest anything of George Zamfir's pan pipe music would be best. Neptune or Uranus from Holst's 'Planet Suite' can be effective. My own favourite for such rituals is a recording by the Zemal Choir of 'I will Arise and go into the House of the Lord'. This is an old record and I am not sure it can still be obtained. The Zemel is a Jewish choir and the other pieces on the record are all ideal for temple work.

Reading List

Ashcroft-Nowicki, Dolores, *The Shining Paths* (Aquarian Press, 1983)

Davidson, Gustave, *A Dictionary of Angels* (Macmillan, 1967)

Highfield, Andrew, *The Book of Celestial Images* (Aquarian Press, 1984)

Matthews, John, *At the Table of the Grail* (Routledge, Kegan Paul, 1984)

Matthews, John, *The Grail, Quest for the Eternal* (Thames and Hudson, 1982)

Samuel and Samuel, *Seeing With the Mind's Eye* (Random House Books, 1975)

The Fifth Month

The Vigil and the Consecration

Date started ....

There is no longer any need to split the month into temple work and self work. From now on each month will take you into areas of knowledge that will be important to you in future work. Rituals for the seasons and the other important feasts of the year must be worked, written, and set down in a special book. You will also be starting to work with the Magical Mirror in the next few months, so start looking for something suitable. Contrary to some beliefs it does not have to be black. Look for one about 18–20 inches (45–50cm) long, oval or round for preference, and with a thin frame all around, do not choose one with just a bevelled edge. Best if you can buy a new one, if not find an old one *but* stand it 'face to face' with another mirror right through a lunar tide if possible before you use it. One mirror will draw out the 'stale' reflections from the other. Identify the cleaning mirror with a piece of ribbon, that is all the intention you need to start the process.

Setting up the Third Seals

Start the beginning of the month by

Date ended ....

setting up the third and final Seals on the temple. Place your four candle-sticks in front of each quarter as shown in Figure 21. On the altar place four new unlit candles of the best quality

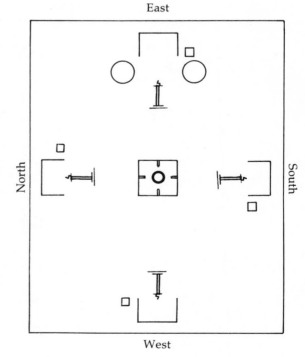

Figure 21 Setting Up the Third Seals

you can afford. Around each one tie a ribbon in the quarter colours. Dress the altar with the centre light and the incense bowl; the incense should be associated with Daath, or the higher mental level. Light the altar light and stand on the eastern side of the altar facing the altar. Take the candle for the East and holding it in both hands, light it from the centre light and move to the Eastern Gate. Think of a cord of light attached to you and trailing behind as you move around. Now turn and walk slowly from the East to the South, on to the West and North and back to the East, always thinking of the trail of light behind you. Lift the candle and invoke:

Oh thou mighty serpents of flame, holy seraphim of the Eastern Gate, set thy guard about this sacred enclosure at its highest level, I call upon thee, I summon thee by the sacred word that was lost, set the last Seal upon this temple.

(Place the candle in the holder and go to the altar. Take the candle for the South, light it and walk to the South, again trailing light behind you. Now walk from South to West, to North and to East and back to South. Stand before the Southern Gate and lift the candle and invoke:)

Oh thou mighty shining ones who defend the gates of paradise with upraised swords of flame, set thy guard about this sacred enclosure at its highest level. I call upon thee. I summon thee. By the first sword made by Tubalcain, set the last Seal upon this temple.

(Place the candle in its holder and go to the altar. Take the candle for the West, light it from the centre light and walk to the West with the cord of light following you. Walk from West to North, to East, to South and

back to the West. Stand before the Western Gate lift the candle and invoke:)

Oh thou mighty cherubim, builders of the Western Gate, set thy guard about this sacred enclosure at its highest level. I call upon thee, I summon thee. By the running of the seventh wave on the seventh shore, set the last Seal upon this temple.

(Place the candle in its holder and return to the altar. Take the North candle, light it and walk to the North letting the cord of light follow behind. Walk from the North to the East, to the South and West and finally back to the North. Stand before the Northern Gate, raise the candle and invoke:)

Oh thou mighty Malachim, kings of the elements, set thy guard about this sacred enclosure at its highest level, I call upon thee. I summon thee. By the highest point of the highest mountain and the lowest valley beneath the sea, set the last Seal upon this temple.

(Place the candle in the holder and return to your original seat. Leave the candles to burn for several hours then snuff them out and leave only the central one to burn out. Note: this sealing, as with the others, can be easily adapted for four people rather than one.)

Your temple is now triple sealed and will give you all the protection you need from now on. One point; a sealing like this is not invalidated by any opening you might do during a ritual. The Seals are activated only when and if something attempts to enter that has no right to be there. Then the shields snap into place on all levels and everything is waterproof, fireproof, demonproof, and if necessary hellproof.

	SUN	MOON	FATHER	MOTHER	EARTH	FIRE	WATER/OCEAN	WAR	WISDOM	BEAUTY/LOVE	MESSENGER	UNDER WORLD	MUSIC	WINE/SACRIFICE
GREEK	APOLLO	ARTEMIS	ZEUS	HERA	DEMETER	HEPHASTEOS	POSEIDON	ARES	ATHENE	APHRODITE	HERMES	HADES	MUSES APOLLO	DIONYSIUS
ROMAN	HELIOS	DIANA	JOVE	JUNO	CERES	VULCAN	NEPTUNE	MARS	MINERVA	VENUS	MERCURY	PLUTO	HELIOS	BAACHUS
NORSE	FREY	GEFYION	ODIN	FRIGGA	NERTHUS	LOKI	NJORD	WODEN THOR	ODIN	IDUNA FREYA	HEIMDALL	HEL		BALDUR
CELTIC	LUGH	ARIANRHOD	DAGDA	DANA	CERUNNOS CERIDWEN	WAYLAND GOVANNON	HANANNAN LLYR	BRAN	GWYDION	RHIANNON OENGUS	GWION	PWYLL	BRIGID TALIESIN	BRAN
QABALIST	TIPHERETH RAPHAEL	YESOD GABRIEL	CHOCKMAH AIN SOPH AUR	BINAH NETZACH	MALKUTH URIEL	NETZACH	BINAH YESOD	GEBURAH KHAMAEL	CHESED DAATH 4 HOLY CREATURES	NETZACH HANIEL	HOD YESOD GABRIEL	QLIPPOTH	TIPHERETH RAPHAEL	TIPHERETH CHRIST
EGYPTIAN	RA	ISIS	ATUM	NUIT	NEPHTHYS	SEKMET	ISIS	HORUS	THOTH	HATHOR	ANUBIS	OSIRIS	HATHOR	OSIRIS
HINDU	SURYA NAKAYANA?	SOMA MITRA	INDRA VISHNU	MAHASAKTI LAKSHMI	ADITI	AGNI	VARUNA	SKANDA KALI SHIVA	GARUDA TVASHIRI	KAMA KRISHNA	GANESHA HANUMAN PUSHAN		NAIARAJA	THE AVATARS OF VISHNU
ASSYRIAN	SHAMASH MARDUK NINAGAL	SIN	BAAL ENLIL AN	MAMI	NINLIL NINTU NINHURSAG	NUSKU	EA TIAMAT	NERGAL ANAT TESHUP SHARMA	NABU EL	TANITH ISHTAR NINSIG	NABU	MOT		ANAT
AMERICAN INDIAN							YOU FILL THIS ONE IN!							
AZTEC	HUITZILO-POCHTLI TONATIUH	NANAHOATL	VIRACOCHA OMETEODUNTU	COATLICUE	CIHUACOATL	UEUETEOTL	TLALOC	GUKOMATZ	QUETZACOATL	TLAZOLTEUTL	NANUALPILI	MICTLANTECUTLI TlAZOLTEOTI	XOCHIPILLI	XIPETOTEC
CHINESE	FU-HSI	HENG-O	HUANG-TI	NU-KOA	P'AN CHU	CHU YUNG FLAME DRAGON	YU CHIANG	CHIYOU		HSI WANG MU	YI THE ARCHER	LORD ON HIGH		
NOTES:	LYRE BOW CHARIOT DISK	BOW VIRGIN CRESCENT TIDES	SKY LIGHTNING BOLT	HEAVEN MARRIAGE FIDELITY	CORN SICKLE	SWORD SMITH GODS	EARTHQUAKE HORSES TRIDENT	SHIELD AEGIS SPEAR	LOOM SPIDER BOOK PEN TREE	APPLE EMERALD OIL LAMP MIRROR BELT	CADUCEUS STAFF	DOG RICHES DJED SHOES	HARP FLUTE LYRE	GRAPE HEADS COLUMN MISTLETOE

Figure 22 The Pantheons

The Opening of the Gates

As you open each Gate at the beginning of a ritual, you will find a series of images building in your imagination. You will start out with the images you have been taught to build. However when the temple has been established a while you may find a new set impinging on your consciousness. No two people have the same picture, but they augment each other and in the usual paradoxical way of the occult, they work perfectly together.

The usual opening of the Gates is done by building either wrought iron gates or immense wooden doors with massive hinges and locks. But you can have anything you like as long as you feel safe behind such gates. As they swing open, the quarter's God-form or Archangel comes forward first, the landscape behind should conform to the symbology of the quarter, i.e. desert or volcanic for the South, lush fields or deep caves for the North, etc. After this figure comes the Elemental King seen in the colours appropriate to his nature. Then add the elementals themselves, and even animals associated with that quarter. It is a good way to remember things by association.

When you come to write your own rituals you may on occasion decide to invoke just the Elemental Kings, or just the God-forms, Archangels or whatever. For this you will need a proper invocation for each one. Sooner or later you are going to have to learn how to write an invocation. The best way is to read poetry because that is in essence what an invocation is. By reading it out loud you will train your ear to the most essential part of poetry, and that is rhythm. It must scan... in layman's terms it must have an 'umpty sound' like a nursery rhyme. Read Longfellow's poem *Hiawatha*, or Coleridges *The Rhyme of the Ancient Mariner*, both have a natural beat to the words. This is the kind of beat a good invocation must have.

At the end of this chapter you will find examples that you can use until you can come up with your own. Get yourself a copy of *The Poet's Rhyming Dictionary*, it will save a lot of time trying to find words that sound the same.

When working with God-forms in the quarters you must have the pantheons at your fingertips. It is no use remembering halfway through a ritual that Vulcan goes in the South and you have him in the East. But there is a way to plan ahead. Buy a large sheet of cartridge paper and mark it off into 1 inch squares. In the left-hand column write the types of the traditions: Greek, Roman, Celtic, Qabalah, Egyptian, Assyrian, Chaldean, Norse, Chinese, Hindu, Aztec, American Indian, and any more you can find. Along the top write the areas of rulership: Sun, Moon, Stars, Earth, Sea, Sky, Smith, Corn, Magic, Wisdom, Time, Love, War, Sleep, Dreams, etc. Now with the aid of an encyclopaedia of mythology from your local library, fill in the names of the gods and goddesses according to tradition and rulership. (See Figure 22)

With this table you will never put the wrong god in the wrong place. It will also act as a memory aid and you will soon be able to remember the right order without referring to the graph. You may find that some gods overlap into various rulerships, this is usual and means you can place the God-form in any of those areas where it is marked. You can do this with colours and symbols as well, if your wall is big enough to carry all the charts!

The Dog of Defence

By now you should have chosen your

Temple guardian and named it. There is an invocation known as 'Raising the Dog of Defence'. It was taught to me by W.E. Butler, and he got it from Dion Fortune who learned of it when she was a member of the Golden Dawn. It appears to have been an adaptation of an Egyptian spell to set a guardian before the door of a tomb. It is still powerful after many centuries and can be used to place your guardian if you adapt the words. Here is the original:

> *Arise Dog of Defence that I may instruct thee in thy duties. Be thou ever watchful to the North and the South, the East and the West, behind thee and above thee, and below thee and around thee. Take thy watch from the setting of the Sun to the coming of the dawn, and stand guard as I have instructed thee.*

The adaptation for the temple might go like this:

> *Arise.....of defence that I may instruct thee in the guarding of this sacred place. Look to the East and the South, to the West and the North, above thee and below thee and from whatever quarter evil may strike. Thy standing is for a year and a day from the setting of the Sun to the rising of the Sun. When thy time is done depart to thine own place and may you be blessed with the amount due to thee.*

A guardian is normally an elemental whose shape has been changed by your intention into whatever shape you decide upon. *No elemental should ever be forced into perpetual work of any kind*, hence the time limit of a year and a day. After that you erect a new guardian. You can use the Dog of Defence if you are away from home and feel the need for protection of some kind. It is highly effective, and if you happen to be even a latent materializing medium, you can end up with something very tangible.

The Vigil of the Five Points

If you have a copy of *The Shining Paths*, set yourself to do the twenty-fifth, twenty-fourth, and twenty-third paths during this month. All have a bearing on the training you have had so far and what you can expect in the future. Do one each week, and leave the last week for the Vigil of the Five Points and the Consecration Ritual itself. Perhaps now is the time to tell you that it is not just the temple that will be consecrated... during the ritual you will leave the title of neophyte behind you, and your priesthood will commence.

The ceremony is best performed on a Friday or Saturday night, so that you can sleep in a little next day and take things easy. As you may have found out, rituals can have some strange effects at times. The work you have been doing on the Quarters and Godforms is really part of the consecration, but because of the shortened time of your training I have, in effect, been easing you into the ritual bit by bit, so that a little of the 'steam' is taken out of its culmination. The last bit of pre-ritual work is to be done a few days before your 'finals'. This is the Vigil of the Five Points. Be warned, it is deceptively quiet and simple!

The intention of the Vigil is to let you and the temple meld into each other. We have spoken at some length about the beings who will be working with you, but the temple itself *is, or will become, an entity in its own right*. You will learn more about this when we come to the lesson on Group Souls and Group Minds.

It is a good idea to miss a meal before doing the Vigil, but do have a hot drink in a flask and some plain biscuits ready to eat afterwards. Record the main details and then go straight to bed. The

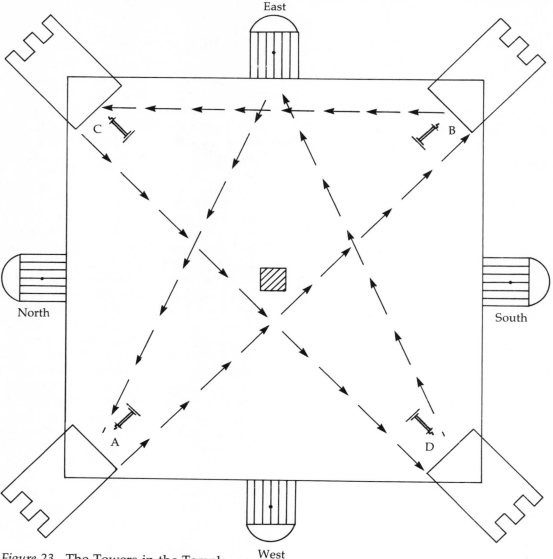

Figure 23 The Towers in the Temple

length of the Vigil depends on you, it can be as long or as short as you like. For what it is worth my advice is not to decide on an hour or two hours, but to take each station as it comes and let your inner feeling tell you when it is time to move to the next station.

A few chapters back I spoke of the temple as having Four Quarter Gates, with *towers* set between them. If you look at Figure 23 you will see how the four of them are placed, with the fifth point being the Gate of the East from where the activating influence enters the temple. You also see that the lines of that influence make a five pointed star. This is not just for use in this particular instant, this pattern can be used as part of an opening ritual as well. Like the better known Ritual of the Rose Cross, it is extremely potent and can activate the power points in a temple very rapidly.

Take a bath and put on your robe, girdle, slippers, and ring. Place the candlesticks with new, unlit candles at the points marked A, B, C, and D in Figure 23. The East does not need a light, for you, the Magus will be representing the light in that Quarter. Dress the altar with the centre light and a single red rose. Have a long wax taper by the altar light. Light the incense (Frankincense) and put a glass of water on the table in the East (you may need it to moisten your mouth during the Vigil). If you like, put on some music, turn it down so that it is just audible.

When you feel you are ready enter the temple and take your seat in the East. Sink into meditation and think upon the temple that you have built over the past months, think about the Eastern Gate and its power as the place of 'First Light'. You are now seated in the position of 'The Light Bringer'. It is *you* who must bring that Light over the threshold of the East and carry it to the Towers so they can act as beacons for those that come after you. Know this also, that in lighting such beacons you become responsible for them being kept alight. Feel the burden that it puts upon your shoulders, examine it thoroughly, know what it is, what it means to be an Officer of the East, more than that, what it means to be a Priest of the Western Mysteries.

When you have thought about these things and sorted them out in your mind, rise and go to the altar. Place your hands flat on either side of the light and look into it deeply. Think about its meaning, who and what it represents, imagine being in that position. Now take up the taper, light it and return to the East standing with your back to the Gate. Now following the path shown in Figure 23, pace slowly to the candlestick in the north-

west, light the candle there, turn and pace to the candlestick in the south-east. Light the candle then turn and cross to the candlestick in the north-east. Light it then turn and go diagonally to the last candlestick in the south-west, light it and return to the East. Put out the taper and stand for a moment, then with the same slow pace move to the north-west again and stand before the candle there. Look deeply into it and build in your mind the image of a great Tower rising into a sunset sky. At its summit a fire has been lit as if to guide the lonely traveller to a safe haven. Think of this Tower as part of yourself, the part that stands ready to help when needed. Cup your hands about the flame and bless it and the service it represents.

Now turn and go to the candle in the south-east. Look into it and build another Tower like the first, standing against the amber clouds of dawn. The fire from its topmost turret leaps upward illuminating all around. Think of this fire as incoming knowledge, and the Tower as that part of yourself that may one day pass on what you have learnt. Cup your hands about the flame and bless that which it symbolizes. Now turn and make your way across to the candle in the north-east. Look into its fiery heart and see the great Tower build up; it stands tall and dark against a night sky lit by a Full Moon. The fire that surmounts it gleams palely in the moonlight. It stands for the Mysteries ancient and awesome, the Tower itself is that part of you that strives to know what is hidden. Cup your hands about the flame and bless it and all that it stands for.

Once more you pace the temple towards the south-west and the candle that glows there. The Tower stands in the full light of the noonday Sun, its crown of flame rivalling Apollo's chariot. This fire is the fire of love given and accepted freely and without barriers. The Tower is the symbol of the spirit that stands true and loyal to its principles. Cup your hands about the flame and bless it and the Tower it conceals. Now return to the East and sit. Sink down into meditation and think on what has just passed, think of the inner meanings and symbols and store up the knowledge that comes to you.

Now for the third time pace out the five pointed star, but this time as you stand before each candle, let the Tower appear and enter that Tower and see what lies behind its door. Follow the same pattern and come at last back to the East and sit in meditation on what you have learned.

Now for the last time make your journey of woven paces. As you come to each candle snuff it out, return to the East to make the pattern perfect, then go to the altar and take the rose and lift it up.

The Vigil of the Five Points has been made, the Towers have been built, the fires have been lit, now I place this rose at the centre of the pattern for it symbolizes perfection, silence, and beauty, let these things come to full flower in me.

Place the rose in the centre of the altar, put out the altar light, make sure the incense is safe, then leave the temple.

You may think from reading this ritual that it is simple and easy. In point of fact it can be more powerful in its effect than the actual consecration. You may feel those effects the next day or not until several days have passed, but sooner or later it will hit you for six. Record as much as you remember before you go to bed, the rest will float to the surface later.

The Consecration

Now all you have to face is the consecration, which will not be as tiring as a lot of the work normally done during such a ceremony has been taken care of already. You may be asking just what a consecration does? It takes and sets apart from the mundane whatever is the object of such a ritual, in this case a temple. It is like a hallmark on a piece of gold, it stamps it 'for sacred use only'. It gives it over to the deity who will preside over it. A deed of gift from Man to God.

The Consecration Rule

Dress the altar with the centre light, incense, water, salt, wax taper, and chalice of wine. Your magical weapons can be placed in the appropriate Quarters. Put the Quarter candlesticks in place complete with candles (unlit). Have music ready if you are going to use it. Make sure the room is pleasantly warm.

Into your pre-ritual bath sprinkle some sea salt and, if you like, some essential oil of your own choosing. Wash your hair as well and make sure your fingernails are clean! As with the Vigil make up a flask of tea or chocolate, not coffee, the ritual will be stimulating enough without adding caffeine, some plain biscuits or sandwiches will help to close down the centres.

Dress slowly and carefully, then sit for a few minutes to collect your thoughts, after all you have been working towards this moment for five months. When you are ready make your way to the temple. As you stand before the door visualize the Guardian on the other side, mentally give the password, then go in and lock the door behind you.

Make your preparations without

haste, light the altar light, and the charcoal, and when it is ready sprinkle on the incense. (A recipe specially created for this rite by 'Incenses of Arcady' will be found at the end of the book). At this time the only light will be that from the altar. Light the taper from the altar light and turn to the East and bow. Now light the candle there and say:

In the East there is Light.
(Move to the South and bow.)
In the South there is Light.
(Move to the West and bow.)
In the West there is Light.
(Move to the North and bow.)
In the North there is Light.
(Move back to the East.)

(Put out taper, take incense and go to the East, waft the incense towards the Gate three times and say:)

In the East there is Strength.
(Move to the South.)
In the South there is Strength.
(Move to the West.)
In the West there is Strength.
(Move to the North.)
In the North there is Strength.
(Move back to the East and replace the incense.)

(Bless the salt and water and pour one into the other, take it to the East and sprinkle it there and say:)

In the East there is Life.
(Move to the South.)
In the South there is Life.
(Move to the West.
In the West there is Life.
(Move to the North.)
In the North there is Life.
(Move back to the East and replace the salt and water.)

(Turn to East, spread arms wide.)

In the name of the one creative source both male and female this Gate of the East is opened to the forces of Light. Come forth ye Holy Ones who have guided man in his search for the truth. Come forth and accept the dedication of this temple to your service. Consecrate this place to your use that we may work in peace and harmony together. Let your powers flow through this Gate of the East and make them available to those working within this sacred enclosure. Let them flow also through those gathered here that these powers may not be abused but contained and used for the good of the Earth and her children. Accept this place and make it your own. Accept those gathered here and help them to grow in grace and truth.

(Imagine a great wave of light and scented air flowing through the East and enclosing you within itself, let it saturate you and enter into your very veins, flowing through every part of your body. Feel it fill the temple not only on the physical level but filling up all the levels that you have so carefully built. Let the force of all this build up inside you until it reaches such an intensity that it forces itself out of you in a shout of:)

Fiat, Fiat, Fiat

(Let the feeling die down a little for a few moments, then pace to the South, spread your arms wide:)

In the name of the one creative source both male and female this Gate of the South is opened to the forces of Love and Courage and Strength. Come forth ye sons and daughters of god worshipped by mankind since the dawn of time, come forth and accept the dedication of this temple to your service. Consecrate this place to your use that we may work in peace and harmony together. Let your powers flow through this Gate of the South and make them available to those working within this sacred place. Let them flow also through those gathered here that these powers may not be abused but used for the good of all mankind and all that lives with him on this Earth and in the fullness of time for those that he may meet beyond this Earth. Accept this place and make it your own. Accept those gathered here and fill them with your ancient strength and love of life.

(Imagine a great flame erupting though the Gate of the South. Let it enfold you and caress you. Open your mouth and draw it down into your lungs and feel the fire spread throughout your body, up through the spine and into the head filling all with its power. Let this feeling of strength and controlled power of love build up within you until it becomes a shout of joy and ecstasy.)

Selah, Selah, Selah

(Rest for a few minutes and gather your strength then move to the West, spread your arms wide:)

In the name of the one creative source both male and female this Gate of the West is opened to the forces of Form, Faith and Silent Understanding. Come forth ye archangels of the crystal spheres. Messengers from beyond time and space, harbingers of knowledge and new thought come forth and accept the dedication of this temple to your service. Consecrate this place to your use that we may work together in peace and harmony. Let your powers flow through this Gate of the West and make them available to those working within this sacred place. Let them also flow through those gathered here that they may not be abused but controlled and used that man may no longer destroy what has been given to him but may learn to live in harmony with all things. Accept this place and make it your own. Accept those gathered here and fill them with faith and understanding.

(Imagine a mighty wave that roars through the Gate of the West and saturates you with its deeps. Let it into your soul, let it become a tide within you that will forever ebb and flow with those other cosmic tides that rule the lives of galaxies. Let it cause a wave of patience, faith, and tolerance to rise within you building up until it becomes a torrent of feeling that turns into a great cry of:)

Amen, Amen, Amen.

(Rest for a few minutes, then go to the North, hold out your arms:)

In the name of the one creative source both male and female this Gate of the North is opened to the forces of Growth and Fruitfulness, of Endurance and Time. Come forth ye mighty kings of the elements. Stand forth and in your hearts forgive the harm that man has caused your kingdoms. Come forth and accept the dedication of this temple to your use that we may from now on work in peace and harmony together. Let your powers flow through this Gate of the North and make them available to those working within this sacred place. Let them also flow though those gathered here that they may be made your emissaries upon Earth. Accept this place and make it your own. Accept those gathered here and fill them with your patience and endurance and your ability to forgive.

(Imagine there comes through the Gate of the North a feeling of great sorrow mixed with hope. All the pain of the Earth and its creatures flows through and fills the temple as if seeking refuge. Take all the pain into yourself, take it and know it fully, know what mankind has done and all for gain. Feel the pain of the torn earth, the agony of the trap, the terror of the abattoir, the sadness as the last of a species dies forever.

Now let the hope come in, the caring and the offer of help. Open yourself to all that the Four Gates have offered and let it lift you up in the arms of hope and trust. Let it come in and let out the cry of:)

Peace, Peace, Peace.

(Make your way to the East and rest there. When you feel ready, go to the altar and take up the wine. In your own words bless the wine and offer it to the East placing a drop on the candle there, then drink yourself. Do the same at the other Quarters. Back at the altar lift the Cup up and again in your own words offer yourself as you have offered the temple, then place a drop on the altar light and drink the rest yourself.)

I summon Raphael from the East, Michael from the South, Gabriel from the West and Uriel from the North. Take this temple dedication and the offer of myself to the highest point of Light and let it be written in the great book of records what has been offered and accepted this night. I invoke the master of this temple.............and ask that ....will make this place one of deep peace of mind, body and soul and that.............will indwell it for as long as it will stand.

(Go the the East and hold out your arms as if to embrace the Beings who stand there and say:)

My brethren accept my love and thanks for what has been offered and freely given this night. Stay with me until the dawn, guarding my sleep and teaching me in my dreams. Farewell, with the coming of dawn, depart to thine own place with my blessing.

(Go to the South and hold out your arms:)

My brethren accept my love and thanks for what has been offered and freely given this night. Stay with me until dawn, fill me with strength to face the future. Farewell, with the coming of dawn, depart to thine own place with my blessing.

(Go to the West and hold out your arms:)

My brethren accept my love and thanks for what has been offered and freely given this night. Stay with me until the dawn and teach me the true meaning of understanding. With the coming of dawn depart to thine own place with my blessing.

(Go to the North and hold out your arms:)

My brethren accept my love and thanks for what has been offered and freely given this night. Stay with me until the dawn and show me how I may right the wrongs of the past. With the coming of dawn depart to thine own place with my blessing.

(Go to the East bow and go to altar. Lift the light high and pronounce the blessing:)

In the name of Adonai the Lord of the Earth I bless all those who have been with me this night. Let all accept their just dues. This temple has been consecrated with Light, Fire, Water, and the fruit of the Earth. Now its work begins.

(Go to the East and put out the light, to the South and put out the light, to the West and put out the light, to the North and put out the light. Pace round the temple from East to South to West to North and East again three times. Leave the altar light burning. You may leave now, or you may like to stay in meditation for a while. If you really want to make full use of the powers that have been summoned into the temple, you can sleep the night there, using a sleeping bag.)

The Temple Sleep is a ritual in its own right, and there are many different ways of doing it. You can end an important ritual such as the consecration by sleeping by the altar. Or you can spend three consecutive nights sleeping there once or twice a year. You can sleep there after doing a request ritual for the answer to a specific question or problem. Or it can be done as a ritual itself, this requires a man and woman and I will be giving more details in the next chapter.

This concludes the consecration ceremony; record the main details so they are not lost during sleep, have something to eat and drink and then go to sleep.

Reading List

Regardie, Israel, *Foundations of Practial Magic* (Aquarian Press, 1979)

Stillman, Francis, *The Poet's Rhyming Dictionary* (Thames and Hudson, 1966)

The Sixth Month

Re-evaluation and the Start of Ritual Magic

Date started ....

Now that your temple is completed, and consecrated, there will be a great temptation to heave a sigh of relief and put your astral feet up. Think again. The time for the greatest effort is the moment when you feel you have earned a rest. That is a maxim you can apply to your daily life as well. All good business men and women set themselves a yearly goal, as do large consortiums and governments. You should follow their example if you want to make a success of your occult work. Establish good habits now, and they will be with you forever. Remember in the beginning I told you that what your learned in your inner work would seep through into your everyday life. This is where it starts to take effect. All that you have been building on the Inner Levels, will soon begin to filter through to the physical world.

Check on your daily work, are you still doing it? If you are, then you are definitely the stuff which magicians are made of. More than likely you will find you have slipped, if only a little. Tighten it up again. Make sure you are doing at least ten minutes a day in relaxing and breathing, breaking it up if need be into three or four lots of three minutes. Keep to your observation practice, learn to observe people and places closely and to remember them. Are you still playing Kim's Game? How good are you? Very good, good, bad, don't do it anymore? Tut, tut!

The Locus Memory Device

In his book *Getting What You Want*, J.H. Brennan offers a centuries old memory device used by Roman orators to remember their key phrases. This is the principle of the locus. As Mr Brennan explains, locus means place, and it is so simple to use, one wonders why it it not more widely known. As a bonus it also helps to train your inner visualization. The method is quite simple, if you have a list of items, numbers, facts, data, names, or key sentences for a lecture, you place them in a precise pattern in and around a specific location, as Mr Brennan says, 'the bigger the better'. You should use a large building with which you are already very familiar, I use my local public library for smallish lists, and the British Museum for the really big ones.

Mr Brennan advises several days of simply visualizing your *locus* and getting every nook and cranny fixed firmly in your mind, he also stresses the importance of using the same route every time. When you can visualize all this instantly you are ready to use your locus.

With a list of the items you need to remember take your usual walk through the chosen building starting with the front door, steps or whatever as usual. Simply follow the route visualizing each item, number, or symbol to your key sentence in the many rooms, places and stairways. Make them stand out against their surroundings, in exotic colours if you like. Fix them firmly all along your usual walk through the locus. Take your time, you may even have to go through it several times at first, but you will soon be astonished at the ease with which you can remember the most complex data. This can be used in your job with great effect as a bonus from your inner world to your outer one. For a more detailed explanation and a lot of sound common sense teaching about using your inner powers to help your daily life read, *Getting What You Want*, by J.H. Brennan.

Re-evaluate Your Records

Go through your records to date and evaluate them, be your own harshest critic. When you have done this, imagine that you are a tutor marking a student for their six-monthly exam and mark those papers out of 100. Allow 20 for consistency of work, 20 for understanding of material, 20 for content and quality of records, 20 for result of ritual work, and a final 20 for growth of integration between your inner and outer selves. As only you will know the results you will have to be painfully honest. You will find an interesting self quiz in the J.H. Brennan book which may help you.

If you want to go deeper into the study of magic, you must establish this habit of recapping and evaluating your work and your progress every six months. Only by doing this can you avoid the bug bear of self taught occultism, which is: not recognizing a mistake in time to correct it. There are always going to be times when you make a mistake, an error in judgement, an idea that is off beam with your chosen tradition even though it *looks* alright, a viewpoint that will lead you on to very dicey ground ritually unless you adjust your thinking, or simply the old 'favourite' the *I'm the greatest* syndrome. By going over your work results on a regular basis you can correct the mistakes, or spot them on the horizon before they actually hit. *Always be tough on yourself* before the Inner Levels get tough on you, it is much easier to cope with.

Setting Tougher Goals

Set yourself progressively harder goals in meditation subjects, more results in ritual work, and in your personal studies. Think back to your first month's training and, 'make them hard enough to strive for, but not so hard that there is a little hope of achieving them'. Set yourself to learn enough Greek to invoke the Quarters in an Orphic ritual, you will be surprised how much of a difference it will make. Design and make a robe, headdress and cloak. Research the Golden Dawn records and make a set of Wands or staffs. Research the British Museum for old herbals and incenses and try them out. Boredom will become a thing of the past, and the nicest part about all this is that you do not have to be young or disgustingly fit to do it all. Magicians, like Stilton and a good claret improve vastly as they age.

Your disciplines must be kept under a firm hand, although if you have kept up the work for this length of time it should have become a habit by now. If this is so, you can allow yourself the luxury of one day off a week. From now on you can lie in on Sunday, if you really want to do so.

It is important to remember when you are setting goals, researching, and increasing your knowledge, that each aspect of your work must be integrated one part with the other. For the very basis of mystery work maintains that there is a level at which all things are *ONE*. To give you an example, let us suppose that you have decided to learn Egyptian hieroglyphic writing as this year's goal. Ally this course of study with some research into early Egyptian religion and the emergence, growth, and many variations on the Osiris legend. Along with this make a study of Egyptian dress, then design and make a set of vestments suitable for a High Priest or Priestess of that period. Write a ritual based on one of the ancient legends or perhaps on part of the Book of the Dead, and create an incense to use with it. Make a particular study of one god or goddess and make a notebook on their legends, attributes, symbols, etc.

That lot may well take you into a second year, if so, carry on until you feel you have achieved the goal, i.e. expert knowledge of a particular era in a particular tradition, with emphasis upon one or two God-forms. This, combined with the experience gained in the research and design of the robes and incense, will give you a very solid basis with which to work in the future, *and*, perhaps to teach to others. Before you can speak or teach with authority,

you must *know* your subject. Don't be content with passing on what you were taught, *add to it what you have found to be true from your own experience.*

How Much Ritual is Enough?

One of the most difficult questions to answer is; how much ritual work should I do in say, a month? There is no hard and fast rule. For one person, one ritual a month can be too much simply in terms of time, preparation, learning, and most of all *pressure* on the psyche. Make no mistake, High Magic can have an upsetting effect on some people, *not everyone can take ritual*. The physical pressures as well as the psychic ones must be taken into consideration. You can, in this instance only learn by making mistakes! Most people can take one a month, but the levels should be varied. Alternate a really intense ritual with a much lighter one. This is the advantage of not tying oneself down to a single tradition.

A high level Egyptian or Qabalistic ritual can be balanced by a more light hearted Greek rite. On the other hand don't think that all Greek rituals are light or that all Egyptian ones are heavy... you must learn to judge by their content, or, you must learn by writing them yourself to conform to certain levels of pressure.

If you feel lethargic and wan for days after a ritual, either you did something wrong, (it usually means a quarter was not closed firmly enough) or it means you should make it one every two months, at least for a year or until you can build up your psyche to take the pressure. Don't feel you have failed because you can't make it through two or three rituals a week! The plain fact is that only a fool would try to do so many. Nevertheless I have in my time received many letters from would-be magicians complaining that they perform a ritual almost every day and cannot get any results, please can I tell them why. Yes I can, they have broken the link with excessive use and they are just not getting through to the Inner Levels.

So what is the answer? For those who wish to do it right and not run into trouble in the future, I advise, at the most, two rituals a month, one of a light nature and one a little deeper and stronger in its effect. This is all part of integrating your study, ritual, research, and work process, and will include seasonal rituals for Spring, Summer, Autumn and Winter, such rituals will be the 'heavys' for that particular month. Add to your ritual work your daily meditation of up to fifteen minutes a day. Not much you may think, but if done on a regular basis this will be far more effective in results than an hour once or twice a week. Your relaxation and breathing can be slipped in whenever you have five minutes to spare, but don't neglect them. Magic works best when the mind and body are in an unstressed state, this can be achieved at will when you practice it daily.

For study purposes calculate how many hours a week you can spare, again a small amount of *regular* time is better than a long spell every now and then. You find this when learning a language, spend fifteen minutes a day learning one verb and ten new words, and in six weeks you have a working vocabulary. On top of this add time for research. This kind of work *can* be done in a lump, say one afternoon every two weeks, or a weekend of work once a month. A lot will depend on how much time you owe to other people. If you have a family they have a right to some of your time, the Path of the Hearth Fire must not be neglected. All

magical work has anchor points that are firmly fixed on the physical level. It is through such points that the results from such work are manifested so do not cut yourself off from the point of manifestation.

Because of the enormous scope of magical work a great deal of your success must rely on your willingness to read and acquire data, and then to put that data to use. One book cannot teach you all that you should know, which is why you have been directed to carefully selected books that will provide knowledge in a digestable form. As much basic information as possible has been passed on to you, and there is more to come, but you will have to fill in the inevitable gaps with practical experience and your own determination.

And talking of practical experience it is time to look at Seasonal Rituals. You should eventually write your own but for now you will find a complete set in several traditions provided in this book. They will serve the purpose for at least a year and then perhaps provide a basis on which you can build your own ideas.

Seasonal Rituals

We have already spoken about the use of rituals purely as a form of worship, working through mythological God-forms, Archangels, and the Elemental Kings but always aimed at the Primal Creator/Creatrix from which they, and mankind, emanate. Such rituals link us with that Primal Force through its ambassadors, stepping down the Power that otherwise might be too much for mere mortals. The tale of Zeus and Semele is more than a pretty tale, it is a warning to those who would aim too high, too fast.

Although they can have some heavy

effects, seasonal rituals are comparatively easy to build and use. This is because a lot of the Inner Level work has already been done for you. The higher astral, like every other plane, has its Tides, and each Tide brings to the shores of the physical world the Great Images of that Tide. Images that we can use in ritual. The Spring Tide brings images of new life, Easter, Eggs, the Death and Rebirth of the Son of the Sun, the goddess Flora, the return of Persephone from the Underworld and a host of other ready-made images all primed and ready to use without any extra effort on your part. The same goes for the other Tides each with their own symbols, festivals, images etc. In fact you can, with the aid of a list of traditional events, (see Marian Green's *A Harvest of Festivals*) use any and all of the images that have been built up, used, and ensouled by the emotions of centuries. Candlemas, the first Light of the Year, in Scandinavia and the Baltic States celebrated by a Maiden wearing a crown of candles. Mother's Day, which can be made the focus of a beautiful and highly effective Ritual of the Earth Mother. Lady Day, Beltane, Midsummer's Eve, Lammas, Harvest Festival, Thanksgiving, the Fourth of July, Hallow'een, etc. There are more than enough to last for a lifetime of rituals.

By using such ready-made images you do not need to expend so much energy, which for someone at the beginning of their ritual work is a great help. Such festivals, both Christian and Pagan can be a rich source of material for future rituals of your own. While you are about it, explore the festivals of Europe as well, don't confine yourself to your own backyard so to speak. The folklore of your county can yield some very interesting ideas. You might contact the British Folklore Society, and subscribe to their magazine. *The Ley Hunter* magazine is another that can open up possibilities, if not for ritual, then as pathworkings. You can take the 'Green Roads of England' and travel them in different times, as you will see in a later chapter.

So look for ritual source material in local, racial and continental folklore and festivals, in mythology, the sacred books of the world, in specialized sources such as the separate vignettes of the Egyptian Book of the Dead, and the Tibetan Book of the Dead, and even in books on anthropology. They all have something to offer when you start writing your own rituals. Later, you will find ideas emerging from your Inner Levels and they will be the most satisfying of all. When this happens you will be faced with a new problem, understanding what the ritual is about and the effects it will bring in its wake.

Until then you will have chosen your ritual material knowing in advance what effect you are looking for. When your own inner, higher, self comes up with the theme for a ritual you have to sit down and figure out: 1. Why it has been given to you? 2. What effect it is designed to have? and 3. The probable results of those effects. First look at the theme itself, meditate on it for a week or so. Look at the symbolism and check it out with other symbols of similar character, again meditate on what you find out. Finally when you have written it, go through it in the form of a pathworking first, wait and check the results. Then go through all your notes to date and you should have a good understanding of the principle of the ritual. Indeed before using any ritual, it is best to read it thoroughly, look up the symbology and generally make yourself familiar with its content. In this work take nothing for granted.

Since Spring is the first quarterly

ritual of the year we will start with that although you may be reading this earlier or later. In that case start with whichever ritual is appropriate for the season. Since this quarter is concerned with new growth after the winter frost and snow you will be making use of all the soft greens, daffodil yellows, pale rose and earth browns as colours in the temple for all three types of ritual. All these rituals have been written specially for this book and have only been performed in order to test their efficacy. Therefore they belong to no Order and are under no restriction of practice. We will take the Celtic first.

The Celtic Ritual of Spring

This is a ritual for four people or it can be done with three and the Spring Maiden in the North can be simply visualized. You will need:

Incense: A mixture of rosemary, damiana, aniseed, and coriander, mixed with a little oil of sassafras, and gopal gum. This can be a little 'heady', so use it sparingly.

Altar: Instead of one centre light use a small ring of greenery and wild flowers into which tall slim green candles have been firmly fixed. Salt and water, a sprig of rosemary and a small bowl of mixed leaves and flower petals. A glass or chalice of mead. Some twigs made into a broom by binding the tops together. A hammer and a piece of iron. A wreath of wild flowers and leaves.

In the North place your Spring Maiden in a green robe and girdle, bare feet, and covered wth a long black or grey veil.

Start your ritual with a few minutes meditation on the coming of Spring. The Magus starts by blessing the salt and water.

Magus:

Salt, creature of Earth, be blessed in this hour and give up all that is evil within thee. In this place be as pure as thy time of creation. Water, child of the Cosmic Sea, be blessed in this hour and give up all that is evil within thee. In this place be as pure as thy moment of creation.
(Return to seat.)

South:

(Sprinkles incense on already prepared charcoal.)
Creature of Fire, burn brightly in this hour and cleanse this sacred enclosure with thy perfume.
(Returns to seat.)

West:

(Tips salt into water and lifts Chalice.)
Sacred Cup filled with honeyed ale, be thou the link between the gods and mortals.
(Returns to seat.)

Magus:

(Stands and faces East, with the forefinger of the right hand he draws a spiral moving from the outer circle to the centre point thus:)
Protector of the East, I name thee Gwydion son of Don. Master of Magic. Shape Shifter I name thee and bid thee haste to this sacred enclosure.
(With finger outstretched, moves to South and draws spiral as before.)

Protector of the South. I name thee Govannon son of Don and brother to Gwydion. Master of the Forge Fire, Slayer of Dylan of the Wave, I bid thee haste to this sacred enclosure.
(Moves as before to West and makes the spiral.)

Protectress of the West. I name thee

Arianrhod of the Silver Wheel. Goddess of the Wave, I name thee and bid thee haste to this sacred enclosure.
(Moves to North and repeats.)

Protectress of the North. I name thee Ceridwen of the Cauldron, Mistress of all that grows. I bid thee haste to this sacred enclosure.
(Returns to Altar and faces East.)

Gwydion, guardian of the Blessed Isles, welcome in this place and hear our plea. Return to us the Maid of Spring that Winter may release its hold upon the Earth and let it blossom.
(Faces altar.)

South:

(Faces South.)
Govannon Maker of Spears, turn thy hand to the making of ploughshares that this land we love may yield corn. Return to us the Maid of Spring that her tears of joy may soften the hard Earth and give life to the seed beneath.
(Faces altar.)

West:

(Faces West.)
Arianrhod of the Silver Bow. Goddess of the Great Tides. Lift the seed in the dark Earth and bring it up into the light of the growing Moon. Return to us the Maid of Spring that her laughter may waken all to love and joy and fruitfulness.
(All face North.)

All:

Return to us the Maid of Spring lest mankind grows cold and hungry. Let not the children cry for bread, nor the bird desert her nest.

North:

Who calls the Maid of Spring from her sleep in the kingdom of Annwn? What do you want of me? Let me sleep and dream.

East:

Waken Maid of Spring, the Isles of the Blessed have need of thee, awake and bring us joy.

North:

What will you do that I will wake and join you upon the Earth.

East:

I will sweep the snows of Winter from thy path and every stone from beneath your foot.
(Takes up the broom and goes to stand before the Maid.)

North:

Perhaps I will come if the snow and the stones are swept away.
(She rises, the Magus walks backwards sweeping the path before her moving right around the circle until they reach the North again.)
No I will return to my dreams.
(East returns to seat.)

South:

Waken Maid of Spring. The fires of the Earth have need of thy sweet breath. Aye and the fires within man also.

North:

What will you do that I will waken these fires?

South:

I will beat the swords into ploughshares and make thee an iron cauldron from my spear.
(Takes up hammer and iron and goes to stand before the Maid.)

North:

Perhaps I will come if there is a plough for the Earth and a man for the Maid.
(The South preceeds the Maid around the temple striking the iron with the hammer until they reach the North again.)
No I will not waken the fires.
(South returns to seat.)

West:

Waken Maid of Spring. The waters of the rivers are iced and need the warmth of thy glance to free them. Let the rivers flow and free the life blood of man.

North:

What will you do that I will free the river of ice?

West:

I will cast salt before thee to savour and sweet water to drink.
(Takes bowl of salt and water and a sprig of rosemary from altar and goes to stand before North.)

North:

Perhaps I will come if there is salt to savour and water to drink.
(The West preceeds the Maid around the temple sprinkling the salt and water with the sprig of rosemary before her until they return to the North.)
No, I will not free the river of ice.

West:

Maid of Spring I will sprinkle petals before they feet if thou wilt return to us. if thou wilt bring us joy, waken the fires, and free the river.
(Goes to altar and takes bowl of petals then returns to the North.)

North:

I will come to thee, and bring thee joy, I will waken the fires and I will free the icy rivers. Cast the petals before me and I will come.
(West throws the petals before her and they come to the East, the Maid throws back her veil and gives the East a kiss. They move on to the South where another kiss is exchanged, then to the West where the wreath of flowers is placed on the Maid's head, the West escorts her back to the North then returns to her seat via the full circle.)

North:

The Spring Maid has awoken. Let the Earth rejoice and be fruitful.
(All come to the centre, join hands and circle three times round.)

All:

Come Maid, come Spring, come joy and life,
Come all and one to hear,
The song of sweet Rhiannon's birds,
That call both loud and clear.

The life awakes in man and beast,
The beltane fires are laid,
The flame that calls the buck to doe,
Does quicken man to maid.

Sun and Moon and Star and Earth,
All have their part to play,
But oh the Maid of Spring is here,
And with us she will stay.

(Everyone should be back at their own quarters, and the Mead is now shared around with a little saved to pour onto the garden or on some area of growth. Now the circle can be closed.)

East:

Let us give thanks for the return of spring, for the new warmth of the Sun, the growth of life and the beauty around us.
(Faces East)
Protector in the East, Gwydion, son of Don, hail and farewell to thee. We give thanks for thy presence, depart to the Halls of Math.

South:

(Faces South)
Protector in the South, Govannon, son of Don. Master of smiths. Hail and farewell to thee. We give thanks for thy presence, depart to the Halls of Math.

West:

(Faces West)
Protectress in the West, Arianrhod of the silver wheel, hail and farewell to thee. We give thanks for thy presence, depart to the Castle of the Moon.

North:

(Faces North)
Protectress in the North, Ceridwen of the Cauldron of Life, Hail and farewell to thee. We give thanks for thy presence, depart now to thy place.

East:

(Turns to face his own quarter, makes the spiral sign but starting from the centre and moving outwards he moves from the East to the South, to West, to North and back to East.)
The sacred circle is closed, peace be between us all, let the guardians depart. All is complete.

Put out the candles, and leave quietly. After an hour or so the temple can be tidied up and the petals etc, removed.

As you can see, a very simple ritual that enacts the enticement of the Spring Maid back to Earth. It requires very little in the way of preparation and is basically just an acknowledgement of a special Tide. There are other far more elaborate Spring rituals but this is adequate for your purposes especially when you are adjusting to the new pressures of ritual work. Simplicity is no bad thing in magical work, there is a tendency among people to over elaborate things and what should be a quiet dignified rite, or just a simple joyous ritual, becomes instead a 'Hollywood Spectacular'. I have said before and will say again, the real magician needs nothing not even a temple, to practice his art.

The Greek Ritual of Spring

The Greek Spring ritual I have made quite different from the Celtic. In the first place, since the former was for four people, I have written this for just one person. Secondly, it will be a good experience in using movement as a means of drawing power into a temple, as you did in the Vigil of the Five Points. You will need:

Incense: For this ritual mix an incense of sanderac, pine resin, benzoin, with leaves of eucalyptus, pine needles, rosemary, mixed with oil of jasmine. You can add a few bits of rosemary as well.

Altar: Move your central altar to just before the Pillars, and place the small Quarter tables in the centre of each quarter but with enough room for you to move around them. Dress each altar with a white cloth, and a small centre light, (a nightlight in a white saucer or bowl is ideal). In between the quarters place your tall candlesticks with greenery around the stems, and alternate green and gold candles. On the Eastern altar put a plate with some pieces of homemade bread, and a teaspoon of honey. In the South put the incense with the charcoal well alight and ready for the incense. There is a jug of red wine and a Cup for the West. Finally put a bowl of fruit in the North (Use only those fruits found in Greece, apples, grapes, figs, pome-granates, with ready shelled almonds, some raisins and a bowl of mixed flower seeds.)

Robe: A white robe made in the style of a Greek tunic is ideal if you can make one. If not, a simple white towel wrapped like a Greek kilt and secured with a leather belt. For a lady a white nightdress with a pale green stole (see Figure 24) can be effective. A wreath of flowers and greenery for the head if you so wish, tie the ends together with green ribbons.

Light a taper and stand facing the East, light the altar candle then with the taper make an infinity sign thus, ∞ build up the figure of Hermes between the Pillars and invoke:

East:

Son of Zeus and Maia, swifted footed messenger of Olympus draw near and fill this quarter with the divine pneuma of the Gods.
(Wait until the image is clear then move clockwise round the altar, in front of the south-east candlestick, then round the back of the Southern altar and face the South ∞ (see Figure 25, route A.) Light the altar light, make the infinity sign, build up the God-form of Apollo and invoke.)

Figure 24 Robe for the Greek Rite of Spring

South:

Son of Zeus and Leto, god of Delphi and of Delos, driver of the sun's chariot, draw near and fill this place with light.
(Let the image build, then move around the altar and on to the West passing in front of the south-west candlestick, around the back of the

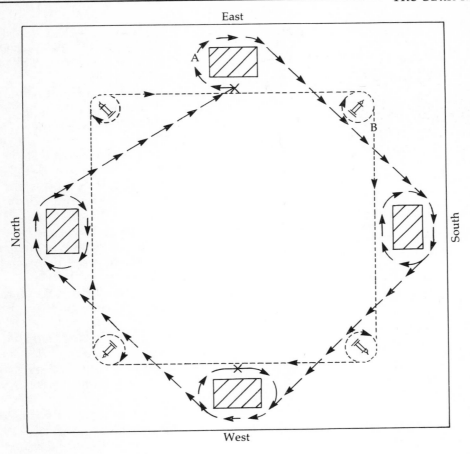

Figure 25 Pattern of Movements for the Greek Rite of Spring

Western altar and face West. Light the altar light, make the infinity sign. Build up the God-form of Artemis and invoke.)

West:

Daughter of Zeus and Leto, night's slender huntress, virgin of the Moon, draw near and fill this place with Tidal power.
(When the image is strong move around the altar and on to the North passing in front of the north-west candlestick, on around the Northern altar and face North. Light the altar light and make the sign. Build up the

God-form of Demeter and invoke.)

North:

Daughter of Chronus and Rhea, Earth Mother and giver of bread, draw near and fill this place with strength and growth.
(When the image is steady move around the altar and return to the East passing in front of the north-east candlestick and going round the back of the Eastern altar to the front and face it. Light a new taper and go to the south-east candlestick, light it, build up the God-form of Iris the Rainbow Goddess and invoke.)

S/East:

Many coloured Iris, servant of Hera, draw near and be ready to take our plea to the halls of Olympus, to the feet of Zeus.

(Circle the candlestick once, then move to the one in the south-west, light it and build up the God-form of Aphrodite the Goddess of Love and invoke.

S/West:

Golden Goddess of Love, Aphrodite of Paphos, draw near and give your aid that we may persuade Hades to return Kore to the Earth.

(Circle the candlestick once then move to the one at the north-west light it and build up the God-form of Hades and invoke.)

N/West:

Dark browed Hades, Lord of the Underworld, give to us your queen, the beauteous Persephone for six short months that the Earth may be fruitful and mankind may grow in strength.

(Circle the candlestick once then move to the one in the north-east, light it and invoke Kore the Spring Maiden.)

N/East:

Sweet faced Kore, Persephone of the white arms, leave your halls of the Underworld and join us here on Earth bringing new life to the Earth and joy to us all.

(Circle the candlestick once then cross to the one in the south-east, bow once and return to the East. Put out the taper. See Figure 25, route B. Take up the piece of bread, dip it in the honey and eat it, offer the plate to the East.)

East:

Great Hermes, take what we offer to great Zeus and ask that Kore may be returned to Earth.

(Move to the South, lift the incense, smell it, then offer it to the South.)
Golden Apollo halt thy chariot and listen to our plea, take this incense to Olympian Zeus and ask that the Earth Maiden be given back to us.

(Move to the West, pour the wine into the Chalice and drink, then offer it to the West.)
Chaste Artemis, Virgin Goddess of the Moon, take this offering to thy immortal father Zeus and plead with him to set free the giver of life.

(Move to the North, take and eat a piece of fruit, then offer the bowl to the North.)
Demeter, Corn Goddess, Earth Mother, like you we mourn the loss of Persephone, ask thy brothers Zeus and Hades to free her that the fields may be blessed.

(Move to the centre of the temple and lift arms.)
Hear me oh ye gods, give to mankind the blessing of the Spring.

(Kneel and place your head in your hands. In your mind build up the sound of running feet, hear them take the twisting labyrinthine path that you have woven in the temple. It is the sacred way of the ancient times and Kore now treads it on her way to earth. Feel the Earth beneath you tremble and the whole of nature holds its breath. Let the feeling of imminent Spring and growth build up inside you until the intensity bursts through in a cry of...)

Kore, Kore, Kore, Kore.

(Stand up and face the quarters in turn giving silent thanks to the gods. Then take the bowl of seeds around to each and hold it up for a blessing. Place your wreath in the centre of the temple and put the bowl inside it. Now go to the East and re-trace the patterns either by pacing, or better still by dancing. Dance until you feel tired, then take up the wreath and the seeds and go to each quarter in turn saying:)

Go in peace and harmony and with thee go our blessings for the work this night. (Put out the lights in the order in which they were lit. Put out bread for the birds, pour the wine on to the Earth, scatter or plant the seeds and share the fruit with family and friends.)

This is a more complex ritual with less to say and more to actually do. But movement is a great power builder and you must learn to be uninhibited about things like dancing in a temple. A man will often say 'I'm *not* going to dance around like a fool', but with a little wine inside you, with the lights, incense, and the energy building up, you may well change your mind. Mankind has danced before his gods for thousands of years, and even David the King of Israel danced before the Ark of the Lord in praise and worship.

In Egypt the seasons were different, they relied on the Nile floods to bring down the rich silt in which they could then plant their crops. So for them the flooding of the Nile valley was a yearly miracle without which they might starve. The first two examples have given you an idea of reasonably complex rituals. The last one is more of a ritual path-working. The Egyptian mysteries ranged from the incredibly difficult to the astonishingly simple type of ritual, and because I want you to have as wide a choice and experience as possible this last one will be for two people only and involve hardly any movement, but a lot of inner vision work.

The Egyptian Ritual of Spring

This ritual involves the two participants assuming the roles of the High Priest and the Goddess Isis in the East and West respectively, while the South and North are filled by the passive and silent figures of Anubis and Nephthys. The East/West axis is deemed to be the length of the Nile river with the High Priest invoking Isis to send down the life giving flood waters. It will require some extra items to be made so give yourself enough time to get everything ready.

If possible a white robe for the Priest, and a pale green one for the Priestess/Isis. If you look at Figure 26 you will see the kind of thing required. The Collars and the Priest's Apron, see Figure 27, are easily made and will be useful for future rituals of this kind. If it is possible, try to have a wooden dais on which the seat of 'Isis' can be raised. This is important as it gives the whole ritual a more formal and Egyptian atmosphere. It should be strong enough to take the weight of the chair and the Priestess, a small footstool will help her ascend.

The Priestess will need an ankh and sistrum, and the High Priest a shoulder-high ceremonial staff. All these things will be used for other rituals so making them is not a waste of time. The ankh and sistrum can be bought ready made from most occult suppliers, the staff is best made by its user, and if possible topped by a hawk or a dog's head. If you are no good at modelling I suggest for the dog's head, buying a cheap china model of an Alsatian dog, break off the head and fix it to the staff. Paint it black and gold and it will look very good. If you cannot do this, make a small Ankh out of modelling wax and top the staff with that.

Figure 26   Robes for the Egyptian Rite of Spring

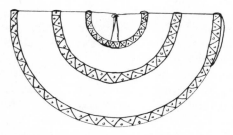

Egyptian collar. Satin over iron-on vilene. Decorate with fancy ribbon and sequins.

Satin over vilene. Turn over top to make loop for belt.

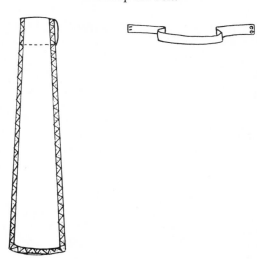

Figure 27   The Collar and Apron for the Egyptian Rite of Spring

Incense: Use kyphi, which can be bought (see occult suppliers) or you can mix your own from a recipe by Gary Farmer. For this you need willow charcoal, mastic resin, myrrh resin, scammony resin, rue, vervain mixed with oil of myrrh or juniper. This makes a very pleasant incense which can be used for all Egyptian rituals.

Altar: Place the central altar in the East between the Pillars so you have a clear run of power between Priest and Priestess down the length of the temple. Place two small tables in the North and South, and one in front of the Priestess. On these and on the Eastern altar place a centre light. Put your tall candlesticks two and two between 'Isis' and the East, see Figure

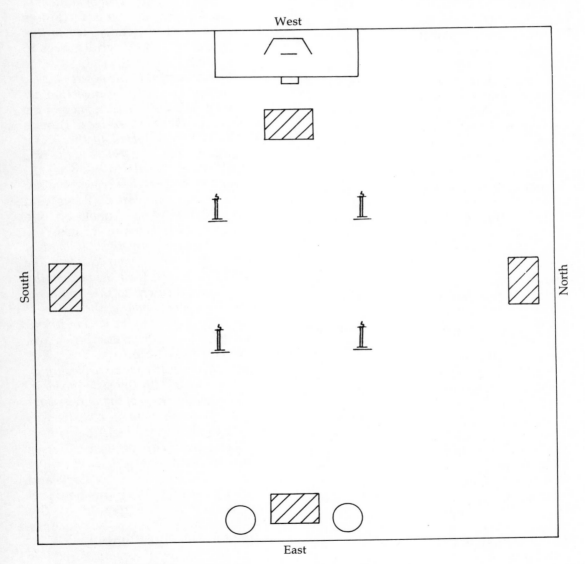

Figure 28 The Temple Layout for the Egyptian Rite of Spring

28. The Priest is the supplicant asking for the 'Miracle of the Inundation' so that crops may be planted. In case it has crossed your mind, no, it will not cause a local flood, the gods are not daft, they know the difference between West Acton, down town San Francisco, and ancient Egypt! This is a Spring Ritual and 'They' know that means crop planting.

There are records and tapes of Egyptian Harp music to be found if you search around. The music department of a good library will be able to help with names, and numbers. On the Eastern altar put a bowl of petals, a bowl of incense, and a Cup of wine. Now you are ready for the ritual.

The Priestess should enter the temple and take her place ten minutes before the Priest. She must then think on the Isis God-form strongly visualizing Her as standing behind the chair. Establish a link with this form through thoughts and emotions, then gradually draw the figure down and into the body. Feel the Goddess becoming one with you. Feel Her dignity and grace fill you totally. Let Her loving concern for mankind be *your* concern also. Let the calmness often seen on the ancient statues reflect on your face, gaze ahead and do not look at the Priest until the ritual requires you to do so. Maintain a mental distance between you.

Now the High Priest enters carrying a lighted taper in one hand, and using the staff to mark his paced steps. He makes a complete circle of the temple then pauses before the East and lays down the Staff. He turns to Isis and bows, then back again to light the altar light. He then lights the altars in the South, West, and North, bowing before each one. Lastly he lights the tall candlesticks, puts out the taper and takes his place facing the East:

High Priest:

Hail to thee great gods. I come before thee as a priest and a man to ask for thy help and succour lest mankind goes hungry and the children cry at empty breasts. Hail to thee Ra of the Hawk's Head, rise in the East of this sacred place and shine upon us. (Raises hands palms out to shoulder level.) *Let our voices reach thee in the boat of millions of years and hasten to our aid.* (Raises hands to level of head.) *Hail to thee Lord of Heaven.* (Bows and moves to the South.)
Hail to thee Anubis of the desert lands. I come before thee as a younger brother asking for help lest the corn fail and the sands cover the bones of men. (Raises hands as before.) *Hail to thee jackal headed one, guide the waters of the Nile to us.* (Raises hands to head level.) *Let our voices reach thee beyond the two worlds of life and death.* (Bows and moves to the West, kneels on one knee and holds arms up to Isis.)
Hail to thee great mother, beloved of Osiris, grant to us your children the boon of thy waters. Hear the voice of thy people when they cry to thee, open the gates of thy mercy and let the waters of the Moon bring life to the land of Khem. Hear us, hear us, hear us. (Bows and moves on to the North.)
Hail to thee gentle dark eyed Nephthys, intercede for us with thy sister goddess, hold the soft darkness of thy wings above us and shelter us from all evil. (Raises hands to shoulder level.) *Be with us oh thou sweet cup of wine.* (Raises hands to head level.) *Be with us and save us.* (Moves back to East and takes up incense. With this he paces the length of the temple to the goddess and offers the incense smoke to Her three times.)
Great Isis, Moon of Egypt, accept this sweet perfume as a token of our love for

thee and thy divine son Horus. Give to us a sign that this gift is acceptable to thee.

('Isis' leans forward and shakes the sistrum three times over the incense. Priest bows and takes incense round the temple. Back in the West he places the burner on the altar. He then goes to the East, brings the bowl of petals and offers them to Isis.)

Flower faced one, look upon these fragile gifts and see reflected within thine own beauty. Accept them as a token of our faith in thee and give to us a sign that our prayers are heard by thee.

('Isis leans over and shakes the sistrum six times. The Priest bows and, walking backwards, sprinkles the petals on either side making a path back to the East. He then takes up the wine and approaches the West, bows and offers up the wine.)

Honey scented one, let thy silver feet be heard in the temples of the two lands. Taste the wine here offered as a covenant between Priest and Goddess. Let the waters flow as the wine flows. Accept and drink with us, give to us a sign that the covenant is made.

(Takes wine up to the Goddess, holds it to Her lips and she drinks, Priest returns to the altar and drinks also. 'Isis' leans down and shakes the sistrum nine times. Priest takes wine round the temple, offers and drinks a sip at each altar. Returns to the West and kneels.)

Isis:

Hear my voice in the temple, hear the voice of Isis, Lady of the Moon. Because thou hast offered to me sweet perfume I have come from the Halls of On, to this place. Because thou hast strewn before me symbols of the Earth's beauty I have heard thy prayers, because thou hast

offered up wine as a covenant between us I will open the waters of the Moon and the land shall be made fertile. But most of all, it is because of my love for thee my children that I will hear thee. Be diligent in thy sowing and in thy work among the crops and I will smile upon thee. Forget not the Earth that feeds thee and return to her a small part of the fruits of your labour. I will enter thy temple and fill it with my presence.

('Isis' rises and comes down from her throne and followed by the Priest she circles the temple pausing at each altar and shaking the sistrum three times. Back at the West she remounts the throne and makes her farewell.)

Isis:

Farewell Priest and friend, I will come again if I am called, see that my children forget not the great mother, come to me that I may bless thee.

(Priest kneels on Her footstool and Isis touches him with the ankh, then she shakes the sistrum over him three times. He rises, bows and returns to Western altar, bows again and returns to East. He makes a cirlce of the Temple putting out the lights except the Western altar. Then he comes to the West last of all and makes a silent farewell to the Goddess, then puts out the light and leaves. The Priestess allows the Goddess to leave her consciousness fully, then makes her own thanks, rises and leaves the temple. This completes the ritual.)

Reading List
Brennan, J.H., *Getting What You Want* (Thorsons, 1985)
Fortune, Dion, *The Mystical Qabalah* (Benn, 1935)

Green, Marian, *A Harvest of Festivals* (Longman, 1980)

Hope, Murry, *Practical Egyptian Magic* (Aquarian Press, 1984)

Hope, Murry, *Practical Greek Magic* (Aquarian Press, 1985)

The Seventh Month

Building the Group Soul

Date started ....   Date ended ....

Openings and Closings

The way you open and close a ritual is very important, such things are the Alpha and Omega of the Rite and as such deserve your full attention at all times. If you do not open the temple in the right way you will not get the full influx of power needed to carry the ritual right through. If you do not close firmly, you will get a sloppy ritual and more often than not, some form of phenomena such as noises, smells, balls of light flitting around, etc. It is nothing to be frightened about, it's just unused force trying to find a way 'home'. So make these points of your rituals very definite and firm in voice, and in action. In fact all the way through a ritual you must be authoritative without being bossy, particular without being a nit picker. Don't creep apologetically around the temple, stride or pace around it with an upright stance and dignity. Don't whisper your invocations into the quarters, speak up and out, and with confidence. You don't have to shout either, but like an actor, judge the acoustics of the room and pitch your voice accordingly.

More trouble is caused during the opening and closing of a ritual than at any other time, so learn them well. By now you should have the Lesser Banishing Ritual of the Pentagram at your magical fingertips. When performed efficiently there is a great deal to be said for it. However over a period of time, as with all things, a certain sloppiness can creep in. Make a point of overhauling your 'performance' from time to time and tightening up the loose ends. The trouble arises if exactly the same words, gestures and movements are used at both ends of a ritual. A banishing rite banishes, *ergo* it cannot be used at the beginning *and* at the end. Few magicians bear this in mind and bumble into ritualistic chaos.

The increasing popularity of the occult can be blamed for the hit and miss methods of ceremonial magic, people with little or no training apply their own ideas and most of them miss. All rituals are divided into three parts, an opening, a closing, and the bit in the middle which is the crux of the whole thing. An opening invites certain powers into the quarters as allies or friends, you request their support or at least try to arouse their interest in what

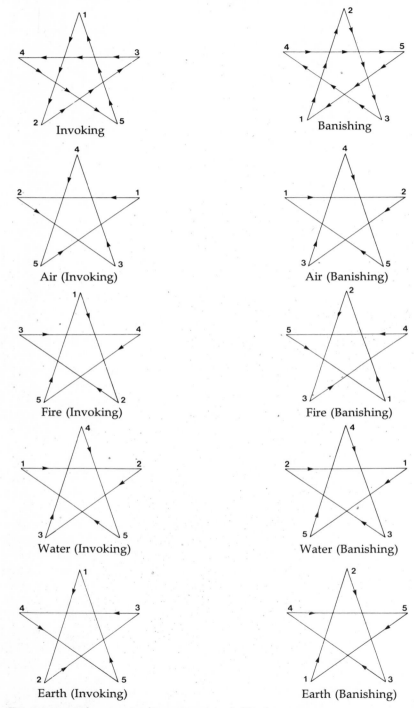

Figure 29 Pentagrams for use in Openings and Closings

you are about to do. The circling of a temple or sacred enclosure is done to define the area, to mark it out as the territory of the Gods, and is usually combined with a cleansing rite such as the sprinkling of salt and water, the carrying round of incense, etc. If you use the Lesser Banishing Ritual of the Pentagram as an opening, make certain you do it *before* you invoke the presence of the God-forms, and not after, otherwise you will have a nice clean temple, but no one in it! Also make certain you know which Pentagram opens and which one dismisses, an important point!

There are different Pentagrams for the different Elements, and they are used when you are working with one element through the Rite. They are useful to know and you will find them pictured in Figure 29. They take a little time to master but the results are worth it. There are many different openings and closings and each tradition has a particular slant which stamps its mark on the work, but all are at the same time an integral part and a separate part of any ritual. Integral because the work cannot take place without it, separate because it has a distinct purpose within the ceremony itself. A good magician will research, adapt and learn as many openings and closings as he can, and this can be integrated with your study programme.

The Ritual in Detail

Let's now take each stage of the ritual and look at it in detail The opening itself can be broken down into separate parts, the marking out of the enclosure, the cleansing and the bringing in of the powers, God-forms, Archangels, whatever or whoever, your ritual needs. In the qabalistic rituals, marking out the boundaries or

the circumnambulations are always three in number. Three because the ritual is taking place on the level of form, Malkuth, and three is the number of form in its highest sense, Binah. This makes sure your ritual manifests in the highest sense of form. In the higher levels of qabalistic ritual you adapt the circles to the level of whichever one of the Four Worlds you wish to contact. It is not often realized that the same ritual can be performed at different levels and with different results, simply by changing colours, symbols and numbers to line up with the higher planes.

Once the enclosure is marked out, the next step is the cleansing. This is usually done first with salt and water, then with incense. The Magus can carry out both duties or the cleansing can be carried out by another officer. Sometimes in the Celtic tradition the cleansing and the marking of the boundaries are combined duties carried out by the Priestess who uses a sprig of herbs with which to sprinkle the salt and water. On rare occasions in the Greek mysteries the temple is marked out by the use of Pan Pipes, a different trill being used at each quarter. A Scottish piper pacing the hall at dinner while the laird entertains, and the piping on the battlements at sunset hold a common origin, as does the sounding of 'taps', and the 'Last Post'. Music can lay down a complicated cone of sound that makes for a very tight magical seal, but it does require a good knowledge of music.

The third stage of opening requires the bringing in of the power. This is done by invoking the God-forms, *or*, by using the inner powers of a Priestess. I said at the beginning of this book that the ideal number in a temple was three, two men and one woman, or two women and one man. It links up with three being the highest number of form. A woman can fill a temple with her inner power and supply the 'ignition' for the ritual invoking of the archetypes. Even when working alone, a Magus uses, consciously, or unconsciously, his anima power to provide this spark. When there is a polarity of sexes in a temple, the Priestess brings in the power and the Priest directs it. Unless this is fully understood you stand a good chance of blowing your ritual to bits.

A Priestess can fill a temple with power simply by entering a few minutes before the others, sitting quietly and visualizing the whole place filling up with a soft violet light. This is a simple and very safe way, there are other ways but they require more training than can be given here. The next phase is the actual opening of the quarters and invoking of the 'helpers'. The symbols, sigils or pentagrams used are many and varied and are drawn with the forefinger, or the Rod/Wand. They can also be drawn by the Athame or the Sword. All the quarters *must* be linked by a continuous line of light, there must be *no* break. Once the symbol is drawn the God-form can be invoked by name, and installed in place. Keep all symbols/sigils, etc. simple so they can be held clearly in the mind as you draw them. The shape should be easy enough to draw in one continuous movement. You can always test a good shape with the help of a friend, a camera, and a torch or better yet, a child's sparkler. Use a slow exposure in a dark room, go through the movements smoothly with the lighted sparkler. The resulting picture should show a picture of the symbol traced in light.

What shape to use? Apart from the ubiquitous pentagram, you can use a spiral, choose which way you want it to turn for an opening, then just reverse it for the closing. A fleur de lys is useful for rituals to do with a feminine archetype, A fourfold petal cross, the infinity sign of an eight on its side, the ankh, the Icthys, the Girdle of Venus, and so on may all be used. Once your archetypes are placed, you can move on to the main point of the ritual which is the intention.

The Ritual Intention

The intention, unless it is obvious, e.g. seasonal rituals, should be stated clearly at the altar, otherwise your God-forms are left in the position of being invited to a party but not knowing who it is for, or even what kind of occasion is being celebrated. The quarters and their occupants are now asked for their help in dealing with the intention, and reminded that their particular attributes are suited to the granting of the intention. All the time the Magus and officers are concentrating on the end result, seeing it as already being in manifestation, pushed onto this plane by the forces you have called to your aid. You will find that a ritual will build naturally to a peak of intensity. Hold this moment for as long as you can, which will be about thirty seconds, rarely longer. Then there is a small pause when everyone, including the star guests can catch their breath. Then the whole thing winds down towards the closing.

The Closing

The closing consists firstly of thanking the Inner Level beings who have attended. Always offer a blessing to them before giving permission to depart. Take them in reverse order and give them time to withdraw, don't gallop around the temple because you feel tired and want your tea. Closing in a hurry *can* be done, but I do not advise it. Take your time. When your God-forms have departed you can make the reverse circles and sigils. Put out the lights, and declare the temple closed.

Outdoor Rituals

In warm weather there is no reason why you should not perform an outdoor ritual, however there are difficulties. First, you *must* have a place where you will not be disturbed or overlooked, this is important for your own peace of mind and well being. A secluded garden away from neigh-bours, the deepest part of a wood, a moorland not likely to be infested by fell walkers, troops of scouts, or marines on manoeuvres, or even the top of a small mountain. You can mark out your sacred enclosure with a length of consecrated cord or rope, and use large stones to mark the quarters. Use your common sense, a Qabalistic or Egyptian ritual is best done indoors, but Greek, Norse, or Celtic rituals can all be done in the open air with great success. It gives a whole new dimension to the work, and should be tried at least once by anyone who aspires to magical work.

A few words of warning, if you light a fire make absolutely certain it is safe to do so and you are not breaking the law. Just because you are outside don't make it an excuse for finishing a whole bottle of wine. Being breathalysed on the way home is no way to end a ritual. Finally, remember there is *always* a risk of someone coming upon you unawares. Do place a lookout so you have enough warning to deal with things. How *do* you deal with it? It calls for good inner vision, clothe your quarters with a golden veil, unless you have brought the entire contents of the temple with you there will be little to give you away; douse the incense and hold the quarters firmly in your mind, frozen in time. Smile sweetly at the intruders and if possible answer any questions in French! With luck they will soon depart and you can carry on from there. In a dire emergency *only*, I offer my own solution. Simply fix your quarters with a stern gaze and say firmly; *You're all closed.* I have only done this on one occasion and I don't recommend it as a regular thing, but it can be done if you don't mind a splitting headache for the rest of the day!

Invocation and Evocation

Invocation and evocation are almost, but not quite, the same thing, but both are used in the practice of magic. *Invoke* to call 'in' or 'down', *evoke* to call 'forth'. When you are filling the quarters in a ritual you *invoke* because you are calling beings higher and greater than yourself to come into the temple prepared for them. But when you are working on a ritual to bring something out of yourself, i.e. you are trying to improve yourself in some way, you *evoke* your own higher self to 'come forth'. Paradoxically when you invoke a God-form, its presence evokes a reciprocal giving out from your inner self. Make sure you fully understand the difference between these two ways of calling.

Using the Magic Mirror

By now you have had plenty of time to purchase a mirror for magical work. Not too large, about 18 inches (45cm) long at the most. An oval shape is best, with a plain frame. Mirrors can be used for scrying, for searching back into your own past, and for divining.

Some people cannot use a crystal ball successfully, I am one of them, but I can and do use a mirror or a bowl of water. There is a body of opinion that says all magical mirrors should be black. Not true. A plain mirror can be used in magical work with no trouble and just a little preparation. First buy or make two squares of black material, one should be large enough to cover the background when you are looking into the mirror. In fact a large sheet of black cartridge paper does just as well as long as it can be fixed firmly to the wall behind you. The second piece should be a square yard with a hole cut out in the middle just large enough for you to put your face, but not the whole head, through and fit snugly. The mirror should be hung or propped up about 3 or 4 feet (1m) away from you, with a small nightlight or candle placed below the face throwing light up into it. The black surround, plus the black background now gives the impression that your face is floating in a black void.

Now concentrate on your face, keep your eyes on the eyes of your reflection. Try not to blink, soon your eyes will slide out of focus the face before you will start to change. Face after face will peel away and you will see it change from man to woman, from one colour to another from race to race, and time to time. Do not extend the first few times beyond five minutes, and never go beyond fifteen minutes however tempted you may be. At first it will be rather scary, even upsetting, in which case stop at once and leave it for a few days. By concentrating on a person it is possible to call them up in the mirror, though it needs a lot of practice, and you *must* understand that this can distract the person thus called with sometimes dangerous consequences. With prac-

tice it is as accurate as a crystal ball, but do not use it to excess, it can become an addictive habit.

Group Souls and Group Minds

As yet we have not touched upon the teachings concerning Group Minds and Group Souls, but it is an area in which you, as a working magician, must have at least some basic knowledge. Along with the knowledge of Group Minds goes the sometimes dangerous knowledge of 'artificial elementals'. They are not the kind of thing to mess with, but it is in your own interest to understand what they are and what they can do.

Group Minds and Group Souls are often confused by the novice, but they are very different in structure and usage. A Group Mind is the result of organized thought by a group of highly motivated people, with its origin in a subject about which they feel very emotional and which arouses deep feelings within them. Never forget that emotion is the very foundation of a Group Mind, therein lies its power for good and evil.

As an example of a Group Mind, take the crew of a ship. These men can, and do, create a Group Mind from the moment they take her out to sea on her maiden voyage, and for some ships their 'elemental' birth can take place in the shipyard. Any ship builder will tell you that a ship is 'born' like a person, with a mind of its own. When the Ark Royal sailed into harbour for the last time, every man aboard had tears in his eyes. To them it was a friend, not just a pile of metal that was going to the scrap yard. All sailors talk lovingly of their ships referring to them as a woman. The helmsman will tell a newcomer, 'she' pulls to left, don't be too heavy handed, 'she' doesn't like that. The ship is a person to them, she looks after them, carries them in her 'womb', they respond by loving her, she responds by building a Group Mind, something that encompasses every man aboard from the captain to the newest recruit.

The modern term for this kind of thing is 'team spirit'. It denotes a group of people with a single, emotive aim in mind. Normally a Group Mind will disperse as soon as the group that formed it disperses, but if they get together again, it will rapidly reform. Sometimes they do not disperse, but are kept alive by the group either intentionally, or because so much emotion has been poured into the Group Mind that it becomes ensouled, and we get an artificial elemental that takes on a life of its own. If its basis was good, it persists as a memory in the racial memory, if it was bad it may go on the rampage.

When this happens with an occult group, mystery school, or religious gathering, it can sometimes happen that the ensoulment comes only partly from the group itself, the greater part comes from a higher level. In short the Group Mind becomes ensouled by the essence of a Master, or an Angelic Being. When this happens we say that the group or school is now 'contacted'. As time goes on, and if the channel for the ensouled Group Mind is kept clear and true to its first principles, the school becomes a channel for new teachings being fed into the world as a whole. It depends upon the potential within the school. The idea of ensouling a group by filling it with a Divine Essence is inherent in the saying of Jesus, 'Where two or three are gathered together in My Name...'. He would have known that even such a small group, given deep faith combined with love for their Master

and Teacher, would be enough to cause a Group Mind to emerge from within them, and that He could then ensoul that Group Mind with His own Divine essence. Once this was done, contact on the Inner Levels with His flock would be much easier.

Any deep faith that is lifted to the higher levels of the spirit by the emotional energy of a devoted group will create a Group Mind and this, by its very nature, will have access to the higher inner planes.

As they work for good, so too can a Group Mind work for evil in a very frightening way. It is to our discredit as a Lifewave that mankind can create a Group Mind for evil far more quickly than for good. Think of a lynch mob and you have a good example, think of the mindless violence of a disappointed football crowd and you have another. The worst thing about it is that you do not have to be violent yourself to get caught up in such a mob. The power of a Group Mind hell-bent on destruction is well nigh impossible to resist. You must have heard people say many times, I can't understand it, our son wouldn't hurt anyone... but he did. They are halfway right, the boy may well be a decent person, but once drawn into the mob mind he would have been helpless.

The real experts in this field are the Ku Klux Klan, who stir up hatred with words of seeming patriotic fervour, music, parades, and strange costumes. Riding at night with blazing crosses held on high they can whip up a Group Mind in a matter of minutes. But they are not the only ones, such things can and do happen in any country, within any race and most are stirred up by experts paid to apply the use of mob psychology for their own ends. They just have to start it, the Group Mind will do the rest. Once aroused, *it* is in command. It literally *feeds* on the violence which it then augments and passes back to the Mob, a vicious circle with destruction and even death at its command.

Once the mob goes, the Group Mind quickly disappears, for it feeds on human energy, then reason returns, and with it horror and self-loathing. The tragedy is that once such a Group Mind has been built, it requires little effort to do it again, *and* with the very same people, Hitler, was devoted to the Lords of the Dark Face, and knew the power of Group Minds and used them well. His public speeches were designed to arouse fear, anger, and finally a venomous hatred that he was then able to direct against those he wanted to destroy.

Always, whatever the reason behind it, the same ingredients are used in the forming of a Group Mind — emotion and energy. This is a good lesson in the basic principle that there is no such thing as black or white magic, just pure power and energy, it is people who colour the power. When a group genuinely seeks a higher purpose for its energies, the results can be as spectacular as those seeking destruction. Fear and a desperate need for hope and comfort produced the phenomena known as the Angels of Mons in the First World War. Pride in themselves, their country and their King gave overwhelming victory to the English at Agincourt. The coronation of a new monarch will produce a Group Mind of superb majesty that far exceeds anything that can be seen on a physical level.

Any kind of group can produce a Group Mind, from the local council to the W.I., from the opening ceremony of the Olympic Games to those that form over long established religious houses and cathedrals such as Winchester. Man has always known of their existence and they have come down to us in legends of winged horses and guardian angels, etc. The Four Holy Creatures epitomize the highest such things can reach, they then become the property not just of a group, but of the whole of mankind. They have become synonomous with the Four Evangelists, a 'group' of more than usual ability to create a Group Mind.

Most Group Minds live only a short while and belong to the category of the office party, a first night at the theatre, a reunion of old comrades, etc. But when they are the focus of continuous thought and emotion from an entire race, they can become a permanent fixture. Among such Group Minds are the racial archetypes, John Bull, Uncle Sam, Marianne of France and so on. Sometimes they have a double form, the second taking a totemic form such as an American Eagle, a British Lion, or a Russian Bear. They are built from pride of race and country and have been invoked for many centuries, now they are part of the race itself and will never die.

Sometimes, when used in connection with a mystery school you will hear a Group Mind referred to as an *Egregore*. This is a highly evolved form of Group Mind built up over many years quite deliberately by the brethren of an Order or School. It combines love, principle and dedication and is the Guardian of that school, *and also of each and every member belonging to it.*

If you are ever caught up in a mob Group Mind what can you do? *Do not try to fight it*, one person cannot do it alone, you need a whole group of highly trained people to do that and even then they may not win. Find yourself a spot out of the worst trouble and surround yourself with an aura of blue light. Get out as quickly as you can. Make for a church, chapel, or a Salvation Army room, anywhere where the atmosphere is clear and made sacred by people aiming for the highest in themselves. Build up an archetype such as St George, or St Michael, or Athene/Horus, any of the protective deities. As soon as possible get home and take a bath with a good handful of sea salt in it. This will cleanse your body and your aura of anything that might taint it. *Do not go into your temple until this is done.* If you find yourself unable to get out of the area, find some kind of protected space and keep your mind occupied with the most trivial nonsense you can think of. Nursery rhymes are the best. Keep repeating them so that your mind is not pulled into the maelstrom of emotion going on around you.

There are very few books about the occult side of Group Minds, but quite a few on mob psychology and behavioural psychology. They will give you some ideas. W.McDougal's *The Group Mind*, W. Trotter's *Psychology and the Herd in Peace and War*, and Jung's *Man and his Symbols* are the best. C. Leadbetter's book *Science and the Sacraments* is out of print but if you see it get it. Now let's have a look at Group Souls, you will see that this is an entirely different thing.

The Structure of a Group Soul

A Group Soul is composed of astral matter out of which an individual beingness evolves by way of experience and the demands made upon it by the organism it represents. That sounds complicated, but it can be made simpler. Man at the beginning of his evolution had not yet individualized, he existed as a 'whole' i.e. as a Tribe. He could think of himself as 'us', but

not as 'I am'. With no separate identity, he was little more than a wild animal. Life was short and reincarnation quick. But each and every bit of experience went back into the soul pool, for man shared his soul in those far off pre-historic times, there was one Tribal Soul. Into this communal soul all experience was placed and shared. Each time a man made a step forward inventing something new, doing something in a new and better way, his knowledge and experience went into the Tribal Soul at death and the experience was shared. As time went on mankind became individualized spirits with individual souls, but deep

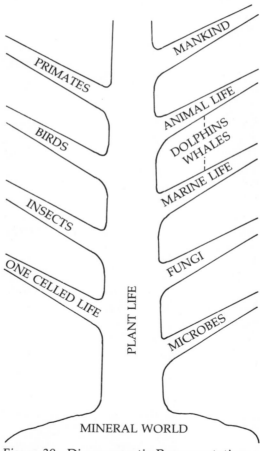

Figure 30 Diagrammatic Representation of the Group Soul

down at a level now buried forever, there is a part of mankind and of *all life*, that shares a united Group Soul. This primitive Life Soul can be tapped under certain circumstances.

In the early days of life on earth, one great soul covered the whole of life's many forms, but later, different species began to impress the astral matter with a definite pattern. Obeying the divine Plan, each life form very slowly evolved its own Group Soul. Mankind's Group Soul went on from there and evolved a soul for each person, but the younger life forms continued to share a soul. We can use the symbol of a tree to show that although each species has its own Group Soul it also shares a Oneness of Life with everything on the planet (see Figure 30).

As each Group Soul grew it evolved an archetypal form on the higher astral and mental levels. This led to the making of a Great Pattern for each species. As man has the archetype of Adam Kadmon, the Divine Man, so there is a Great Dog, a Great Cat, a Great Horse, etc. Each and every life form has its 'pattern', its Group Soul, to which the majority return at death. Each return enriches the Great Pattern or Archetype with the experience the individual animal, bird, fish, etc, has undergone. Thus, if the life has been one of deprivation, starvation and ill treatment, the Group Soul will assimilate this and new animals will be born with a built in wariness towards man and other predators. This explains the way in which young birds taking their first flight south 'know' the way though the older birds fly later. The pattern of their flight is born as part of an inherited memory.

If, however, the life has been spent with those who have understood their role as the designated initiator of the animal kingdom. If they have been

given love, understanding, and the freedom to be themselves and not makeshift children, then the essence of that animal at death takes back an enormous contribution to the Group Soul of its species. Thus did the dog become the friend of man, though man does not often deserve the name of friend to any animal.

Sometimes an animal is given so much understanding that it will tend to return to the same environment. People often remark how like a former dog or cat their present one behaves. Sometimes an animal essence will have a succession of such lives, then something happens to that essence. It individualizes *out* of its Group Soul and becomes a separate pattern. At death it returns to its Group Soul only to pass on its experience, then it returns to its new pattern and to another life *on a higher scale*, or it will await the coming of the person(s) who helped it achieve its new individualization and seek to accompany the soul in order to learn more from their mutual companionship. Sometimes they will incarnate in circumstances that will bring them together again. Such an animal's essence will eventually, after many lives, incarnate as a human being on a low scale of life, or one destined for a very short life, in order to gain the new experience of a personal soul.

Orthodox religions teach that only man has a soul and can hope for an 'after life'. It seems to make a mockery of 'God's Love', that an animal can be tortured to death for the sake of science, then denied a just reward. The Bible tells us that 'He knows when a sparrow falls', in which case 'He' seems to care for them more than man with his personal soul can do.

This does not mean that the animal does not have to earn its personal soul, it does. But unlike man, an animal has not deviated from the path laid down for its species in the beginning. Savage in the wild they may be, but they obey an ordained way of life. Too often mankind forgets that his life and the other forms of life on this planet are interwoven, destroy one and inevitably you will be destroyed in your turn. As the overlord of the planet, man will have to account for his stewardship one day. The 'younger brethren' are fellow travellers on the road of evolution. Remember that each Group Soul has a nucleus, a divine spark of life, God given, that makes it a holy creature and as much a part of the Great Divine Plan as man himself, more so since it has not left its place in the Plan.

The Celtic Ritual of Summer

We come now to the Seasonal Rituals for Summer. By now you should be able to write your own so I will give only two examples from now on. The first is Celtic in its choice of God-forms, though it owes more than a little to the much maligned but richly symbolic Craft tradition. And although it can be performed in the temple, I have written it primarily as an outdoor ritual for a change! This means that you will need few of the usual 'props'.

Summer is a time of well-being, of rejoicing in the promise of the growing crops, relaxing in the warmth of a summer sun. All these things should reflect in your ritual since ritual is a mirror to life in many ways. So this ceremony is purely one of enjoyment. It carries none of the urgency for the return of spring, or the gratefulness of the autumn and the harvest, nor the need for protection against the dark of winter. Summer is for life, love and laughter.

As you will be outdoors, wear something summery and freshly washed. Choose a place where, if possible, you can go with bare feet. You will need a long coil of rope or thick string. A bottle of mead, or some real ale, homemade bread, cakes, cheese, and fruit. A large old-fashioned basket, made from traditional materials, not plastic. This will take the place of the Craft cauldron. You will need something to drink the wine from, pottery goblets are nice for this kind of ritual. Flower wreaths for the women, ivy for the men. This is a rite to share with friends. You will also need a small bag of corn and some honey.

Wherever your chosen place is, make sure the last half mile at least is on foot. The ritual is the first thing on the agenda. It is likely to be very dry and too risky to build a fire, instead look around for something to use as an altar, a stone or a tree stump. If not, then use a white cloth and spread it in the middle of the working place, on this put all your needs for the ritual. Take your rope and tie the two ends loosely together, then the four who will be the officers take hold of it and make it into a square which is then laid down on the ground. The Magus steps into the enclosure, picks up some corn and takes it to the East. He throws a small amount onto the ground outside the circle.

Magus:

Cernnunos, Cernnunos, Cernnunos, sacred stag of the Blessed Isles, hear my call. Come from thy deep forest, leave the doe and the fawn and come to us who call thee. Watch over our Rite of Summer and rejoice with us. We will remember the old ways and the old gods. Take up the guarding of the East, and accept the

offering.
(Throw a few more grains of corn on the ground, then turn and face inwards.)
The East is protected.

The Officer of the South takes the honey and goes to his quarter, there he pours the honey onto the ground outside the circle.

South:

Artor, Artor, Artor, bear guardian of the Isles of the West, of old hast thou been worshipped and given offerings, we have come to make the Old Ones live again. Leave the lair, leave the stream, come to us who call thee. Watch over our Rite of Summer and rejoice with us. Take up the guarding of the South and accept the offering.
(Pour a little more honey, then turn and face in.)
The South is protected.

The Officer of the West takes some corn goes to West and throws it on the ground.

West:

Epona, Epona, Epona, white mare of the western hills, leave the sweet grass of the cwm* and come to us who call you. Too long have you been absent from our lives, join us in our Rite of Summer. Take up the guarding of the West, and accept the offering.
(Throw a few more grains on the ground then face in.)
The West is protected.

The Officer of the North takes up some corn and goes to North and throws it on the ground.

* Pronounced 'coom'.

North:

Mona, Mona, Mona, sacred cow of the dark isle, most ancient of our gods hear us when we call to thee. Come down from the shadowy tor and join us in this Rite of Summer. Come and hear the old words of worship, take up the guarding of the North and accept the offering.
(Throws a little more corn then faces in.)
The North is protected.

(East goes to the place where the rope is knotted and unties it. If there are others with you, they may now enter the circle at this point and no other. As each one enters, a dab of honey is placed on their tongue. All come together in the centre holding hands and start to circle, step three times to the right then twice to the left, three times to the right and two to the left again. Repeat this as many times as you wish. It is nice to have some music, English madrigals and round songs are best. Shakespeare's songs set to music are very appropriate especially the lovely, 'Summer is a-coming in'. When you feel you have danced enough, all sit down in the centre with the basket in the middle. Take off your wreaths of flowers and ivy and put them in front of you, the food you take from the basket is placed within this circle of plant life. The Magus, or as he should be called in this type of ritual, the 'Lord', and his 'Lady' stand with the basket held between them.

All:

Bless the food within the cauldron, bless the wine within the cask, bless the ones who surround us with love and protection, bless the Lord and the Lady who serve us.

Lord and Lady:

Bless the great ones here with us, bless those who are with us, bless the life around us, bless the life within us.
(The Lord now serves the food and the Lady serves the wine to all. It is an added touch to take along some extra wine and corn and when it is blessed to scatter the corn, and pour the wine around edge of the circle.)

When the summer feast is done, gather up all the bits and pieces so that no litter is left to mar the countryside. Leave the wreaths on the earth and use the circle of rope and flowers as a dancing circle. As far as possible everyone should take part, either singing, dancing or playing. Let the feeling of summer seep into your bones. When you feel the time is right call everyone together inside the circle, and stand silently for a while blessing the life around you and sharing your inner joy, happiness and contentment with that life.

Lord:

Let us make our farewells to our ancient gods.
(Goes to the East.)
Bless thee great Cernnunos, proud stag of this fair isle of Grammerye. Go to thine own place in peace, but know this, we hold you dear in our hearts and while we live you will know honour and be recognized as Lord of the Forest.

(Lady goes to the West.)

Lady:

Swiftfooted Epona, mare of the western hills, go now to the thine own place in peace, take with you our love and our blessing, thou art precious to our race and we honour thee while our life shall last.

(Lord goes to the South.)

Lord:

Artor, lord of the Britons, blessed be thy name, return to thine own place in peace, we offer you our love always, guard us, be with us in all our troubles. Share your strength with us and be honoured for all time in this land.

(Lady goes to the North.)

Lady:

Mona, thou of the dark isle, hear me as I bless thee, of all thou art the most ancient of our gods, fill the land with fruitfulness as thou hast done through the centuries. Bless all here and receive in place our worship of the greatness thy shape conceals. Mother of the race be blessed.

All join hands and remain silent. Then hang up the wreaths on the trees and prepare to leave. Walk in single file singing softly as you go home through the twilight thinking of the ancient Gods you leave behind.

This may seem too simple to be a ritual, but you will find more effect from this than many a full temple ritual with lights, incense and robes, etc. Simplicity is the keynote where effectiveness is concerned. You will share a moment of complete oneness with the lost Gods of Britian, and that is worth a lifetime of the more glamourous rituals.

The Greek Ritual of the Summer

Now we come to the Greek Summer ritual which is a little more formal. This is for two people, who represent Hermes and Flora the Goddess of Flowers. The white robes made for the

Egyptian ritual without the collars will do nicely. Add a flower crown and a silver girdle for Flora. A pair of wings cut out of card and covered with silver foil and stapled to a ribbon worn round the neck for Hermes. If you wish you could make a Caduceus as well (see Figure 31). Use a wooden rod as a base, and make a pair of wings as above. Top with a pine cone. Use modelling wax

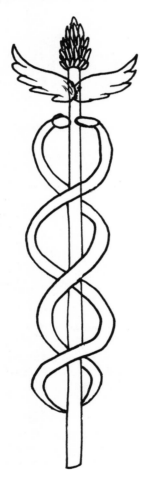

Wooden rod topped with pine cone. Cardboard wings covered with foil. Snakes made of modelling wax sprayed silver.

Figure 31 The Caduceus for the Greek Rite of Spring

for the snakes, or you can buy plastic ones from a novelty shop. Fix them in position with a good adhesive and spray the whole thing silver.

Colours for summer are rose, green, gold and blue. Place the altar before the pillars, and the small tables before the other quarters. On each put a small cup of wine and a piece of bread or a honey cake. In addition, the South should have a burner with lighted charcoal but no incense, the West should have a growing plant, the North an empty vase of water, and finally the East a small mirror. Flora has a small basket with some incense, a bottle of water, and some mixed flowers. All the altars should have centre lights. Flora waits by the door, while Hermes opens the temple. He faces East and with the Caduceus makes the infinity sign ∞.

Hermes:

In the name of the All Father, Zeus, lord of Olympus, I open this temple. Grant to me thy son, messenger of the Gods, the power to open the doors of summer and flood the Earth with warmth.
(He goes to the South and makes the sign.)
In the name of Apollo my brother, I open this temple. Grant to me thy brother the power of the sun that I may ripen the corn.
(Goes to the West and makes the sign.)
In the name of Poseidon, my father's brother I open this temple. Grant to me thy nephew the power of the oceans that I may feed mankind with its fruit.
(Goes to North and makes the sign.)
In the name of Hades my father's brother I open this temple. Grant to me thy nephew the power of the inner earth that I may bestow its riches upon mankind.
(Goes to Flora and takes her by the hand and leads her round the

temple in a circle and then to the East.)

Flora:

Hermes of the swift foot, you have summoned me and I am here, what do you wish of my powers?

Hermes:

Goddess of summer, share with me and with the Earth thy gift of warmth and sweet perfume. Come with me to the Gate of the South and bless it with thy presence.
(Takes her to the South, here she sprinkles incense on the charcoal.)

Flora:

I bless this gateway with sweet perfume and warmth. Bright Apollo share with me and with thy brother the wine and bread of the Sun.
(Hermes breaks the bread and shares it with her, also the wine. He then leads her to the West.)

Hermes:

Sweet Flora pour out thy love upon the life of Earth, bless the Gate of the West with the moisture of thy breath.
(She pours the water on the plant.)

Flora:

I bless this gateway with moisture, great Poseidon share with me and with thy nephew the wine and bread of the west.
(Hermes shares the bread and wine with her as before. Then he leads her to the North.)

Hermes:

Blessed Flora grant the Earth the colours of thy beauty, deck her with loveliness and brighten the hearts of mankind.
(She places flowers in vase.)

Flora:

I give my colours to the Earth. Let summer reign as queen. Dark browed Hades open up the richness of the Earth and share it with all men. Share with us also the bread and wine of the North.
(The bread and wine is shared as before, and Hermes leads Flora to the East.)

Hermes:

Light footed Flora, Golden skinned goddess of summer, let us praise the sky father together and ask his blessing upon the Earth.
(They join hands and lift arms up.)

Both:

Great Zeus we praise thee, and that which was before thee, we ask for the blessing of summer upon the face of Earth.
(Stand silent for a few minutes.)

Hermes:

Daughter of Zeus, sweet sister, have you no gift for the Gate of the East?

Flora:

To the East I give myself, that I may be one with the Earth and all that lives upon her. Sweet brother take my kiss as a gift for the East.
(They kiss, and share the bread and wine. Her crown of flowers is placed upon the altar as an offering. Now they circle the temple, Hermes going clockwise and Flora anticlockwise, they cross at the West and continue round and back to the East. Flora goes to stand in the centre and Hermes closes the temple.)

Hermes:

With the power of my father Zeus, I close

the temple. To thee great one our thanks and blessing.
(Goes to the South.)
With the power of the sun and my brother Apollo I close the temple. To thee our thanks and blessing.
(Goes to the West.)
With the power of the oceans and my uncle Poseidon, I close the temple. To thee our thanks and blessing.
(Goes to the North.)
With the power of inner earth and my uncle Hades, I close the temple. To thee our thanks and blessing.
(Back to the East and to the centre, Hermes and Flora kiss, and together put out the lights.)

Reading List

Brennan, J.H., *Astral Doorways* (Aquarian Press, 1980)

Stewart, R.J., *The UnderWorld Litiation* (Aquarian Press, 1985)

The Eighth Month

Into the Deeper Levels

Date started ....   **Date ended** ....

Astral Doorways

The book *Astral Doorways* by J.H. Brennan created quite a furore among occultists when it was published, mostly because for the first time genuine practical work was put before the reader. It remains one of the best down to earth books on the subject, and despite what popular novelists and off-beam journalists would have you think, the way of magic is a very down to earth subject.

If you have read the book as requested in the last chapter, you should have a reasonable grasp of what is meant by the term Astral. That first chapter is worth ten of the more 'spiritual' books on the subject. Many people assume that the Astral is a *place*, an exotic location like New York, Khartoum, or Basingstoke. It is and it isn't. It is to the beings who have their existence on that level. It isn't to beings like ourselves who live on another level of perception. To them *we* are the ghosts, to us *they* are the nebulous figures of dreams.

Unless you can use your imagination, the Astral Plane is barred to you, because that is the one and only doorway into the land beyond the Rainbow Bridge. Sadly we are beginning to lose our imaginative gifts as we have lost so many other talents. The killer is the printed word, the symbols of script have taken over and we are gradually accepting them in place of the pictures within the mind. Imagination, emotion, and energy are the basic talents a magician needs to succeed on the Path of High Magic. Without them you are better off using the second-hand dreams of television.

Some of the techniques in *Astral Doorways are* dangerous, which is why you are just now using the book after several months of hard work. They are not to be taken lightly nor are they to be treated in the manner of a video game in your head. This is why you were asked to read the book thoroughly before starting to use the magical techniques contained within. I recommend to you the author's own statement, '...if you run into something nasty on the Astral, it is because something nasty already exists in your mind'. This is true, not the whole truth, because nasty things already exist in some parts of the Astral levels, but it is the truth as far as a novice is concerned.

This book contains the most sensible and down to earth explanations of just what the Astral is and how it can be used that has yet been printed. I urge you to read it, use it and try out the exercises described within for they are well tried and tested. In addition to your basic meditation routine try the exercise of concentrating on a simple geometric shape for as long as you can without letting other thoughts stray into your mind. Do this three or four times aiming for at least ten seconds each time. Then go on with your usual meditation. It helps if you cut the shape out of brightly coloured paper and look at it for a few minutes before closing your eyes. This brings me to the use of the 'flashing colours'.

The Flashing Colours

Most people are familiar with the phenomenon of a television image persisting on the eye after it has disappeared from the screen. Few people know that this is used as an occult training technique to relax the eye muscles and enable any latent clairvoyant sight to develop. The image on the screen is repeated *in its complimentary colours* by the human eye. This will soon begin to 'flash' from the first colour to its complimentary shade and it can persist for several minutes getting gradually fainter. You can test this by placing one of your bright geometric shapes on a plain white background allowing at least a 4 inch (10cm) border all round. Stare at the shape for a few minutes without blinking, then shift your focus to a plain white piece of card. The image in its secondary colour will seemingly imprint itself on the plain card. It is this secondary image that can be used as an Astral Doorway through which you may enter the unseen world within.

The Doorway is an Astral one, real on its own level, but not on this level. Such simple techniques can quickly improve your ability to create internal images.

It is very often the case that a true clairvoyant image is seen not as it were, face on but from the corner of the eye. When this happens it is important to observe the phenomena quietly and as if you were looking 'through' it rather than at it. Practice with flashing colours and images will sharpen this ability. To help you in this exercise you will find several examples of imagery in Figure 32. You may like to re-draw and colour them with felt pens, then they can also be used to practice the colour changes as well.

The Dangers of Glamour

Returning now to Astral Doorways, try the exercise of using a short story to sharpen both your visual imagery and your audile memory. Try to find the time to do this at least once a day. If need be, use the time spent in travelling to do this rather than your relaxing and breathing exercises, which should be now be an almost automatic reflex that snaps into action when needed. Vary this by trying to 'hear' your favourite record without putting it on the record player.

Next, test your ability to recall tastes and scents. Use strong herbs and condiments at first then progress to lighter more delicate tastes, then do the same with odours. All this may seem a waste of time, but it is gradually training you for much deeper levels of pathworking where much of your future training will take place.

Within each one of us there is a kingdom of the mind that combines the Laws of both Chaos and Order. In most people that kingdom is without

Figure 32 Images for Flashing Colours

its rightful ruler, a 'Logres' without its Arthur, an 'Avalon' without its Morgan or Nimue, a 'Camelot' without Queen Guenevere. Only when the crown is reclaimed will that inner kingdom be restored to its true state of perfection. For most of us, even if we are fairly advanced magicians there will always be corners of our kingdom marked, 'Here Be Monsters'. If you intend to devote yourself fully to High Magic then the ruling of this inner kingdom will be one of your greatest concerns, and a constant battle against the monsters must be waged.

This does *not* mean that you must be preoccupied with the inner world all the time. That would be falling into the glamour of High Magic, and your work would degenerate into a dream of dungeons and dragons and become a mockery of itself. That inner kingdom is where you form your ideals and hopes, and the dreams that can come true. It is where the higher self is trained, as Arthur was trained by Merlin at the castle of Sir Ector before he claimed the throne. The only way this inner kingdom can be found and claimed is through the deeper levels of pathworking.

The Deeper Levels of Pathworking

You have already done some of the lighter types of working, but now you must learn to go deeper into this strange realm that is never the same two visits running. Instead of pathworking in your favourite armchair, you will be using the temple as a departure point. For the moment it will be enough just to formulate the entry points and make yourself known to the Guardians. Later you will be given specific pathworkings that will take you to the most important locations, but for now you will be learning to go

deeper within yourself than you have ever gone before.

At the beginning of this book you learned that it was possible to meditate whilst upright and moving, now you will learn that there are positions other than simply sitting down in which to do your pathworkings. Many of these are depicted in the statuary of Ancient Egypt and were used in the training of the temple novices. The Egyptians never did anything without a purpose behind it, so learn to look and probe behind the placing of a statue's hands and feet.

Put the altar in the East, then in the centre of the floor put a firm but comfortable cushion. Sit down in the position depicted in Figure 33 with your arms folded across your knees. In museum catalogues, such figures are referred to as 'block statues', it is supposed that it was much easier for the craftsman to carve hard granite with the body in this shape. True, but there are other reasons for it to be so formed. In this position your breathing is slightly restricted resulting in a more shallow breath at each intake, now bend your head and lay your forehead on your folded arms, closing the eyes. You are now exerting pressure on the so called 'third eye' point. In actual fact the third eye, or pineal gland, to give it its medical term, is much further inside the head and is part of the limbic system, sometimes called the mid-brain. However, the centre of your forehead is extremely sensitive and any pressure there causes a reaction in the pineal. With your head down you tend to breathe less oxygenated air and this combined with shallow breathing, plus the pressure on the third eye, produces a mildly soporific effect that will deepen the experience.

Try out this position for a few minutes several times before actually

Nakhtef-muti, presenting
the divine image of Ptah.
22nd Dynasty, Karnak,
Cairo Museum.

Block-statue of the high
priest Hor.

Squatting man. Predynastic
period. N.Y. Memorial Art
Gall., Rochester.

Front view

Figure 33 The Seated Pathworking Position

using it for a pathworking. Make sure that it is not too restrictive for you, not everyone finds it comfortable. If this is so, then use the position in Figure 34, bending the head down towards the chest. This is slightly less effective, but will still produce a deeper experience than sitting in the God-form position which is the better known.

Building the Body of Light

When you are satisfied that you can cope with this position you are ready to do the working. Set up the temple guardian to its 'protect' station, i.e. to guard you while you are in trance. Take up your position and relax into it letting your breathing find its own level. You may find that you slide from a light trance into sleep at the end of the session, this is normal and indicates that your body has adjusted well and is relaxing in its own way. Project the image of the Eastern Pillars into your mind and 'summon up' the entrance to your inner kingdom.

After a few moments your subconscious mind will provide a picture of the Gateway. Allow it to form at its own pace, make no attempt to enter yet. Watch it grow and take shape.

Repose Position

God-form Position

Royal Judge Position

Osiris Position

Offerance Position

Priest King Position

Suppliant Position

Figure 34 Other Positions for Meditation

When it has fully formed, memorize the details and then look through it, to the landscape beyond. In the far distance you can see a shape coming towards you, it draws nearer and nearer until you can see it quite clearly. It may be an animal, real or imaginary, or it may be human, whichever it is, it will be the guardian of this Gate and loyal to you. Salute it, and have it return the salute. Now look at the top of this Gate, and by an act of your will engrave upon the lintel the symbol you chose to put on the reverse side of your Pantacle. By this act you have claimed this Gateway as your own. Name this entrance the Royal Gate. Now you may return to the temple and full consciousness.

As soon as you have had something to drink, and have closed down fully, draw a picture of your Royal Gate and place it in your magical diary. In a few days repeat this exercise with the altar in the South, and you facing in that direction. Follow the instructions as before and let the second Gate build up. It will be quite a different type to the first, but once it is formed, and you and the guardian have exchanged salutes, again carve your symbol over the lintel, name it the Temple Gate, then return to the temple, draw the Gateway and put it away.

Repeat this at the West and North, naming them the Star Gate and the Gate of the Quest repectively. Make sure each guardian recognizes you and that the Gate bears your symbol. Do not try to deal with all four Gates in too short a time. One Gate every three or four days is enough. When this is done you are ready to enter your kingdom. Sit facing the East and build up the Gate and its guardian. When it is ready, walk through the Royal Gate. You will be given a cloak and a staff. With these you may set out to explore.

Remember, as yet you do not rule this land, you will have to prove yourself first. Resist all the temptations to glamourize this part of your training. This is not a video game or a fantasy movie... you are looking at a landscape that reflects the state of your inner self. If there are monsters, evil creatures, volcanos and wastelands, it is because *that* is how your inner self is at the moment. You will have to learn how to change it.

How do you change it? That is something you will have to learn. I can bring you to the Gates of Yourself, but I cannot change you, only you can do that. Work on all of the Gates, going slowly and with caution. Do this for a month then leave it for a while and allow any changes you have managed to make seep through into this level. When they appear on the physical level make a note of it and put it with the others.

When working in this way you are using the astral body, and you know already about your Magical Personality which has been quietly growing in strength with each month's work. But there is another form used by some magicians, the Body of Light. Some think it is the same as the astral body, but it is in fact quite different. The astral is an etheric form common to everyone, a Magical Personality is acquired through practice and concentration. The Body of Light is deliberately built for a purpose, another term used for it is 'cowan'. It is not easily formed, some people never manage it, or at least not fully, and once it *is* formed it can be troublesome, and requires firm handling.

Sit in the God-form position as if in meditation. The building is best done within the temple as this prevents the cowan from roaming around. Close your eyes and build in front of you, with as much power and concentration as you can, the shape of a robed and hooded figure. Build it facing *away* from you, but with the intention that it is a simulacrum of yourself within the robe. Build it slowly and carefully, do not hurry the process, keep at it for a few minutes each and every day without exception until you feel you have built it as clearly as you find possible. This may take several months, or longer, but the most important thing is to do it slowly and carefully. Once the figure is clear, start the second phase. Focus your attention on the back of the head. Now imagine a thin beam of light emerging from your forehead and extending slowly towards the focal point on the figure. When it touches, see and feel it flare like a match head. Now draw it back again. Do this no more than three or four times a day. Once this has become easy to do you may proceed further.

Join yourself to the cowan as usual, but this time let a tiny seed of consciousness travel down the beam of light and into the head of the cowan. Feel as if *you* were inside the figure but still with the eyes closed. Now withdraw it again. Do this two or three times a day, but no more. Finally, when you feel able to send and withdraw the seed of consciousness at will you are ready for the final phase. When the seed has entered the Body of Light, allow it to act as an extended sense of self, try to open the eyes of the figure and look at what is in front of you from the viewpoint of the cowan. You may feel dizzy, if so close your eyes and try again in a few moments. Gradually build up the sense of being in two places at once, but I repeat, *go slowly*.

The use of a Body of Light when fully operational is that it can be sent over long distances as a look-a-like courier

to those who see it. It is a technique widely used in Tibet by high level lamas and there are many records of these cowans being used by them as a communication device. It may sound fanciful but it can be done. However few western magicians have been able to master the technique fully. Which is no reason for you not to try it out at least. A word of caution. With the constant implanting of consciousness, even the tiny amount used here, the cowan will eventually gain a half conscious mind of its own. You will in fact have partially ensouled it. At this point it will almost certainly make a bid for freedom. Something you cannot allow for it has no protection against the darker forces who will take it over and use it against you and even against those with whom you are involved. They will think it is you and trust the appearance. Therefore the moment it feels as if the cowan is getting above itself, give it a good psychic shake, and in no uncertain terms remind it who is boss. Withdraw all contact and do not attempt to build it up for at least a lunar month. This will metaphorically bring it to heel. Do not start feeling sorry for it and allowing it to do as it likes, you will be playing into the hands of forces darker than you can possibly know.

Using Mythology

By now you will be fairly well acquainted with mythology on one level or another. The school in which I was trained insisted upon a working knowledge of two, and if possible, three different pantheons and their mythos. It is a pity that more modern mystery schools do not follow suit for the myths contain much in the way of training and snippets of ritual that give us deeper insight into the mind of ancient man. It also gives training in the science of correspondences and symbolism. With a basic knowledge of mythology you will always have a 'map' with which you can orientate yourself on the astral levels.

When working in altered states of consciousness you are bound to come across the forms and symbols of the ancient world and they can be of value if assigned to their correct place in the Scheme. Frazer's monumental work *The Golden Bough* is the best source of material but it runs to several volumes in its original state. However there are several abridged versions which will give you all you need. Just a glance will show you how alike all religions really are. There is a basic truth that runs through all of them, it appears to be a central point of Absolute Truth from which all faiths emanate. To each race came the prophet, or saviour, or sacrificed god best suited to their needs at the time.

As you read you will begin to see echoes of the Mystery Religions in the world faiths of today. Thus the old myths are not fairy stories told when the world was young, but tiny fragments of truth that have been much distorted over aeons of time, but the particle that remains at the centre, is as true as it always was. Many 'continuing' tales like the Labours of Hercules, the story of the Argonauts, the Voyages of Odysseus, and the tale of Theseus and the Minotaur, are always initiation cycles. They depict the many levels through which a priest or priestess had to go before emerging at the highest level of their calling. Wherever the suffix of 'eus' is found you can be sure the bearer of that name is in reality a man or woman undergoing tests of a prolonged and severe nature. This 'eus' is the name of the King of the Gods, Zeus, and it was to his wisdom and Divine qualities that the priests aspired.

Theseus and the Minotaur

One of the most intriguing myths to unravel is that of Theseus and the Minotaur. Briefly, the storyline is as follows: Theseus was one of the 'legendary' heroes, although he seems to have been based upon a real person of the same name. The 'eus' identifies him as one who seeks a higher form of consciousness. He had many adventures before the best known story of his battle with the Minotaur, but he eventually offered himself as part of the yearly sacrifice sent as tribute to King Minos. The victims were driven into a labyrinth and there devoured by the Minotaur, half bull and half man. Theseus, however, won the heart of the King's daughter Ariadne, and she gave him a ball of thread with which to find his way out of the labyrinth and a sword to kill the Minotaur.

Once the monster had been killed the two lovers escaped to the island of Naxos. Here Dionysus appeared to the young prince in a dream telling him to leave Ariadne and sail away. The God then took Ariadne to Olympus where he made her his wife. That is the bare bones of the story, but now look at it in detail.

Because of his name (ThesEUS) we know we are dealing with someone undergoing an initiation involving an altered state of consciousness. We can think of Minos as being the more earthly side of Theseus, and the Minotaur as his basest self. The wise men of the past used many ways to push home a point of teaching, including parables using the names of real people and past events, so although Theseus and Minos were real, in this story they are being used as symbols for a deeper and more complex teaching. The Minotaur who bears part of the name of Minos is the lower bestial part of man whose desires are uncontrolled to the point of the degradation of the sexual act (the Minotaur was said to be the child of Pasiphae, wife of Minos and the local Bull God).

The symbolism of the half man, half beast is as follows. If the body is that of a man, and the head, an animal, it means the baser part of man is taking precedence. If the other way round it shows the higher aspect of the reasoning mind lifting itself above the bestial. When it also has wings, as in the Winged Bull, then the mind has lifted itself towards the Gods.

So far in the story we have an initiate aspiring to a higher grade, in which the earthly desires are to be purified, not thrown away, but purified through all levels. Those levels include, the lower — the Bull man, the ordinary man — Minos, the initiate — Theseus, and we also have the Higher Anima Self — Ariadne. It is this Anima who with the Feminine Wisdom supplies the initiate with a ball of thread — the conscious link between all the levels, and a sword — the trained will. Armed with these the initiate enters the labyrinth — the ritual experience of higher initiation, and faces his deepest and darkest self. This part of himself he 'kills' — transmutes through his sword of will, and now, completely whole, he finds his way out of the darkness and into the light. But the initiation is not yet over. First he must give up part of this new found wholeness, Ariadne must be offered up to Dionysus — the Divine Spark. This final act of sacrifice of self (Dionysus was himself one of the sacrificed God-forms) brings about the ultimate initiation, the complete *at-oneness* with the Godhead.

Who said mythology was dull?

Using Art and Poetry

Not all myths are remnants of rituals, some are merely tales that have been embellished over the years but which still have a bright grain of truth at their core. Search it out and study it, you will always learn something useful.

Myth is not the only way to search the past for clues to past occult training. Art and poetry can also be of use to you. Painters have long used occult symbolism in their work to speak across the centuries to those who know how to interpret the signs. Many of the Old Masters were men of great learning, some of it occult in the extreme, and left many clues in their work showing where their sympathies lay. The same goes for the builders of the great churches of Europe, stories in stone in their own right. I recommend to you the book by Fred Gittings, *The Hidden Art*.

Poets also have, by tradition, always had entrée to the world of the spirit. If you read Coleridge's *The Rime of the Ancient Mariner*, you can trace the Major Arcana right the way through. It is in fact as much a story of initiation as that of Theseus. Walt Whitman, Longfellow, Thoreau, Byron, Tennyson, Shelley, Keats, Yeats and A.E., all can open the doors of your inner world with the silver key of the written word. All you have to do is turn it.

All this may lead you to think of the occult as something wonderful, exciting and mysterious, it is all of those things, but not always in the way you might think. The cost is high in time, concentration, study, and above all in the dedication of self. In the past some of the famous magicians have been depicted as recluses, living in small dark rooms, hardly stopping to eat, or over-bearing and egotistical. All are true, but you are aiming for the *middle* way. The greatest danger you will have to face is that of being 'fairy addled', falling into the trap of occult glamour. The Path of High Magic is not glamourous, it is long and hard and few make it all the way. It is said that magicians are born, not made ...partly true, the greatest *are* indeed born, but you can be shaped into a competent magician. But only if you can avoid the many temptations that will come your way, including that of discussing what you are doing with all and sundry. Remember your book mark, the first exercise you did in this book? Take it out and look at it, read the words, think about them, Are you still heeding them?

While you have it in mind... make a new one!

Temples Need to Rest

You are now two thirds of the way through your year. Time to give the temple a rest. Clean it thoroughly, wash the curtains, then lock the door and leave it for two weeks. It has worked hard, a lot harder than you have in fact. It may be inanimate but it has taken a lot of battering while you practised your art. Make it a rule to give yourself and your temple a month off every year. Break it into two lots of two weeks if you like, but do it. You and the temple will be much better for it.

The Qabalistic Ritual of Autumn

Time now to look at the rituals for Autumn. A time of harvest, of reaping what you have sown throughout the year. It is also a time of storing up against the cleansing Tide of Winter, when everything that is no longer of use is swept away. The first rite is mainly Qabalistic, and is for one person.

Put four small tables in the Quarters, and the candlesticks between then as shown in Figure 35. In the East put a loaf of home-baked bread, in the South some apples, in the West some wine, and in the North a bundle of wheat, corn, or barley. On the main altar put some small cakes, and the Chalice, plus the incense burner. During the days before the ritual meditate on your year and on your work. What have you achieved, and what still needs to be done? What is your aim for the rest of the year? Write it down, then read it over and condense it as far as possible onto a piece of paper, fold this up into as small a piece as you can and put it on the altar. Have a bath, wash your hair, and cut a piece of your hair and put it with the paper.

Robe up as usual and enter the temple. Light the altar light, and from this, light the other candles working from the East and going round clockwise. Now, standing facing the East, make the Qabalistic Cross.

Ateh, Malkuth, Ve Geburah, Ve Gedulah, Le Olahm, Amen.
(Make the sign of the pentagram and open in the name of....)

Adonai

(Do this all the way around the Quarters. Face the altar.

In the East, Raphael. In the South, Michael. In the West, Gabriel. In the North, Uriel. Welcome to this place in the name of Melchisedek, the High Priest of the Godhead.
(Move to the East, lift up the bread.)

Raphael, Lord of the Winds of Heaven, bless this bounty born of Sun and Air and Earth. Let it feed the hungry and bless the hand that gives it.
(Break the bread in two. Go to the South and offer up the apples.)

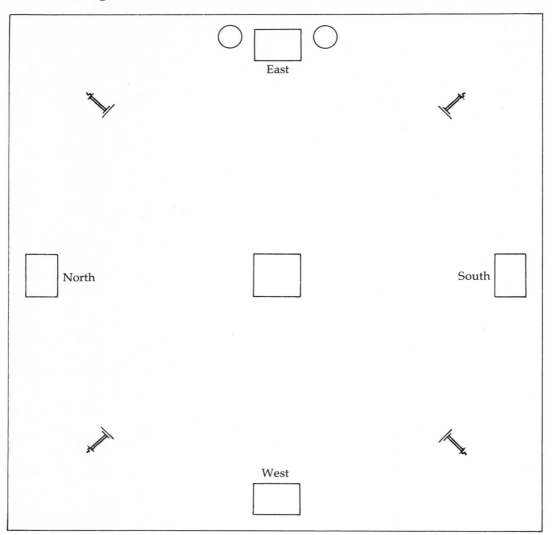

East

North

South

West

Figure 35   The Temple Layout for the Qabalistic Rite of Autumn

Michael, protector of the weak and the oppressed, bless this sun-ripened fruit and let it be not the fruit of temptation but the fruit of knowledge of good and evil that we may know the difference and avoid temptation.

(Replace the apples and go to the West, lift up the wine.)

Gabriel bringer of the word of God, bless this wine to our bodies that we may take into ourselves the wine of life shed by every saviour since the world began.

(Take a sip and put the wine down. Go to the North and offer up the wheat.)

Uriel, Lord of the Earth and all its bounty, bless this crop that it may be plentiful all over the Earth, that this may be a year when all mankind will know the comfort of a full belly.

(Lay it down and go to the altar.)
(Light the charcoal and put on the incense. While this is burning bring a small piece of bread from the East and the wine cup from the West. Pour the wine into the main Chalice and dip the bread into it.)

Melchisedek, priest of the most high God, in the desert after the battle with the kings of Edom thou didst bring bread and wine to Abraham. In this communion shared between man and the priest of the most high God, a covenant was made. I beseech thee in thy wisdom and care for mankind, let this coming harvest make bread for the world. In token of the ancient custom I take this bread and wine into my body.
(Eats.)

Now in this sacred place, guide and teach me, show me how to use my knowledge for the power of good. Help me to grow in wisdom. Bless me, bless those who share my life, bless those who work with me, and bless those unseen beings who stand with me in this place. Bless the Guardian of this temple and the elementals who work with me, bless the house and the earth on which it is built, let it be a doorway to love.
(Take up the Chalice, go to the East, dip a piece of bread in the wine and place it on the table, do the same all round the temple. Move back to the altar and pick up the hair.)

This is a symbol of what I have become in this year and what I hope to achieve in the next. This is my offering of self.

(Cast it into the burner and move to the East.)

Blessed be Raphael who has been my friend and my companion.
(Move to the South.)

Blessed be Michael who has been my protector and my shield.

(Move to the West.)

Blessed be Gabriel who has been my advisor and my teacher.
(Move to the North.)

Blessed be Uriel who has been my provider and my strength.
Blessed be all creatures who share this earth with me.
Blessed be the growing things and the rocks beneath my feet.
(Now close the temple in the reverse order, verbally declare the temple closed, put out the lights, all except the altar light, leave that for an hour or so. In the morning put out the corn, apples and bread for the birds, and pour the wine on to the garden. In this way the blessing is offered to all life.)

The Celtic Ritual of Autumn

This Celtic ritual is for four people:
The Elder, he carries an incense burner already lit.
The Hunter, he carries a silver arrow.
The Maiden, she carries a small cauldron filled with small cakes.
The Wise Woman, she carries a silver sickle.

The arrow can be made from wood and painted, a cauldron can sometimes be found made of brass, designed to carry pot plants. The sickle can be made of card and covered with foil.

(Enter one by one, each taking their seat before the next enters. The Elder to the East, the Hunter to the South. The Maiden to the West, and the Wise Woman to the North. The altar is set with salt, water, a cup of wine and a small sheaf of corn.
Each one places their symbol on the table by them, then the Elder rises and lights the candles placed by each

Quarter, using a taper, the flame being taken from the altar light. When this is done he returns to the East. All sit quietly meditating on the Harvest Sheaf on the altar. After a few minutes the Elder speaks.)

Elder:

The time of gathering is here, the corn stands high and we must give thanks to Ceridwen the Earth Mother for her care of us. How may we do this?

Hunter:

I will hunt a white deer for her and place it on her altar.

Maiden:

I will gather honey and grind barley and make cakes for her.

Elder:

I will gather the sacred mistletoe and fragrant herbs to burn for her delight. What else can we offer to Ceridwen the Earth Mother?

Hunter:

I will hunt the wild boar for her and decorate her altar with its horns.

Maiden:

I will cut my hair and wind it about her sacred tree.

Elder:

I will make a sweet song for her and play it on the harp. How else may we honour Ceridwen the Earth Mother?

Hunter:

I can offer myself on her altar.

Maiden:

I can offer my virginity to her service.

Elder:

I can offer my bard's crown to another and go down to Anwwn for her.

Wise Woman:

(Comes to altar.)
I am she on whom you call, I am she to whom you offer all these things. But you do not offer that which I most desire.
(Goes to the East.)

The Burning of sweet incense is a delight but better by far to see the sweet herbs growing or healing the sick. A bard's crown is a great thing to offer, but who will sing as sweetly if you take the road to dark Anwwn. Better by far that you lift your voice to delight young lovers and stir the hunter's heart.
(Goes to the South.)

The white deer is the shape in which I roam the forest, would you slay me and offer me to myself? Better to keep the arrow for the old and sick that suffering may be short and death merciful. The wild boar is the form in which my horned lord takes his run, would you leave me grieving and with only his horn for memory. Better to wear the horns yourself and learn their power. Your life is sweet, I do not desire that it cease, rather to increase.
(Goes to the West.)

Sweet maid eat the feast cakes yourself, for my fare in Tir Nan Og is better still. Keep your hair to bind the heart of a man, and give to him your secret self. All that I ask is that you love my children and my growing things. All that I need are your hearts, all that is needful to offer is your joy in my presence.
(Returns to the North.)

Elder:

Sweet lady wise and good, we are but mortals who forget how dear these

things are to your heart. We did but seek to show you of our respect.
(He takes the incense and circles the temple from East to North, places the burner on her table and returns to his place. The Hunter brings the arrow from the South to the North, places it at the Wise Woman's feet and returns to the South via the East. The Maiden brings the cauldron and places it before the feet of the Wise Woman and returns via the East and South to the West. The Wise Woman accepts each gift with an inclination of the head.)

Wise Woman:

Blessed be those who give these gifts, and blessed be this sacred place.
(Touches each gift with the sickle.)
Let the smoke arising take the prayers and the feelings upwards to the Cosmic One. Let the arrow's flight be one that lifts the mind to inspiration. Let the cauldron give food for body and mind. This is the blessing of Ceridwen.

Elder:

(Goes to the altar and collects the wine. The Maiden fetches the cakes from the cauldron and puts them on the altar.)
Food offered here.
(All come to the altar and the Wise Woman offers the wine around, and then the cakes. The Wise Woman remains at the altar while the others retrieve their symbols from the North and return to their places. The Wise Woman circles the temple blessing each Quarter in her own words, coming back to her own seat.)

Elder:

We have made our offering and it has been accepted with love. A blessing has been laid upon this place and those who are here. Now let us meditate upon the bounty of this Earth and offer ourselves as her protectors.
(All meditate for a few minutes.)

Wise Woman:

Let the blessing of Ceridwen be upon the Earth.

All:

We receive the blessing with joy.

Elder:

Let us now depart taking with us the harvest that has been granted to us.

Hunter:

My arrows will be used with discretion and mercy.

Maiden:

My cauldron will be offered to the hungry.

Elder:

My learning will be taught to those who seek.

Wise Woman:

I am well pleased with my children.

(All lights but the altar light are doused and all depart leaving only the Wise Woman who stays for a while letting her altar persona of Ceridwen depart slowly.)

Reading List

Coleridge, Samuel Taylor, *The Rime of the Ancient Mariner* (Chatto, 1978)
Frazer, Sir J.G., *The Golden Bough* (Macmillan, 1936)
Richardson Alan, *Dancers to the Gods* (Aquarian Press, 1985)

The Ninth Month

Mantra, Mudra and Movement

Date started .... **Date ended** ....

Racial Archetypes and the Faerie Folk

Until now you have worked in the ritual sense with both God-forms and Archangelic forces, but there are other forces and forms that the trained magician can call upon in the temple. The Faerie Folk are to be found throughout the world and can be both good, bad, and neutral in their interaction with humankind. But first we will look at the great forms that appear within the Racial Group Souls and see how they may be used within the sacred circle.

We can think of an archetype as being the original model of an ideal. So if we meditate on them and study their symbols and the ideals they represent we can get appreciably nearer to the source of their power. You will find such symbols in every country, some are human in form, others are animal or inanimate shapes, some are simply abstract ideals, but all are containers of power for their particular race and are used for propaganda in times of war or whenever national pride needs to be stirred up. It has become fashionable of late to decry national pride, but

without it a nation has no shield on the Inner Levels and can suffer defeat on those levels if an attack was made. Some of these symbols for the races within England, Scotland and Wales are listed below.

Britain: Lion, John Bull, Tommy Atkins, St George, the Rose, Beefeater, Guardsman, Three Lions Rampant, Prince of Wales Feathers, Bulldog, Excalibur, Tower of London, Houses of Parliament.

Scotland: Unicorn, Claymore, the Pipes, the Tartan Plaid, Lion, the Standards of the Scottish Clans, the Bonnet, Heather.

Wales: Dragon, Welsh Harp, Welsh Hat, Cader Idris, Snowdon, Song, Male Choir, Coal.

As an exercise you can search out and list the many symbols that pertain to other countries. Such symbols can be usefully placed in the Quarters of the temple as guardians or as sources of certain types of National Power. They can also be linked with certain days such as St George's Day, Armistice Day, Trooping the Colour, St Andrew's and St David's Days, Burns'

Night, etc. Such times are useful because you can use the 'form' already built up by national feelings for your magical work, with little effort on your part.

A little study and meditation will help you to put them in the right station and in certain types of ritual they can be of more use to you than the usual God-forms. Remember, a good magician will use anything and everything to hand to strengthen, improve and widen his magical ability. He believes that every single thing in the Universe is part of everything else and that it all exists within the ONE. That being so, he is as much a part of such a symbol, idea, God-form, archetype or Archangel as he is of his race, the animal and plant kingdoms or the general life energy of his planet. This includes the other forms of being more nebulous than our own, for instance the Faerie kingdoms.

For the most part the people of Faerie have little to do with mortals, but sometimes their paths do cross. This mostly happens if you are peculiarly sensitive to their vibrations. In Scotland this ability is stronger than it is in England and 'The Sight' is often passed down in a family through the bloodline. It can be both a blessing and a curse. It is common to hear people wish that they had second sight, but the reality is not always either convenient or pleasant. As one so 'gifted', though not as deeply as some, I can say in all truthfulness that there are things I would rather not be able to see especially among the less friendly of the Faerie Folk, (A word of advice, if you have been born with the Sight, do not spread it around, people can more or less live with the idea that you can see 'ghosts etc.' but tell them you can see fairies and you are in a lot of trouble.)

You are most likely to see, or perhaps to invite the Faerie to join your rituals if you are working out of doors. It is rare indeed that they can be persuaded to work inside a house, though there is a type of being that actually delights in living with humankind. Also do not confuse the Fairies of the Wild Places with the Faerie, or Elfin kind, such as Aengus Og and Midir the great Kings of Tir nan Og. If you can believe in parallel worlds then you can believe in Tir nan Og. For the most part leave the Faerie to their own devices, they can be difficult to deal with and have a nasty habit of forgetting their promises!

Having said that, they and their world are still part of that all encompassing Universal Oneness of which I have already written. The magician believes implicitly that he is an important part of this Oneness, can touch it, be one with it, can communicate and influence it, and be influenced by it, which is where astrology comes in.

Natal Astrology in the Temple

So many books on astrology have been written that it suffices to say here that a competent magician should at least know the rudiments of erecting a chart and the basics of interpretation. At the same time you should never allow the 'stars' to rule your life. They indicate trends or the possible outcome of a certain situation, but are not irreversible events. Have your chart drawn up by a competent astrologer, if you can afford it have it progressed for a three year period as this will give you a broad base on which to make plans. I have given a few names in the summary. This does not mean I think they are the only good astrologers around, merely that I have personal experience of their work and regard it as excellent.

Ask for the declination of the planets in your chart, this will tell you which are above or below the horizon. This information can be used for a type of meditation or ritual different from any you have done so far.

Know Thyself, this is the maxim by which all occultists, be they magicians or mystics, strive to live. It is the aim of the great Qabalistic Ritual whose intention is 'The Knowledge and Conversation of the Holy Guardian Angel', it has other names in other traditions, but this is the best known. That ritual requires a lot more experience and training than you will

accrue in one year, but you can make a start on that same intention by use of a certain type of meditation. It will require all your skill in creative imagination, and every ounce of concentration you possess.

We will take it in stages. Prepare yourself with the usual breathing and relaxation exercises, then begin to visualize. Imagine that you stand in deep space, at first you can see only a few faint stars, then gradually there comes into being around you a great shining ring, and then another outside it. When this double ring is quite clear it should surround you at about waist

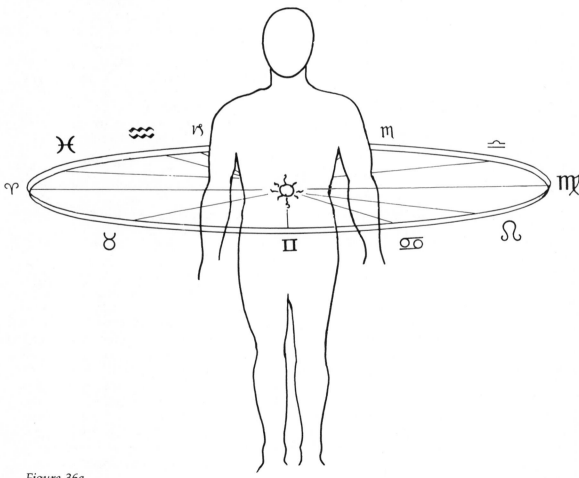

Figure 36a

height, but it will seem to be at some distance from you, giving the impression of great size. When all this is clear you will begin to see lines of force emanating from your body (see Figure 36a).

These lines of force flow out towards the double circle dividing it into twelve sections. For the moment this is as far as you should go in the meditation. Stand for a while in contemplation of the sectioned ring, then return to full awareness. Practice this combined meditation and pathworking until you have received your natal chart, or, if you already know how your chart

looks and the position of the planets, you may go ahead to the next stage.

Build up the scene as before, allow the ring to come into being first as a single circle, then the outer ring forming around it. Now build the divisions, count them as they appear with each line of force as it emanates from your body. There is no 'direction' in space, but the way you are facing we will call the horizon. Recall to mind the sign of the zodiac that is in your first house, if you do not know your true birth time, then place your sun sign in that house.

Now turn slowly, facing each section

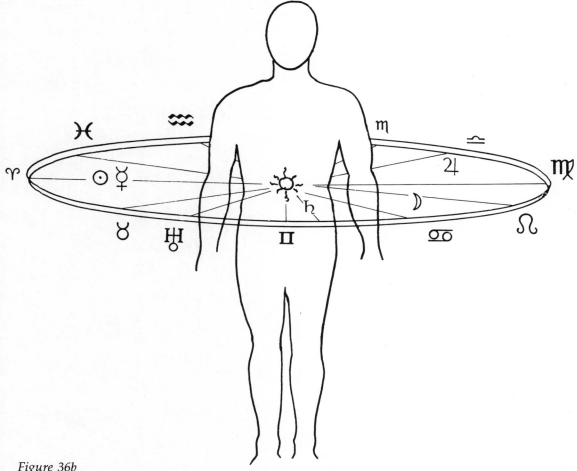

Figure 36b

in turn and visualizing the appropriate sign in that house according to your chart. Take your time and build it as clearly as you possibly can, you may have an intercepted sign in your chart, if so, just place it exactly as it is placed in your chart. If your creative eye is good enough you can attempt to align the lines of force to the exact degree of the houses but do not worry if you cannot manage it, just allow the 'chart' to form, giving 30 degrees to each section. Hold this picture steady and meditate on it. This was how the zodiac looked when you were born. Look at each house, turning as you do

so, think about what you know of each sign, and each house. That is enough for now, return to full awareness and write down what you have realized about your zodiac.

Now for a few days make a study of your natal plan and of the meaning of the houses and signs, when you have done that commit to memory the placing of each planet as it is placed in your chart. When you can remember it all, do the meditation again, starting as always with the build up of the rings and the lines of force, and progressing to the full zodiac. This time face the sign and the house in which your natal

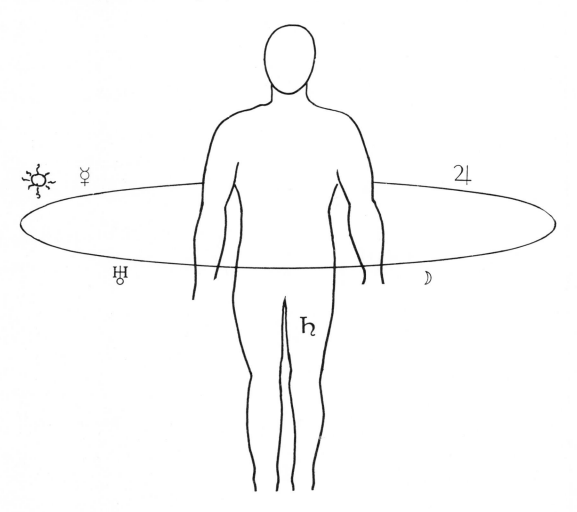

Sun has its place, think about the influence this has upon you, now look for the planet Mercury and see how close or how far it is from the Sun. Now look for Venus and Mars where you know they should be according to your chart. Each time think about what influence they will have upon you, working from that area. Gradually move around until you have placed each planet in its correct house and sign (see Figure 36b). That is enough, return now to full awareness and write down what you have learned.

Leaving a day in between each meditation, do this for the rest of the month. Each time try to learn a little more about how each planet acts and reacts upon you from its natal house and sign. In the days between study your chart and a good book on astrology in order to gain more insight. Halfway through the month, look at the declinations of the planets, and next time, visualize them not all on a level with each other, but as they really are, some low on the horizon, others high up (see Figure 36c). Now you will start to feel their influence in earnest, now you will begin to 'Know Yourself'.

When you are really good at this, you can build another zodiac above the first one which will 'progress' the planets so that you can observe how they are now, compared to how they were when you were born. This is an ongoing meditation that can be used to observe astrally the state of your chart at any given time. It can be taken further and performed as a ritual in the temple with the aid of a few homemade props, as follows.

Take a piece of black cartridge paper and draw on it the outline of the sun with rays emerging from it, now do the same on another piece of card but with the shape of a crescent moon. Cut out the shapes very carefully with a sharp

blade. Do not use scissors or you will spoil the outline, see Figure 37.

Now make stencils of the other planetary sigils, Mercury, Venus, Mars, Jupiter, Saturn, Uranus, Neptune, and Pluto. They should be no more than 6 inches (15cm) high. Now bend back the sides of the card so the stencils can stand up, see Figure 38. With more card, white this time, make 12 squares approximately 12×12 inches, (30×30cm) and mark them in black marking pen with the signs of the zodiac, see Figure 39. With your natal chart to help you, arrange your temple as follows. Move your altar into the East, you will not need it for this working, now place the signs around the temple in a circle as laid out in your birth chart starting with the sign on your ascendent in the East, (*not* your sun sign, unless you have no exact birth time in which case you will *have* to use your sun sign.) The South should hold your midheaven sign, the West your descending sign, and the North your nadir. The other signs go in between as placed in your chart.

Equip yourself with nine candles in steady holders, you do not want them tipping over. Place them just behind the sign which your chart indicates was the correct position at your birth, and place the appropriate planet card in front of them so that the light shines through and you can see both planet and sign comfortably, see Figure 40.

Seat yourself on a cushion in the middle of this circle, facing your sun sign and meditate on the influences the sun, sign, and house will have upon your life. Then turn to your second house, and even if there are no planets there, the sign and the house will still influence you to some degree, for remember, every person receives the impact of every sign, not just those which hold a planet. Continue to turn

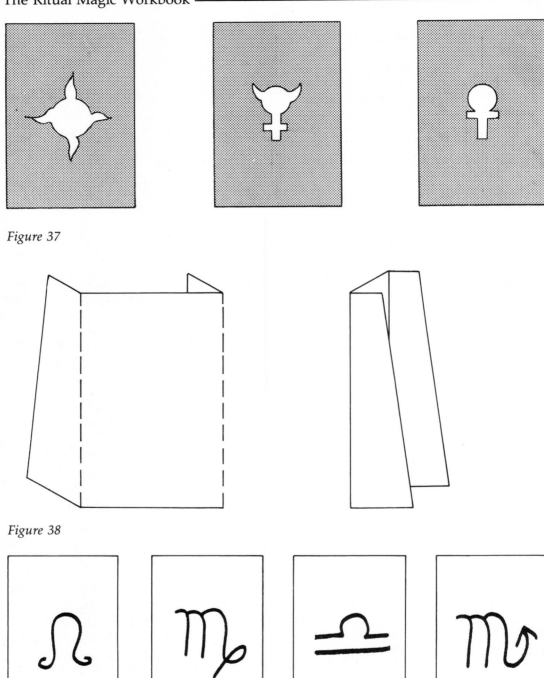

Figure 37

Figure 38

Figure 39

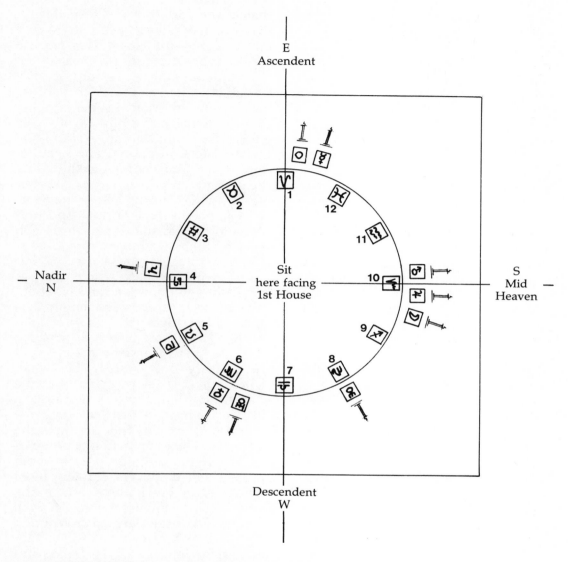

Figure 40 Temple Layout for the Natal Astrology Ritual

and to meditate on each sign until you have made the complete journey. Do this several times during the month and at the end write up the sum total of your meditational findings. Later on you can increase the value of this exercise by using extra stencils and candles to indicate progressed planets, and how this affects the basic chart.

Dancing to Raise Power

Dancing to raise power in a sacred place has been the custom for thousands of years. The figure of the dancing shaman dressed in a deer skin was drawn on the cave walls of Les Trois Freres in the Ariege district of the Dordogne in the dawn of man's history. The power of that dancing figure still draws people from all over the world, in the old days it was drawn to bring animals within the reach of a tribe's spears. Untold centuries later it *still* draws animals, human animals to be sure, but still animal in a sense, and *that* after all the intervening time is a potent example of shamanistic magic.

The power given out by a body moving with ritual intent is immense. The people of the Craft still use dance and movement as a means of raising power, and do it very successfully. But the main obstacle is in being able to lose your self-consciousness about gyrating round the temple. It can take a long time for even the most dedicated would-be magician to shed enough inhibitions (along with clothes in certain circumstances) and tread the ancient measures of ritual dance. But if you want or need to raise a considerable amount of power quickly and safely, then dancing is the way to do it.

The Greeks, Egyptians, and the Hebrews all used dance as a form of worship. It is said in the Bible that David danced before the Ark of the Lord... so you will be in distinguished company. Early man was a being of action, therefore he worshipped his Gods with equal activity, i.e. dance. This has been so all over the world and in every tradition at one time or another. Up until the late middle ages, on certain Feast Days the local priest would lead his parishoners in a dance round the church and out into the village, then back again. It is a fact that dancing under ritual conditions has a strange effect not only upon those dancing, but also upon those watching.

It could be said that the experience is purely emotional, but as Colonel Seymour says in his essay 'Ritual and Religious Experience', 'the fact that an experience is emotional does not make it any the less *real*'. He goes on to say that in the early days of Christianity, Bishops led their flocks in sacred dances before the altars. This practice was forbidden by the Council of AD 692, but it did not stamp it out. Certainly as late as the 1930s dancing before the High Altar was permitted in the cathedral in Seville on Corpus Christi Day, and at the Feast of the Immaculate Conception, and again at Shrovetide. One cannot but think that the present day church would be better off for a little dancing before the altar!

If you obtain a copy of the Apochrypha and turn to the Acts of John you will find there a complete ritual that is danced and which may be used in your temple with excellent results. It was originally intended for an initiation, but equally it can be used simply as a ritual of worship.

What is it that makes dancing so magical? There are many reasons, but the primary one is that, like wine, dancing intoxicates the spirit and the constant twirling and leaping causes a dizzying sensation that lets loose the imprisoned psyche. The rhythm of the dance has a lot to do with it, it becomes almost hypnotic and affects both dancers and onlookers drawing them in until all are one in the ecstacy of the dance. This phenomenon is well understood by the Dancing or Whirling Dervishes of North Africa. They dance themselves into a state of trance and believe that the Divine then speaks through them

The American Indian still dances many of his rituals, and in Eastern Europe it is not uncommon to see a peasant farmer leaping high among his growing corn in the belief that the plants will grow as high as he can leap. The old ways do not die, they simply lie dormant until someone discovers them again. The old Greek word for a ritual was 'Dromenon' meaning 'a thing done'. They understood that in order to get something done i.e. the intention of a rite, *you* also had to *do* something. Hence dance. But can you utilize this in a modern temple? Yes you can, but you have to learn to let go and allow your inner self to surface before you can use it to full advantage.

You have already used movement in the temple to raise power, dancing is the next logical step. Take your recorder into the temple and put on a cassette of disco music, no need to worry about the effect on a consecrated temple... disco music is fairly equivalent to the frenzied drumming and piping and cymbal clashing of the ancient Greeks during a Dionysian ritual. *Do not* have it too loud, you want to be able to hear it, but not to deafen your temple guardian!

Now dance... simply dance, as you please, as you feel, and as you will. Even if you are into your middle years, let yourself go, remember you never lose your younger years, they still exist under the later ones, so let them out. You don't have to be athletic, just as graceful as you can. Dance before your Gods, and let your body worship as well as your mind and heart. If you like keep your Gods in mind, or the One if you are monotheistic, think of them and let your dance be your hymn of praise. Dance until you are nicely tired, but not exhausted, then stop and have something to eat and drink, and probably a shower.

For the time being do this once or twice a week, just get used to the idea of dancing in your sacred enclosure, so that you feel relaxed in doing so. Then change your music to something light and classical so that your mood and your steps must change, then dance with an intention in mind so that you are actually dancing a ritual. First use it

simply as a form of praise and worship, then try it as a form of request, just dancing out what you desire. Go on from there and work out your own basic steps to use with different types of ritual. A frenzied stamping and leaping to build power for courage and enterprise, a softer lilting step for more gentle pursuits. You can use the stately measures of formal Egyptian gesture and movement for knowledge rituals, and leaping steps for the growing Tides of spring and summer.

If you get the chance on either stage or television to watch dance in any form, do so, it will give you more ideas to use. If your child goes to dancing class, do not be afraid to ask the teacher to show you a few basic steps of Greek dancing. You will be pleasantly surprised to find how easy it can be. When this has become second nature to you, you can take the next step. Take off your clothes and dance naked. The human body is not a thing of which to be ashamed, it is the most beautiful piece of engineering known to man. It may not look too much like John Travolta's body, or have the sleek lines of Bo Derek, but it is still beautiful at any age and in any condition. So take 'em off and *dance*. You can cover your magical mirror if you feel that bad about it. But dammit, strip and dance and let yourself feel the music coming through from your toes to your fingertips. Let the God/Goddess come through you and be one with you. Until you have tried it, you will never know how good it can feel when you have left all those stupid ideas behind you and danced before your Gods in the full knowledge of your own Godhood.

When you can do this without feeling embarrassed or ashamed you will be capable of raising a Cone of Power by dance. Everytime you open a temple by invoking certain God-forms or Archangels into the Quarters you are in fact raising a Cone of Power. But if you can open your temple for say, a Greek ritual by using a dance pattern in each quarter and around the temple itself then you will have a doubly powerful Cone of Power with which to work. Raising power out of doors in this way is much safer and more positive than invoking in the Quarters. Incidentally you don't have to dance outside in the altogether, at least you can if you want to do so, if the place is secluded enough and if the weather permits, the latter condition in the British Isles is the most unlikely.

If you are in a group then try a round dance holding hands and going first one way and then the other, or men facing in and women facing out, or try a maze dance in which the leader dances into a tight circle and then out again, all are acceptable ways of raising power. See my book *First Steps in Ritual* for a full outdoor ritual involving a group.

From this you can devise your own ritual movements when you make up your own rites. Never be afraid to try out something new, if no one ever tried we would never have grown this far. By dancing you are imitating the Great Dance of the Zodiac, of Creation, and of Evolution.

Mantra and Mudra

Working along the same lines we come to the use of mantra and mudra, both have a strong link with the dance. Mantra is a mandala of sound, a group of syllables or words that is chanted over and over again and, which in the end produce the same kind of effect as dancing, spinning round and round, or, in the case of a Dionysian ritual as a glass or two of strong home brewed wine. That is to say it separates the etheric from the physical and heightens the finer sense. The best known mantra is possibly Aum Mani Padme Aum, followed by, Hare Krishna, Hare Rama, although we do have mantras in the West used mostly in the Catholic Church.

Mantra has a basic part to play in magic since it is part of the concept of the Creative Word that caused all things to be. The Word, and the God or Goddess who spoke it are for all magical purposes the same thing. It can be regarded as that part of the Primal Creator or Creatrix in which we, and all life everywhere, have our being. Therefore the repeating of a mantra induces within us a sound link with the beginning of the Universe.

In freeing the mind from the physical, the mantra can be made part of the preparation for a ritual, especially if the words link up with either the tradition or the ritual itself. It is not only a group of words that constitute a mantra, a single word, or the name of a God-form can be repeated until a form of trance is achieved. Your own first name can be used. Alfred, Lord Tennyson, the Victorian poet, used to do this and found it a very effective way of achieving an altered state of consciousness.

All this links in with what you have already learnt about sound and its use in the temple, and about the finding and using of a body note. You should also learn something about the Pythagorean system of numbers and how they relate to sound and particularly to music. You have been told about the importance of voice, and again this links in with the use of mantra, so do the daily breathing exercises that you have been doing regularly.....you *have* been doing them regularly haven't you?

There is another aspect to the power of mantra that may have escaped your notice but which affects every part of your life. Political slogans rely as much upon the power of the mantra as do the chants of a Tibetan lama. The advertizing slogan that you can't get out of your head is another aspect. Back in the sixties a toothpaste advert with a totally asinine jingle swept across our television screens, but twenty years later most people will remember it as, 'You'll wonder where the yellow went when you brush your teeth with Pepsodent'. Such is the power of a catchy repetitive phrase, such is the power of mantra.

Mudra

Mudra is the use of gesture, hands and mime, the use of the hands in Hindu dances that describe so graphically the lives and loves of their Gods. The speaking hands of the Hula dancers of Hawaii use mudra. The Praying Hands so beautifully portrayed by Durer are another example. The ritualized gestures used in High Mass have come down to us from the early Christian ceremonies, and in the paintings of the old Masters great emphasis is placed on the hands and the gestures made by them or the objects held by them.

Many pictures of saints show them with a finger placed against their lips and one foot slightly advanced. This is a mudra stance and gesture intimating that the person so depicted was of a certain degree of advancement. The finger on the lips was a sign widely used in ancient Egypt. Another well known mudra is the pose of the Dancing Shiva, and that of Mercury, poised lightly on one foot as if ready for flight.

The moment you lift your magical wand or sword you are using mudra, this means you are moving with intent,

using gesture to say something forcefully. Returning to the Catholic High Mass, if you watch carefully you will be able to distinguish a whole series of beautiful, graceful, and extremely powerful mudras. Get a book on mime from your local library and study it, try out the gestures as exercises. See if you can make up some mime exercises for yourself. Practice using your magical weapons without actually holding them. Then sit down and try forming your hands and fingers into symbols and meditate briefly on each one. A book on Ninja philosophy will give you a whole series of mudra with which to work, so will a book of photographs from great ballets. You must never forget that observation is a magical tool as important to you as your chalice or sword.

There are also mudra for psychic defence, such as the folding of the thumb over the two middle fingers, with the forefinger and the little finger extended like horns. Insulting mudra like the finger placed to the nose, the accusing pointed finger, and the enticing beckoning finger are all mudras that we use every day. So observe the way that people use their hands and bodies, they say a great deal, if you are interested in learning more read the book *Manwatching* by Desmond Morris. It will give you a lot to think about, though it may make you keep your hands in your pockets for a while!

Divination in the Temple

Now we come to the use of divination and talismanic magic in the temple. I am not going into the ordinary use of the crystal, I Ching, the tarot or geomancy in the usual sense. I want to look at them as temple implements and their use within the sacred enclosure.

Every magician should be fairly expert in at least one form of divination and preferably two. It is up to you which you choose. The crystal is one that most people try at one time or another, but not every one can use them. I cannot use a crystal at all, but I can use a bowl of water, a pool of ink, or even the palm of my hand with a light shining on it. So if the crystal chooses not to work with you do not be discouraged, try some variations on the theme and you may be lucky. The symbolism of the tarot cards is fairly easy and quick to learn, but the deeper levels take time and effort. W.E. Butler's book, *How to Develop Clairvoyance*, is good for beginners in crystal scrying, and a companion book to this one, *The Tarot Workbook* by Emily Peach, is the best to use for either beginners or old hands when it comes to the tarot. As an added bonus the latter book goes into the Qabalah as well.

The I Ching is an ancient and valuable form of divination as is geomancy, but both are very hard to master fully. You might try the runes. Tony Willis', *The Runic Workbook*, is an excellent introduction to them and their history. Whatever you choose remember that they are as much a tool for temple use as any other. By all means use them in everyday life, but learn to develop their power within the lodge as well.

Because they are the best known we will just take the crystal and the tarot as our examples, if you are using other methods, try adapting them to the suggestions that follow.

Crystal Scrying

You already have the black furnishings that you made for the magic mirror work, these can be used in temple scrying with the crystal. Set up your temple as follows. Hang your mirror on the Eastern wall, and cover the Western wall with the black cover in such a way that when looking into the mirror you can see only the blackness behind you. Set a small table in front of the mirror with a black cloth over it, and on this place your crystal with a small candle between it and the mirror. Put on your black headdress and take your seat facing the crystal and the mirror.

Now relax and start your breathing exercises, keep them going until you feel ready to start. Look deeply into the crystal and make a contact with it. Now look into the mirror and assume the God-form of Thoth if a male, or Isis if female. Draw the form down on yourself with all the power you possess and feel it settle into your seat. Make an invocation to the God or Goddess that you may 'see' clearly and with truth. Now you can proceed in one of two ways, you may ask your question of the crystal and look into the mirror for the answer, using your own face as a scrying mirror, or you can reverse this and ask the question of the reflection and seek the answer in the crystal. I prefer the latter myself for this means you are asking the question of the assumed God-form and seeking the answer from within your own psyche in the reflective surface of the crystal.

Wait quietly and patiently for the image to form, it may not appear objectively in the crystal, it may appear in your own inner eye, or it may appear in highly symbolic form. Have a small pad and pencil near and quickly jot down the essence of what you have 'seen'. If you have the courage, and it takes a great deal of courage, you can dispense with the crystal and ask the

God-form to show you the answer to your question reflected in the mirror before you. There are some provisos for this variation on the crystal theme, 1. You must *never* look behind you, and 2. once you start the process you *must* finish it no matter *what*. This is not something to attempt out of sheer bravado. You may be lucky and get away with a pounding heart and a splitting headache. If you have even a modicum of the materializing medium in you, you could possibly get an actual appearance, not something to look forward to I assure you.

If you wish to get the best out of your crystal leave it uncovered in the temple whenever possible, it will absorb the influence of the temple oversoul and be refined in the process. You can also invoke a favourite God-form in the appropriate quarter, ask the question and leave the uncovered crystal on the table or chair in that Quarter. In the morning or the next evening, sit and look quietly into the crystal for your answer. You can if you so wish dedicate your crystal to such a God-form and ask that an atom of their 'essence' be spared to fill the crystal so that you may link in with that God or Goddess and scry under their protection so to speak. In the same way you might like to place your magic mirror under the protection of Hathor whose symbol it is, or Aphrodite if you prefer the Greek pantheon.

Tarot

Using the tarot in the temple is a little different and can be approached in two ways, that of using the Major Arcana simply as a ladder to lift your consciousness to a higher level, or as a divinatory aid. In either case the Major Arcana is all you will need.

To use the trumps as a means of achieving an altered state you will need to set out the cards on the floor in a circle round the temple. You will also need a tape recorder and a copy of the tape 'The Journey of the Fool' which is available from Sulis Music Tapes, BCM Box 3721, London WC1N 3XX. The tape is a spoken journey through the Arcana, recorded by bone fide occultists as it was performed at the SOL Conference in 1983. As each trump speaks move to stand in front of it and listen intently, the temple should be lit only by the altar light, and a proper opening should have been performed prior to the start of the tape. Preface the journey by a brief meditation in which you assume the role of the Fool about to start on the great journey into manifestation. The combination of the temple atmosphere, the solitary light and the sense of 'taking a journey' will react upon you quite considerably. You can also lay the cards out in the pattern of the Tree of Life and walk the paths of the Tree as each trump speaks, drawing its influence up into the Chakras of the Middle Pillar of your Body.

For divination by tarot under the temple influence, arrange your temple as shown in Figure 41 using an extra small table between the altar and the West to act as the station of Yesod. Sit in the East and meditate on your question with the cards held between your hands. Now shuffle them thoroughly. Stand and lay the first card face down on the chair, say:

This it the beginning of my journey to the truth.
(Move to the station of Chockmah and place another card, face down, say:)
This is the line of thought that leads me on.
(Move to the station of Binah and

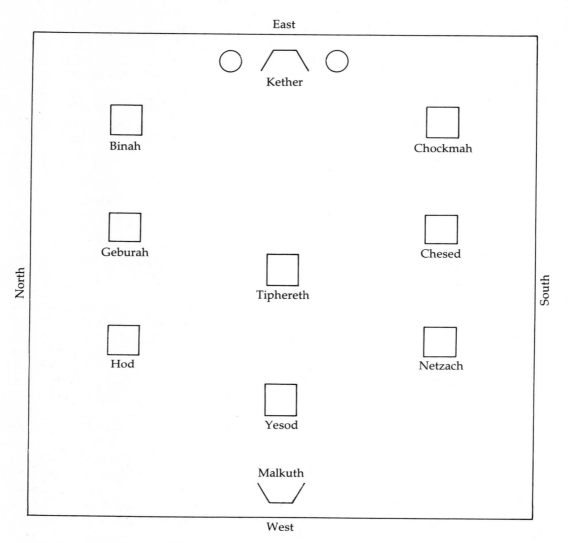

Figure 41 Temple Layout for Tarot Divination

place the card face down and say:)
This card shows the root of my problem.
(Move to the station of Chesed, lay the card down, say:)
This card shows the plan I must follow.
(Move to the station of Geburah, lay down the card, say:)
This card shows that which must be changed or eliminated.
(Move to the station of Tiphereth and place the card, say:)

Here is my stability, my strength in the matter.
(Move to the station of Netzach, put down the card say:)
Here is the way to understanding and success.
(Move to the station of Hod place the card, say:)
Here is the way to communicate my wishes.
(Move to the station of Yesod and place the card, say:)

This is the direction most likely to succeed.

(Move to the final station of Malkuth and lay the card down, say:)

This shows the probable outcome of the situation.

(Now move back to the first card and turn it over, interpret the meaning and move to the next card, turn it over and consider it along with what has gone before, in this way work through all the cards to the final outcome. It is a good idea to have a small notebook with you and to note down the cards and their position so that you can enter the spread in your diary and meditate on it later. You can of course vary this lay out with any other you may prefer to use.)

Talismanic Magic

There is a lot of confusion between talismans and amulets. There need not be, they are quite different in the work for which they are designed. A talisman as defined by Golden Dawn magician, MacGregor Mathers, is 'a magical object charged with the actual force it is meant to represent'. It is an active object filled with an equally active force designed to bring a certain set of magical laws into being around the person for whom it was made. It is like a sign post over one's head saying, 'Here, this is the one'. In modern terms it is similar to having a post code which directs mail to your house.

If made properly it will go on working for as long a period as was designated without needing anything more being done, self-perpetuating in fact. An amulet is more like a safety helmet, it is mostly protective and deflects bad influences from its wearer. Something worn continuously like a St Christopher as a shield against accident during travel, or a cross/crucifix against evil of any kind, an ankh, a pentacle, or any kind of symbol hung around the neck is basically an amulet against something or other, even though the wearer denies it, it is there subconsciously. Often it is given as a gift and therefore carries the wishes and prayers of that person for your safety and continued well being.

A talisman is most often a series of sigils, names, and/or numbers or Hebrew letters contained within a circle. Traditionally they are drawn on virgin parchment or vellum in ink that has been ground and made by hand. However because of the Law of Intent, which is paramount in magic, they can be drawn on ordinary paper with felt pens and will be just as effective. If you want to use real parchment I should warn you that it is expensive, so practice drawing your talisman on ordinary paper first, then when you have it off pat, make a final drawing on a piece of parchment about 4×4 inches (10×10cm) for a large talisman or 2×2 inches (5×5cm) for one that you want to carry around with you.

The first rule in making a talisman is to sit down and decide what you want it to do. This is actually the hardest part, you will find six or seven ideas coming into your head and all of them as important or so you think, as each other. By sifting them all through you will eventually come up with one that will either encompass most of the others, or which will seem to be the most important. The next task is deciding under which set of influences this project will be best placed. This is where your knowledge of symbology will be of use. I hope you are taking note of the fact that all the 'boring' hours of study in the early part of your year of instruction are beginning to bear fruit!

Talismans come under planetary

influences so you will need to know the list of correspondences associated with each one. For example:

The Sun and **Jupiter** work along similar lines and control things like; honour, riches, clothing, position, fortune, gold, rulership and things like nuclear energy when *not* used for warlike purposes. Law. Justice.

The Moon rules dreams, sea, change, birth, delusion, growth, magic, women and women's mysteries.

Mercury: all forms of communication, books, learning, gambling, travel mathematics, theft, science, computers and calculators, television.

Mars: war, weapons, imprisonment, fire, forge work (smithy), men's mysteries.

Venus: love, music, pleasure, luxuries, beauty.

Saturn: earth, agriculture, legacies, death, inheritance, consolidation, banking. Just dues, either money, or repayment in other forms.

In their book *The Techniques of High Magic* the authors advise the making of an earth talisman for use with others, in order to 'earth' them. This is a good idea and one that you might profitably follow.

There are a number of good books that will tell you how to go about the making of a talisman, they will also give you long lists of the symbols that correspond to other symbols, plus things like the sigils of the Planetary Intelligences and the Kameas or magical squares for them, but when it comes down to the crunch a talisman is meant to act for *you* and on *your* behalf. So it is you who will have to search out a symbol that means something on a

personal level. For example, you are an engineer, you are sitting for an advanced exam and you want to pass well, what symbols would you choose to put on your talisman?

First and foremost you want a basic Mercury talisman because Mercury rules all and any form of communication, books, sciences, and learning, all of which blend in with what you want. But what type of engineering are you interested in, constructional, mechanical, marine, or even genetic..? What tools do you use in your type of engineering? Choose one that it typical and incorporate it into the design. Failing that see if there is a God-form specifically for your type. For marine, try Poseidon and include a trident in the design, for bridges, what about a rainbow? the first bridge of all, or a god like Heimdall who guards the bridge of Bifrost, for constructional, use the god/architect Imhotep. The more work and effort you put into the research and preparation of your talisman the better the result. It is the symbol that embodies the desire behind the talisman to *you* that matters far more than using the correct Kamea or angelic sigil. It is good to start off using other people's ideas, but when you can start to substitute your own, things will work faster and better. So get into the habit of thinking for yourself, checking back to see if it is workable, trying it out, modifying where needed and trying again.

One of the most important things to decide is just what it is that you *do* want, but once you have decided stick to it. Practice drawing your talisman on an ordinary piece of paper a few times, then, when you think you are ready, make the real thing. Most talismans are drawn within a circle, and use symbols pertaining to the requirement for which they are being made. Using the table of correspondences you already have, choose the planet who rules the area. Place the planet's sign within the circle plus the symbol you think best describes what you are asking for, then write around the edge of the circle the name or names of the God or Archangel connected with that planet. Then take the initials of your first name and surnames and make a sigil from them. To do this you first draw out the two letters then gradually reduce the

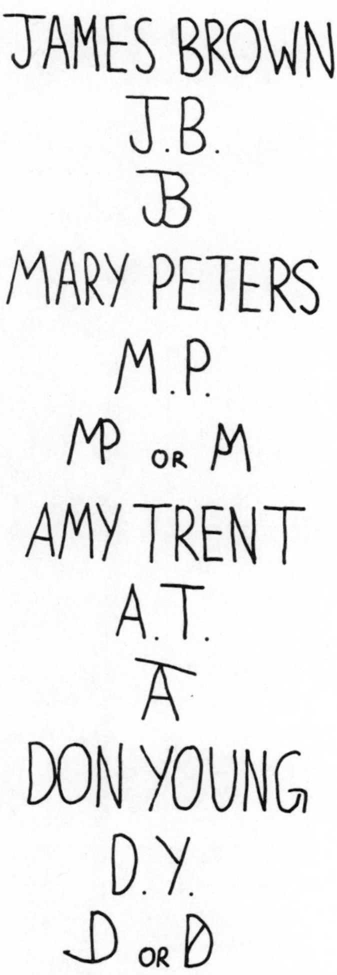

JAMES BROWN
J.B.
JB

MARY PETERS
M.P.
MP OR M

AMY TRENT
A.T.
A

DON YOUNG
D.Y.
D OR D

In all of these combinations the lines of each letter can be traced.

Figure 42 Making a Talisman

number of stokes needed to make them, see Figure 42. Get it down as far as you can, this then becomes your personal sigil, it means *you* on the Inner Levels. Now place this sigil within the circle with the other symbols. Use a different colour for each one, or if you prefer a colour associated with the planet concerned.

Now turn the talisman over and draw a circle around the edge, you now have to seal your magical circle. There are a number of traditional seals, and you will find them along with their magical squares and sigils in Figure 43, you can use any one of these to seal your work, or, you can devise your own seal. Again it is question of what *you* think of as being a symbolic picture of a seal. A key, a closed door, two crossed swords, the 'No Go' sign from the Highway Code, a closed eye, if want to add a touch of fantasy, draw an animal type seal! The main thing to remember is this, what *you* think of as a seal, will *be* a seal..

When making your talisman there are certain rules which should be obeyed. The making should be done on the day of the week ruled by the talisman's planet, i.e. Sunday for Sun, Monday for the Moon, Tuesday for Mars, Wednesday for Mercury, Thursday for Jupiter, Friday for Venus and Saturday for Saturn. You can also go so far as to make it during the appropriate hour for that planet, but you can make a satisfactory talisman without the extra work.

When you have made your talisman the next thing to do is to energize it, and fill it with the appropriate force. This should be done at the same time and on the same day only seven days later. The consecration can be done in several ways, the most popular being the Four Elements, or using the Middle Pillar exercise of the Tree of Life, or by

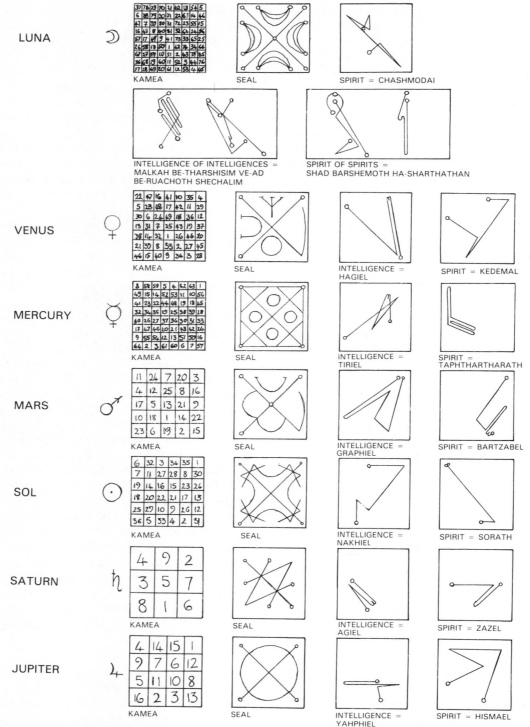

Figure 43 Seals for Talismans

the Ray of Light method.

By referring to your index chart of Gods and their attributes, or to your copy of the *Introduction to the Mystical Qabalah*, you will be able to find out which sphere of the Tree to use. Once you have done this you can go ahead.

For the Middle Pillar method proceed as follows:

Dress your altar with a cloth of the sphere colours, and place the talisman on this. You will also need the altar light, and some appropriate incense, (please refer to the chapter on incenses for the correct kind to use.) Open your temple with the Lesser Pentagram Ritual, then take your seat in the East. Visualize a ball of light just below the ceiling of the temple, make it the same colour as the sphere upon which you are calling. Visualize the same kind and colour of sphere above your own head, this is easier if done with the eyes closed. Now draw in a breath, hold it for two seconds then as you let it out intone the name *Eh-heh-ee-yeh*. As you do this feel the sphere above you slide down and rest on the top of your head, now 'see' the sphere about a foot above the altar. Take another breath, hold it, then let it out to the name *Je-ho-vah El-o-him*. Feel the sphere slide down over your head to your throat. The sphere over the altar also comes lower.

Now a third breath, hold it, let it out to *Al-lo-ah-va-daart*. This time the sphere comes down to your solar plexus, and the sphere over the altar follows suit. The fourth breath is used to intone *Shadd-i-el-hi*, and the sphere now rests in the genitals, the sphere over the altar is almost but not quite touching the talisman. The last breath intones the name of *Ad-o-ni-har-ar-ret-z*, and the sphere settles over your feet, while the altar sphere now covers the talisman.

At this point rest for a few minutes, then intone the last name again and imagine the sphere rising from your feet to the genitals, intone the Tiphereth name and feel it rise to your solar plexus, now send a line of energy out from this centre towards the talisman and feel it connect with it. Now repeat the intention of the talisman like a chant, making it as short and intense as possible See this 'chant' pulsing along the beam of light that joins you to the talisman. Keep this up until the repetition induces a light trance, then draw on the energy from the Kether and Malkuth spheres directing it to the solar centre and throw it into the talisman. 'See' the talisman glow with it, then the glow dying down to a steady pulse beat of light. It is now activated.

Allow what is left of the energy to flood your physical body with healing energy. Sit quietly for a few minutes, then get up, close the temple, and leave the talisman on the altar for twenty-four hours, then put it into a silk bag or cloth and keep it in a place where it will not be disturbed. If it is small it can be carried on your person. Now just forget it and let it do its work. Don't go poking at it or unwrapping it every few days.

An Elemental consecration can be done by a simple ritual. You will need your altar light, salt, water and some planetary incense. Place a seal of your own choice on the temple, then lay the talisman on a piece of silk and proceed. Consecrate the salt and water as you were shown at the beginning of this book, sprinkle the talisman with a little water and say:

I .... do hereby consecrate this talisman with the element of water and ask that Nixsa the king of that element empower it for the purpose of ....

(Sprinkle the talisman now with the salt and say:)

I .... do hereby consecrate this talisman with the element of earth and ask that Ghob the king of that element empower it for the purpose of ....

(Pass the talisman over the smoke of the incense and say:)

I .... do consecrate this talisman with the element of fire and ask that Djinn the king of that element empower it for the purpose of ....

(Lift the talisman and breathe on it and say:)

I .... do hereby consecrate this talisman with the element of air and ask that Paralda the king of that element empower it for the purpose of ....

(Now prick your finger with a sharp, new needle and place a tiny drop of blood on the talisman, don't let this part put you off, you haven't made a pact with the devil, you have just made the talisman part of you, providing a link in the same way that the ray of light coming from your body made a link. Now wrap the talisman in silk and put it away safely.)

The Middle Pillar method is just as simple. You use the same method of intoning the names of the spheres as you did in the first talismanic ritual, but the talisman is placed on your chair so that the genital area is directly above it. It is time you realized that *all* magical power is generated in the sphere of Yesod, the genitals. That is, in Qabalistic terms, where the Machinery of the Universe operates, that is the centre of the creative power of mankind. In ancient times all oaths of special significance were sworn on or by the male testicles, hence the term 'testimony'. So you are working real

magic, and not indulging in some form of perversion. If you have serious sexual hang ups then magic is not the kind of thing you should be studying anyway.

Now visualize the sphere of Kether as a brilliant white light just resting on your head, as you intone the Godname. 'Pull' a thread of light down from it through the centre of your head, passing through the mid-brain (which incidentally controls most of your sexual powers and therefore can be said to be the magical control panel) down to the throat area of the thyroid. Intone the Godname for Daath, and again draw the thread of light down along the spine to the area behind the solar plexus and intone the next Godname. Pull the thread down along the spine and into the genitals and intone the Godname of Yesod. If you have done it correctly you will feel the whole spine tingling and this sensation will centre on the talisman. At this point start the chant of intent as you did before and keep the 'light' focussed on the talisman all the time. Do this until the object of this consecration starts to throb against your body. Then you will know it has been activated. You now withdraw the thread of light in the same way, finally dismissing the Kether sphere.

For the inherently lazy magician who wants his talismans to work quickly, try inscribing the symbols on rice paper and eating it... it does work, but only for the amount of time it 'stays' with you!

The Qabalistic Ritual of Winter

We now come to the last of the seasonal rituals, those for winter. The winter Tide is sometimes called the 'Cleansing Tide' all occultists expect this Tide to 'take away' those things in their life which are no longer serviceable or useful. This is one reason for the tradition of the New Year's resolution. So we would expect any ritual for this Tide to be an opportunity to get rid of anything we feel we no longer need, a bad habit like biting your nails, or smoking, or laziness; or you might have been trying to sell your car for ages, or your house. Use the Cleansing Tide to 'carry it' away. A word of warning, *don't* use it on living creatures, you can incur much karma that way, and more trouble than you can handle.

The first ritual is Qabalistic in type and for a solo magician. You will need for the altar, the usual light, a bowl of consecrated water and a few sprigs of the herb hyssop, failing that some thyme. Have your incense burner already lit and a Saturn incense ready to hand. A piece of folded paper containing the time you wish to see taken away by the Winter Tide. In the four candlesticks at the four Quarters place candles, blue, red, green and gold.

Take a bath using either salt or a ready-made ritual bath sachet, and put on your robe, leave your feet bare, and go without your girdle which encompasses you when it is worn, for this ritual you need to be outside of time and space. When all is ready enter the temple and take up the repose position before the altar. Meditate upon the thing you wish to cast away from you, is it right to do so, are you sure it not longer has a use or a value? Learn to question yourself always as to your motives.

Look deeply into your deepest self, how has the year been for you? Has it given you something new in your life, or do you feel you have missed something? Think of your year as a set of accounts and draw up the debits and credits. How have you been to other people, could you have helped more, have you helped too much and in doing so taken away someone's right to find things out for themselves? Take your time and weigh up the last twelve months. When you have done this, think about the item that is to go with the Tide. Look at it, be sure it is the right one. Then rise and take your place at the altar.

(Put the incense on the burner, then with a taper, light the four Quarter candles. Now open the temple with the usual Qabalistic opening in the name of Adonai. Take your piece of folded paper and go to the East holding the paper between your hands, and say:)

Adonai, lord of heaven, behold your son/daughter who comes before you seeking enlightenment. I have chosen to allow this Winter Tide to take out of my life this item I hold in my hands. Let it go from me without restraint, bitterness, or hurt to any other creature. Let it go to the four winds of heaven, may it be so, Amen.

(Take the candle from the holder and seal the paper with a drop of its wax, then replace it, and move to the South.)

Adonai, lord of the inner fires of earth and of man, behold your son/daughter who comes before you seeking courage for the year ahead. Let this winter tide burn away that which I hold in my hands. Let it go from me without any burning of the heart. Let it find its place in the fires of earth, may it be so, Amen.

(Take the candle from the holder and seal the paper with a drop of wax from it, then replace candle and move to the West:)

Adonai, Lord of the great tides of life that surge across the starry seas, behold your son/daughter who comes before you looking for the understanding of the life that surges within with all its complexities. Let this Winter Tide carry away that which I hold in my hands. Let it be borne upon the starry waves far out to the shore of an unknown place, may it be so, Amen.

(Take the candle from the holder and use it to seal the paper a third time, then replace the candle and move to the North:)

Adonai, Lord of the fruitful, patient earth, behold your son/daughter who comes before you looking for the fulfilment of life and the harvest that comes when the work is completed. Let the sweet earth take that which I hold in my hands and transmute it into her own substance, may it be so, Amen.

(Take the candle and make the fourth seal with its wax on the paper, then replace candle and return to altar. Take up the water and the hyssop and circle the temple sprinkling the four quarters:)

Thus do I cleanse the holy Quarters of that which they have sealed, thus do I cleanse the East, thus do I cleanse the South, thus do I cleanse the West, thus do I cleanse the North.

(Return to altar and replenish the incense, then take the paper and cast it onto the burning charcoal.)

Thus all is to ashes, and is gone from me, the fires of earth, the smoke of heaven, cleansed by the sweet water, and received into the earth, all is fulfilled.

(Sprinkle a little water on your head and hands, then close the temple extinguishing each Quarter candle as you do so. Leave the altar light for

about an hour before putting it out. Let the incense burn right down through the night and in the morning take the ashes and scatter them in some place that you like.)

The Celtic Ritual of Winter

The next ritual is Celtic and a little lighter in style. It is for five people, taking the parts of the High King, the Warrior, the Lady, Arawn King of Annwn, and the Crone. The King should have a Wand or Sceptre, the Warrior a Sword, the Lady the Chalice, Arawn a necklace. The Crone must have a black cloak with a hood and a white robe beneath. The altar should have its usual light augmented by an extra candle on either side. Put an unlit candle in each quarter, and each person should have a box of matches ready. The Chalice should have red wine, or if possible mead.

This ritual works best if learnt by heart, but it can be read if this is not possible. The four Quarters go in first and the Crone last, placing herself between the North and the East. The High King speaks:

The winter's tide flows swift and cold, once long ago the year was young and full of promise, now the leaves forsake the tree that bore them and the world grows dark.

The Warrior:

Once I fought on sunlit turf and vowed my strength in mighty deeds, but now the earth has turned and winter's chill descends upon the land.

The Lady:

Once the young men came to me vying with each other to go a Maying, now there are no flowers to gather, the meadows are bare and the young men come no more.

Arawn:

Long ago I sent a young maid to wander the sweet fields of earth, she took with her my heart, but mankind needed her and I let her go from me. Now my heart calls her back to be with me and leave the earth to winter's chill.
(The Crone comes forward, pauses to right of King.)

Long ago I lived in a land where time stood still and everyone was young and beautiful. But I sought to know the world of men and begged my lord to let me go. He loved me dear and begged me stay, but my eyes were dazzled by the flowers and singing birds. Now my youth has gone and I must return to my own land or die forever.
(High King lights his candle, the Crone makes as if to pass him and he stops her:)

You were the young maid who brought the spring with her, I remember you although your beauty now knows winter's touch. Your laughter gave me pleasure, your singing made my heavy duties light, for this I owe you much. Stay here with me and I will see you treated gently and with care.
(Crone shakes her head:)

I may not stay though gentle are your words and loving is the thought that carries them, let me pass and I will come again.

High King:

Nay pass me not and I will give you furs and soft silks, and maids to do your bidding. Stay and I will give you a castle and power over its people.

Crone:

Power is fleeting and a castle will one day be vanquished by the hand of time, furs and silks are for the young, and I must go my way, but I will bless you for your thoughts and in return will take from you your love of power, then will you rule in perfect justice.
(She passes to the South. The Warrior lights his candle and stops the Crone as she passes.)

Warrior:

You were the maid whose favour I displayed upon my arm, it was to you I gave the Tourney's coronet. You made me knight of knights and for this I owe you much good dame. Stay with me and I will treat you like my lady mother. Soft beds and gentle voices be your lot, my sword will guard you with as much courtesy as when you were young and fair.

Crone:

I may not stay, though well I will remember your fair words and hold them dear. Let me pass and I will come again.

Warrior:

Nay pass me not and I will give you a knight to do battle for you and bring you wealth and land by right of conquest.

Crone:

Conquests breed fear and hatred, and my knight would bring a blood price upon his head just for my pleasure and my wealth. These things are for the down-cheeked youth who knows not the rules of chivalry. Let me pass and I will grant you peace of mind and take from you the nightmares that haunt your dreams.
(She passes on to the West. The Lady light her candle and stops the Crone as she passes:)

Lady:

You were the gentle lady who did aid me when my child was born, but for your skill I would have lost my son. Then you were rosy cheeked and comely, I grieve to see how quickly time has seared your face. Stay with me beldame, and I will give you shelter in your ending, as you did give me hope in a beginning.

Crone:

I may not stay, though I remember that birthing day and rejoice that you and the babe did live. But I may not stay, let me pass and I will come again.

Lady

Pass me not and I will give you care of my child that he may grow in wisdom and understanding, mayhap his hands will also heal as once yours did for me. Stay and I will give you high station in my house and jewels to hang about your neck.

Crone:

Your child will need no wisdom, I gave him that when first I held him, and understanding he will learn by trial. High station is naught to me who once ruled a kingdom far from here, and jewels are best about a throat that's young and fair. Let me pass and I will give you joy in your children and take from you the fear of age when time sets its finger on your cheek.
(She passes to the North. Arawn lights his candle and takes her hands and kisses them:)

Arawn:

My lady and my love, long have I waited for you in this land of the ever young. Has your heart now had its fill of earth and have you come to be my love again?

Crone:

Alas I am no beauty now and Earth's time has touched me with his finger yet many were kind to me along the way and I have come home to be at rest, the only aged dame among the Sidhe. Yet I would have you take from me the things I took as a grace from the world. They would have held me in honour, but I wished to see you just once more.

Arawn:

My lady know you not my powers even now? I did but let you go that you might learn, and in that learning teach the world of men some good. Now draw near and let me kiss your lips, so,
(Kisses her and she drops her cloak and is once more young and fair.)
In this fair land we called you Eithne and now you have returned to me once more as you were. Stay now and let me be your love and lord, the earth shall no more hear your name.

Eithne:

Nay my lord, I promised I would come again, give me leave to spend half my year with you and half with mankind that I may ease their lot with my poor arts.

Arawn:

As you will my love, it shall be so, when spring is near you shall go once more and I will wait heartsore but loving still.
(All douse their candles and progress from temple.)

Summary

This is a good time to go over your day and make sure you are still keeping to the disciplines of relaxing, breathing, and meditation. Do not let up on these things, they are the basis of a magician's continued ability. Draw up a list of the national days, feast days, old festivals etc, you should be able to find one for almost every day of the year. You will find Marian Green's book *A Harvest of Festivals* of great use and very informative. Any S.P.C.K. shop will have a saints' day calendar, between that and any local history book you should have a good idea of what to celebrate on which day, and what 'forms' to use.

Write off for your astrological chart. I recommend the following professionals:

Mr Peter Clarke, 17, Abbey Gardens, St Johns Wood, London NW8 9AS.
Mr Tony Willis, 61a Brownhill Rd, Catford, London S.E.
Mrs M. Anderson, 11, Parkwood Rd, Wimbledon, SW19 7AQ.

These are people whose advice I have sought myself and whose work I have found to be accurate and extremely helpful. Work on the chart meditation/path working at spaced intervals during the month, making sure you have the information to go on before you start the actual chart visualization. If this work spills over into another month don't worry, it can be carried over.

Reading List

Ashcroft-Nowicki, Dolores, *First Steps in Ritual* (Aquarian Press, 1982)

Baker, Dr D., *The Seven Rays* (Aquarian Press, 1977)

Butler, W.E., *How to Develop Clairvoyance* (Aquarian Press, 1979)

Butler, W.E., *How to Read the Aura* (Aquarian Press, 1979)

Harrison, Jane, *Ritual Art and Magic* (Butterworth, 1913)

Morris, Desmond, *Manwatching* (Cape, 1977)

Peach, Emily, *The Tarot Workbook* (Aquarian Press, 1984)

Willis, Tony, *The Runic Workbook* (Aquarian Press, 1986)

The Tenth Month
Extending the Magical Range

Date started ....   **Date ended** ....

I would like to bet that you are agreeably surprised to find you have made it this far.... so am I! So let's go a bit further and push our luck.

Mediumship and Mediation

Mediumship is a word you will hear a great deal in occult terminology. Mediatorship is comparatively new. Both operate in the same area, but in very different ways. The former is a term used most often in spiritualism where it describes a man or a woman with the ability to contact a level of existence associated with the dead. This ability has been recognized and recorded for thousands of years and is not, as some seem to think, of fairly recent origin. According to Homer, Odysseus communed with the dead on his way back from Troy. He dug a deep trench in the Grove of Persephone and filled it with fresh blood. This drew the souls of the newly dead, among them the seer Teiresias, from whom Odysseus wanted information. Shakespeare uses the idea of communication with the dead in many of his plays, among them *Macbeth* and *Hamlet*. Dr Dee the Elizabethan magician used the mediumistic power of Edward Kelly as a means of obtaining information. Closer to our own era there have been many famous, and infamous, mediums. Some have used their undoubted powers for the comfort of others, others with more limited powers have had to 'stretch' them by artificial means, and in doing so have lost the little they did have.

In the area of High Magic, mediumship has been used in the past, and is still used, to contact the Inner Plane Adepti, the term by which higher level beings are known. This involves trance mediumship of a very high quality and a long hard training. Dion Fortune used this method very effectively, to contact her 'Teachers'. It usually entails at least one other person to take down the teachings as they come through, and sometimes a 'watcher' whose job it is to guard the empty shell of the medium's body.

This method has been very successful for centuries, but it does have drawbacks. The medium is totally unaware of anything going on around her/him, also, if disturbed the backlash can cause varying degrees of shock.

Then there is the inconvenience of having to have a sitter and/or a watcher with them. Because the conscious mind is out of action there is the added danger that whatever comes through may be garbled by the intrusion of material floating free in the subconscious.

This method of contact is now beginning to die out and a new form of contact has been making itself felt since the beginning of this century, though the older method will continue for some time yet. The new method is called mediatorship, and its real value lies in two main areas. The first and most obvious is that the communicator never completely loses consciousness, though there are varying degrees ranging from fully conscious, even startlingly so, to a very light trance more like a daydream effect. This means that whatever comes through from the higher levels has considerably less chance of being flawed by interference from the subconscious mind. There is also very little danger of shock if the mediator is disturbed, very often it is possible if one is well trained, to pick up the threads of the communication again once the disturbance has been dealt with. There is no need for a sitter, the conscious mind retains the message(s) and with a fully trained memory, can hold large tracts of material for fairly long periods.

The other new factor is that once a firm contact is made between an Inner Level teacher and a mediator, it often becomes a permanent link-up. This is like having an intercom in your centre of consciousness, or an ex-directory phone number that only one person knows. It can lead to an even deeper link, one that is rare at this time, but which will become increasingly the norm as we enter the next century. This is the establishing of a symbiotic mental link between a high level entity, one of the teachers who serve the Lords of Light, and a human channel who has been able to contain such a link without damage to themselves either mentally or physically. Such a person is known as a Cosmic Mediator.

This kind of link means that the channel often becomes capable of communicating with more than one being, thus the term Cosmic Mediator. When this happens the human channel no longer needs to sit quietly in meditation or be by themselves for certain periods of time. They need no special place or atmosphere in which to establish contact, it is already there on a permanent basis.

The seeds of this kind of contact were sown by the great mystics of the past like St John of the Cross, and Teresa of Avila, and Ignatius Loyala, and not only Christian mystics, but those of other faiths and traditions. They were, in the terminology of time 'possessed' not by demons or suchlike, but by an essence that had once been a human being and who had risen beyond the need for a human body. Sometimes the essence was even higher in level and had never had a body, but then the human channel quickly burnt out because of the strain. There is nothing demonical about this kind of possession, it is the highest part of a human being reaching out to something even higher and finer and truer than itself and offering its service. If anyone condemns it they also condemn the visions and communications of St John the Divine, for he was above all a Cosmic Mediator, maybe the first one of all.

Such a being will not contact just one channel, there may be many with whom that particular master will work at this level, or, on varying levels according to the channel's ability. This may seem improbable when the link is a deeply personal one, and the essence of that master seems embedded within the channel. W.E. Butler saw the explanation in this way. The amount of particles in a human body runs into untold numbers. When the physical body passes beyond time and space and becomes a master, it still retains the same number of particles, though of an infinitely refined kind. Each of these particles, like a holograph, holds the entire being within itself. Thus, once such a particle attaches itself to a human channel, it is as if the whole master was with that channel. But it does not impose upon its host. The human being lives a normal life, most of the time unconscious of that which has taken root in its psyche. Only when the time is deemed right does the internal essence shift into conscious mode and relay its material. At such times it feels to the mediator as if a burst of creative energy has hit them and they can work long hours without feeling tired, that is until they stop!

At other times, especially when the channel may be speaking either to a small group or to a large company, there is a sudden feeling of 'listening to oneself', the talk or lecture keeps to the original intention, but the quality of the words and meaning deepens beyond the normal ability of the speaker. There is a need to listen in to what one is saying, and often a feeling of 'I wish I had thought of that', or, 'I wonder how *he* is going to tie this lot in with the rest of the talk'! Then as suddenly as it came the contact has gone and the speaker is left to carry on, often with a little hesitation as they try to re-establish their own full identity in front of a crowd of people who have no idea of the little internal drama.

Unless you are a rare exception, or you are training with a personal teacher, there is little possibility of such a contact happening, which does not mean that you cannot make a contact of a less intense kind, and one that will be helpful to you or to the group with which you may be working. But the higher contacts need a long, arduous, and very demanding apprenticeship, of a kind few are willing, or able to give because of other commitments.

However it is essential that you know about and are able to fully understand how such communications work, occasionally, that rare individual turns up and with little or no training gives clear indications of mediator ability. They should be encouraged to join a school, or to find a suitable teacher with whom they can train their ability to full power.

Any group, no matter how small, if dedicated and hard working will be able to make a contact. It may not be one of the masters, but it will certainly be a teacher working under the aegis of such a master. When Jesus said, 'where two or three are gathered together there also am I'. He was explaining that no matter how few a group consists of, if that group has complete involvement and dedication it will call to itself a higher essence.

How do you get a contact?... there is no set way, no rules or pattern or ritual. I can only tell you that come they do, and when they do, you will most certainly know. The difference in your work, in the results of that work, and the effect it has upon the group and their immediate environment will be hard to ignore.

Your main concern if and when it does happen will be to ask yourself if it is a genuine contact, an intermittent contact, or just a burst of psychic power that has built up over several months and like a lightning flash, discharged itself through the group.

This brings a short sharp bout of high voltage psychic activity that can feel like a contact. In actual fact it is because the Inner Level awareness of the group has been boosted for a while.

The best thing to do is wait, watch, and record everything for several weeks. Very probably one of your number will be the focal point if it is a genuine contact. *Always ask for checks on anything that may be 'given' to you.* This is your right, and the Inner Levels will expect it. If it does not check out, wait and see if anything else comes through and ask again.

If it doesn't happen don't become disheartened, it could be a simple psychic block. In any case the achievement of a permanent contact is not given to every group, this does not mean their work is no good, or that nothing worthwhile will come out of that group. Everyone and everything has a limit within this physical world, when you come up against that limit, accept it, it is easier. Not every group can be a Golden Dawn, nor would it be a good thing if that were possible. But every group can add its weight to the Divine Plan.

Temple Healing

We come now to the subject of psychic healing, or rather temple healing since it will be done for the most part within the sacred place.

Most of you will be interested in psychic healing, most of you will want to know if you have any healing power, some will want to know how far it can go. In answer to the first, as a trainee magician you will have to at least understand how it works. Nearly everyone has some power to heal, it is instinctive, as witness the impulse to put your hand over a pain, to suck a finger that has been cut, to rub away a headache. We do it without thinking about it.

How far can it go?... well this is where I stick my neck out and say, with the exception of rare, unpredictable and seemingly random cases, psychic healing has its limits. I am afraid I have little patience with someone suffering with acute appendicitis who thinks that a psychic healer can cure it without resorting to an operation. By the time they have found out it cannot be done, it is too late. Yes, it *is* possible, but highly improbable. It is no good putting marigold petals on gangrene. You have to put psychic healing into perspective.

Where it is of enormous help is in actual healing, i.e. helping people over serious operations, getting the wound to heal quickly and without complications. It can help in things like depressions, breakdowns, assisting the body to help itself so that it will respond to the medical treatment being prescribed. I know that some of the drugs given are harmful, but if the body is encouraged by psychic healing to respond quickly, then the drugs need not be used for very long.

The time to take homoeopathic treatment is for the minor illness in life. Times when there is no need to take the drugs handed out by overworked doctors. Then, when the time comes and you *do* need these drugs, a smaller amount will suffice because you have little or no build up in your system.

I agree that certain natural medicines are as good, if not better than some of the things you are offered in a doctor's surgery, however try telling that to someone struck down with the excruciating pain caused by kidney stones. Without warning you are rigid with pain and you need something to alleviate it, plus something to dissolve the stones, and you need it right now. I speak as one who knows believe me. But, once the bout was over and the stones dispatched, I was happy to take natural remedies to *prevent* another occurrence of the same kind.

Psychic healing works on a different waveband to natural medicines. It is a gift that in some people reaches almost unbelievable proportions, they can certainly cause ultra quick healing, they can help with back pain and things like arthritis and inflammations. Some people can work over quite astounding distances and achieve the same results. Again I can speak from experience, when an SOL supervisor in the U.K. was able to help a student undergoing a long and highly complex dental operation in New York. By rights the patient should have come out of the theatre black and blue and unable to open her mouth.... in point of fact the only bruise she ever had was where the drip feed had gone into her arm.

On rare occasions miraculous cures have happened, and I am quite prepared to accept them, but I think it is unwise to think that a psychic healer can *always* help, especially when the problem is already full blown, perhaps even terminal. In these cases where the power of the psychic healer *can* help is in assisting the body's own healing powers to assert themselves, to wake them up, get them going and in directing them, plus the healer's own power to cause full healing where this is possible, and if not to help the natural pain killers present in the brain to take over.

I would not want the reader to think I am against healers, far from it, two of my best friends, people I hold dear, are very powerful healers, but I think it lays too much of a burden upon such people to expect them to perform miracles to order. All healers are empathic and extra sensitive, when they fail to do as much as they would wish, the backlash is tremendous. Ask them to do as much as is possible, but do not ask them for the impossible.

Do you have healing powers? Well one simple test is this; if you place your hand(s) on someone when they are in pain, do your hands get very hot, or very cold, or do they stay the same? Most, though not all healers have great heat in their hands and this is felt by the people they are healing. A few, feel their hands go cold as the healing power leaves them for the patient.

My advice is this, if you feel you have some healing power, go along to a reputable spiritual healing group and let their clairvoyant have a look at you on the Inner Levels. If you do have some power of this kind work with them to develop it. Some healers, those who are born to it, need little or no training, they 'recall' what they were taught when they were trained by the ancient Therapeutoi, but they are very much the exception.

If one of your group, or a member of your family requires healing you may certainly try invoking the appropriate God-form. Aesculapius, Apollo, Cheiron, and Hippocrates will all work within the Greek tradition. Isis or Thoth in the Egyptian, Jesus of Nazareth, or Raphael within the Qabalistic.

If it is a member of the group, or yourself, you can try sleeping in the temple on the Pastos, a narrow couch used for such purposes. Invoke the God-form you have decided upon, cover yourself with a blue sheet or blanket, and sleep immediately after the invocation. Sometimes a dream will clarify the root cause of your problem, and this will enable you to deal with it at ground level.

If you have been asked to do

something for a person you do not know, or who is far away, you must have something of theirs on which to focus the healing power. Lay the item on the altar, or the Pastos, open the temple in the tradition you intend to use and invoke the healing God-form. It is a good idea to use the powers of the South, West and North to reinforce those of the East. For instance, you might place Aesculapius in the East, invoke Apollo in the South and ask him, as the father of Aesculapius to increase his power to heal. You could place Athene in the West and ask that her wisdom be granted to enhance the power of the East. In the North you could place Hades the Lord of the Hidden Aspects, and ask his help in finding out just where the problem has its root.

Before I get a mail bag full of letters telling me that no one heals by their own power, that it is the power of God that heals, let me make one thing clear. Men and women are the children of that unknowable Prime Cause that has a thousand names, only one of which is God. As a child of this Great Entity, he or she is entitled to use any and all the powers or talents they have been given. Those powers and talents have been given freely, as gifts, to use for the good of others, the healer is well aware who bestowed those gifts, and aware that they were given to use as was thought fit. Free Will was the last, and the most precious of all gifts given to man, he should not be afraid to use it. Many healers heal in the name of God, but as I said he has many names, all of which are valid, so if a healer chooses to heal in a different name, that does not make it any the less holy, or effective. Healing powers are not only the perogative of those of the Christian faith.

Recalling the Past

Those of you who have read the novels of Joan Grant will no doubt at some time or other think about the recalling of past lives. The psychic talent of Far Memory is not as common as some would have you believe. It is a fairly rare gift in its pure form and can be used together with mediation to recover lost knowledge. It is rarely used for the deliberate recalling of past lives. It is my personal opinion that unless there is a real need to recover a past life, they should be left alone. At this moment you are the sum total of the experiences encountered and dealt with, good and bad, in all your previous lives, odd memories will surface as and when they are needed, you do not need to search for them. There must be several thousand Nerfertitis around, and you can multiply that amount by several tens of thousands in the case of Tutankhamun, though why anyone would be anxious to prove they had lived a bare eighteen years under enormous personal stress and probably died painfully from poisoning defeats me.

You *will* have spontaneous memories returning as you increase your ability to understand their place in this life, or if you arrive in a location that holds strong links for you. There *will* be times when you will need to recover certain memories, and you will need to learn how to do this and practice the technique. But to spend large chunks of your time 'researching' your past lives simply to try and prove you were someone famous is ridiculous. It can also be traumatic. Remember this, true far memory means total recall with full sensory perception. You cannot control which area of that life you will tune into. Do you fancy finding yourself on the rack at a particularly painful moment, or watching someone set light to the wood stacked around you, come to that how would you feel if you were the one doing the lighting? When you work on recall as a group you often find that you touch on lives when at least some of you will have incarnated together. Can you imagine what it could do to your present day friendships to find your best friend, wife or son was the one who had betrayed you to the Inquisition, or had gone over to the Roundheads while you were still a Royalist? Such memories can stir old quarrels as well as loves... which is another thing for you to consider. And it is no good telling yourself that you can overcome such things... maybe you can, and maybe not.

If you are returning to mystery school training having experienced it before, you will probably turn up several incarnations as a cleric in holy orders as well as those earlier lives which are concerned with the ancient religions. It is said that it takes three lives of actual training within a mystery school to make an initiate, but there will have been lives spent simply as 'a drawer of water and hewer of wood' as Dion Fortune said.

What is it like to remember a life lived before? I can only offer my own experiences as an example, for each one it feels different. There are two ways in which it can happen. You may have intermittent flashes of memories, no more than a vague feeling of recognition of a place or a person, but as more time is spent either with that person, or in that location the memories become more pronounced, but rarely go beyond that stage. This can happen in many places or with many people during your lifetime. It can account for the immediate friendship with one person, and an

irrational dislike of another for no real reason. This is as far as most people go in the process of far memory.

The second way is a slow awakening to a different reality that seems to overlay the present world. At times it produces a dreamlike state through which one moves, observing and feeling at the same time, while your own time is still present. As you can imagine this can be a bit of a problem, however, as I have said, not everyone experiences things in the same way, and when I am 'observing' for a specific purpose and under ritual conditions it is much sharper and less crowded by the present.

One of the clearest personal far memory sequences I have ever had came to me at Winchester. It is a place I have always loved even before my first visit, in this life. On a cold spring day in the mid-seventies I met with Ernest Butler in Winchester. I had just finished a series of lectures in London and had decided to stay overnight in Winchester and phoned ahead to ask Ernest if he would like to spend the day with me and have lunch. He was delighted and we spent a happy day in each other's company, one of those quiet days that you remember for years after. We walked round the cathedral and spoke of many things, past and present, something that probably started the train of events that came later.

At about five o'clock Ernest took the bus back to Southampton and I, with the evening on my hands, returned to the cathedral to wait for Evensong. It was the beginning of Lent and the Bishop of Winchester was to give the first of a series of Lenten lectures. I sat quietly until the service. As there were so few people attending we were invited to move from the nave of the cathedral into the beautiful carved stalls. I began to feel a shift of consciousness and closed it off for it was neither the time nor the place. After the service I spoke with the Bishop for a few minutes requesting a copy of the lecture which was to be published, then left by a side door and made my way round to the West Front. It was almost dark, a clock began to chime the hour, and I stood looking up at the West window and thinking how much I loved this old place. It then happened so smoothly I did not realize at first what had taken place.

Nearly all the familar houses were gone, those that were there were very different. I was no longer a woman, but a man, middle aged and none too bright, in fact this other me was very confused. I knew everything about him, his name was Walter, and he had been in the monastery since he was quite young, left there by parents too poor to keep him. He was a simple soul and had never amounted to much and spent most of his monastic life in the kitchen helping to prepare the meals. I remembered quite clearly his opinion of Brother Cook and his overwhelming awe of the Bishop. The cathedral was his only home and he loved it with a passion that in his heart he was afraid might border on the forbidden. His confusion arose from a discourse he had just heard in the refectory. Something to do with the possibility of a man living not just one but several lives.

This had frightened him, he could not imagine living anywhere else and was too simple to understand the mechanics of the argument. All he knew was the fact that *this* was home and he wanted to always be here. He stood before the great window looking up, shivering with cold and as I 'slipped in' he was muttering somewhat desperately, 'If I come back again I will stand here and I will remember, I will remember, I *will remember*.' Then I was back, standing and shivering with the cold looking up at the great West window, telling myself desperately, 'I *will remember*'. The clock was still chiming, and I was left with fast fading memories a few of which have remained. I know, with a certainty beyond words, thoughts, or reason that somewhere under the stones of Winchester lie the bones of a none too bright little monk who wanted nothing more of life than to be where he was, in Winchester, We are the same person, we still love Winchester, and each time I pass through on my way up to London I look to catch the short glimpse of the cathedral.

Among the other 'memories' that have been most clear is that of watching my mother and father walking away and leaving me with a strange woman, kindly, but strict, who was to be my guide and teacher from now on. Ahead of me were long years of hard work and study, I felt resentful and afraid and the thought uppermost in my mind was '...if only I didn't have those dreams I would still be at home with my brother'. There was a lot more but its telling is for another time.

If such experiences should come to you try always to check as far as you can, it will seldom be very far, but at least check on the costume, tools, houses, etc. With that part of you that is still in this time, try to note as much as you can, especially the time of year and if at all possible the date.

There are techniques for the recovering of past lives, but I urge you not to use them indiscriminately. If you hit a bad experience shut down psychically for at least two weeks and let it clear from your subconscious. Don't use the techniques more than once or twice a month, keep detailed records of everything you do, see, hear, or remember. Also remember this, most of the 'best' incarnations seem to have been taken already... so you and I will have to make do with what is left!!!

J.H. Brennan's book, *Five Keys to Past Lives* is one of the 'Paths to Inner Power' series published by Aquarian Press. In it you will find all that you need to enable you to acquire the basic techniques of recalling past lives. The only one with which I disagree is the use of a Ouija board. I dislike these things intensely and will always speak out against them. In the hands of trained psychics they may have some merit, but 99% of those who use them are *not* trained, nor anywhere near being trained and that makes it dangerous. When people get unpleasant results, or even experience mental shock through such unwise experimentation, it is always the occult that is blamed, never their own stupidity. That makes me angry because many mystery schools are conscientious, open and run their courses according to the ethics of the Occult. To be blamed because of the carelessness of others who ignored repeated warnings is galling.

Having said that the other techniques in this book are ideal and written with Mr Brennan's impish sense of humour. His chapter on hypnosis is simple and direct and can be followed safely even by a newcomer.

You can of course follow his instructions sitting in your living room, but the atmosphere of the temple may well boost the experiments. I would advise that you always have at least one other person with you, or at least a tape recorder. Certainly if you plan to use hypnosis another person is vital.

Some years ago a book came out called *The Christos Experiment* giving techniques for the recovery of past lives. That it worked was undeniable, that it caused quite serious problems in some people is also true. It is not a completely safe technique in my view, and I would advise against its use. Stick with the straightforward advice of Mr Brennan and you will not go far wrong.

One last word on this subject. The Akashic Records is a term you will no doubt hear when researching past lives. Let me make it quite clear, while it is possible to use them, it is *not* permissable to go rooting about in them searching for other people's past records. I have lost count of the number of people who fall for the old 'I am a high initiate and I can read your Akashic Records' line. A true initiate will rarely admit to being one at all, and as for reading other people's records.....! Occult ethics would prevent that for a start, and you should do your own searching anyway. Such offers can end up with you 'owing' a karmic debt, according to their interpretation, usually to *them*. Past life research can be made a serious study, but it can have a few drawbacks as well. Try it by all means, but tread warily and don't fall for the undoubted glamour of it all.

The Aura and the Seven Rays

The human Aura and the Seven Rays have been the subject of countless books over the years. When you have a plethora of choice like this my advice is to stick to two or three recommended books and read them thoroughly, get to know your subject. If possible attend some lectures on the subject.

The aura is held by occultists to be an area of light, usually banded in different colours and surrounding the body of all living creatures to a greater or lesser degree. It seems to be most prominent in man and can give an indication of many things. Health, both mental and physical, state of spiritual awareness, type of Ray, and in the case of certain degrees, it will bear the sigil of the Inner Plane master under whose authority that person is working.

It has been depicted by artists through the ages as a nimbus of light around the head of saviours and saints. We know for a fact that all living creatures have a field of electrical force around them, it seems logical therefore that this field could be seen to have colour, and be capable of indicating certain areas where disease is present by reason of fluctuations in strength and colour.

It is a vast subject, too much for more than a cursory glance at the main aspects, but it is important that you understand what it is, what it does, and how it can be seen and interpreted. Not everyone can see an aura, and when you do, you have to be careful not to mistake what W.E. Butler described as 'a false aura'. This can happen when you have been looking at someone for a long time, as in a lecture, the eye muscles relax and the focus shifts giving a momentary flash of colour, or it causes a band of light to surround the speaker. It is easy to check since this band of light will always be in the complementary colour to the person. It can be quite impressive especially as the light is usually white or pale gold in colour. But it is not an aura.

But on occasion you may see a sudden flash of brilliant colour leap out from the head or body of a person, this is genuine, a sudden burst of electrical activity in the aura makes it fleetingly visible. I have seen this phenomena several times and it is quite breath taking.

Normally the aura extends to some 4–6 inches (10–15cm) around the body. When in bad health this can shrink to more than half that amount. The more spiritually aware a person is the wider the aura and the greater its impact upon those near. At this level the person themself is physically aware of the force field surrounding the body and can tell if someone enters its circle, especially if that person is sick, or in need of help. Hence the reaction of Jesus when the hem of His garment was touched in the crowd.

We all have a personal space and when someone encroaches into this space we feel upset and resentful. Races differ in the amount of space needed. The English need a lot more space on average than say an Italian or a Spaniard. The latter races tend towards a closeness that allows another person to stand very close without them feeling uncomfortable. This is not so with the English. You only have to watch them in a packed train or bus to see that such close proximity makes them extremely uncomfortable. They will avoid each others eyes, and draw themselves into a corner to avoid the contact. The same kind of thing would not bother an Italian in the least. But this is built into the racial Group Soul and it affects the individual in this way.

It could be argued that we all live within the Cosmic Aura of the Creator. The first lesson in the SOL course gives as a meditation subject the phrase, 'The Cosmic Sea in which we live, move and have our being'. Being within this force field of God, makes the Creator aware of everything that moves within it and causes a reaction to the movement.

It is possible to contact the other

forms of life upon this planet by touching their auric field, this is so with anything from a falcon to a piece of ancient granite. This is the basis of psychometry, the ability to read the experiences imprinted upon the auric field of an object.

It is impossible to go into this vast subject with so little space. Again I have to resort to saying read a book. Like the recalling of past lives, the aura also has a small but vital booklet in the same Paths to Inner Power series, *How to Read the Aura* by W.E. Butler is simple, direct, and full of information. It goes into detail concerning the use of auric vision, etheric healing, re-charging the etheric, the vital flow, and techniques for developing the auric sight, everything you need in fact. Butler had perfect auric sight and knew exactly what to tell students and how to train them; you can do no better than to follow his instructions as I did for many happy years.

As you go further into your occult studies, you will read about the Seven Rays. Like the aura there have been many books written about them, many of which are incomprehensible. I will try to give you a basic outline and give you the titles of two or three books that I think will give you the widest scope of information.

It is said that the Seven Rays emanate from the seven stars of Ursa Major. Each Ray is an expression of a Quality, a type of teaching if you like, and each one is overlooked by a master. These Rays are channelled through the Solar Logos and then passed on to the Seven Planetary Lords, they in their turn pass it on to those who are working along the lines of their particular Ray.

Most people will have a mixture of Ray types in their make up, a few people are only of one Ray and when they come into work of an occult nature their Ray type determines the type of work they will choose. Although there are seven, we hear much more about just three, the Blue or Hermetic Ray, the Green or Creative Ray, and the Violet or Love Ray. Their other titles are Wisdom, Power, and Love. Most mystery schools will try to pass their highest office from man to woman, and from Ray to Ray so that all is balanced as far as possible. The predominant Ray in this solar system is the Violet Ray of Love, the others are sub-rays to this one.

Each of the seven is associated with a musical note, a colour, and a jewel, there are other correspondences but these are enough for now. It must be said that not everyone sees the three main Rays either as the same colour or with the same attributes, and you will have to learn to choose that which you feel you can follow. Remember your bookmark with the words Discretion and Discrimination? Well now is the time to start using the former. You must begin to listen, read, study, and then choose the way you think is best. In doing so you are activating your own ray colour. When you are a student you learn from your teacher, you question, listen some more and file it all away. But the time comes when the student becomes the priest, and then you must choose your own path. You must never accept without question, never be afraid to ask *why*, or to ask for a check.

So as you read the books I will recommend remember that the colours and the attributes may be stated differently. This does not detract from what they say, nor does it mean that I don't know what I'm taking about, we have been taught differently that is all. Nothing is ever straightforward in the occult.

Below you will find some more information about the Rays and their attributes, it is a subject that requires much study and a lot of hard thinking. But like all occult studies it bears fruit, and it is a part of the vast expanse of knowledge that you must have at your command.

First Ray — Will
Virtues: Strength, Courage. Steadfastness. Truthful. Ability to handle People.
Vices: Pride. Ambition. Hardness. Arrogance. Anger.

Second Ray — Love
Virtues: Calm strength. Patience. Endurance. Faithful. Intelligence. Serene Temper.
Vices: Coldness. Indifference. Contempt of Mental Limitation.

Third Ray — Higher Mind
Virtues: Wide view for the Abstract. Sincerity, Intellect. Concentration. Patience.
Vices: Pride of intellect. Coldness. Isolation. Obstinate. Selfish. Criticism of others.

Fourth Ray — Harmony through Conflict
Virtues: Affection. Sympathy. Devotion to Duty. Courage. Quick Intelligence.
Vices: Selfish. Worrying. Strong Passions. Indolence.

Fifth Ray — Lower Mind
Virtues: Accurate. Justice but without mercy. Tenacity. Independence. Common Sense.
Vices: Narrowness of mind. Arrogance. Unforgiving. Lack of Sympathy and Reverance.

Sixth Ray — Devotion
Virtues: Devotion to Duty. Love. Tenderness. Loyal Intuition. Single-mindedness.

Vices: Jealousy. Partiality. Self Deception. Anger. Prejudice.

Seventh Ray — Ceremonial Magic
Virtues: Strength. Perseverance. Care for Detail. Courage. Courtesy. Self Reliance.
Vices: Too Formal. Bigotry. Pride. Narrowness. Opinionated. Over Indulgent. Superficial.

Remember few people are all of one ray, usually two or three, and few people can accurately judge their own Ray. The two books I have found most helpful, though giving different information in some ways, are *The Seven Rays* by Dr D. Baker (Aquarian Press) and *The Seven Rays* by E. Wood (Theosophical Publishing House). It needs detailed study if you are going to go deeper, and can lead you into a much wider area of thought.

Invocations

Chants and invocations are an integral part of ritual work and you should learn to write your own but there are some very old invocations that every magician should have for special occasions. You will find a collection of these in the Ritual Series of the SOL Knowledge Papers, entitled simply 'Chants and Invocations', obtainable from the SOL Jersey address. But here is one that was taught to me by my teacher W.E. Butler. He told me that it was recorded by a group with whom he worked in Glastonbury in 1926. A very strong contact was made with those he termed, 'The Masters of Britain' and with the Elemental Kingdom. It is more than a chant, it is in effect a powerful ritual/pathworking in its own right.

The Chant of the Elements

An Elemental Power manifested and

said to us. 'Greeting, in the name of the Power of the Tor, greeting and welcome', and then another Power manifested and said 'Greeting and welcome within the Gates, the Gates are open, pass ye through, and ye shall see the vision of the opening of the mountain. The house is guarded, the ring of fire is about the house. The vision of the Hill is yours. By day and by night the house is guarded with a force that shall keep off your enemies, the force of the fire of the Tor. For this is the Hill of Fire and the Forces of Fire are about you, the protection of Fire is upon you.' He then went on to give us what he called the Chant of the Elements:

> The Wind and the Fire work on the
>   Hill,
> The Wind and the Fire work on the
>   Hill,
> The Wind and the Fire work on the
>   Hill,
> Invoke ye the Wind and the Fire.
> The Wind and the Fire work on the
>   Hill,
> The Wind and the Fire work on the
>   Hill,
> The Wind and the Fire work on the
>   Hill,
> Trust ye the Wind and the Fire.
> The Wind and the Fire work on the
>   Hill,
> Hail to the Wind and the Fire.
> Draw down the Power into
>   yourselves,
> Work with the Wind and the Fire,
> Sun and Air, Sun and Air, Sun and
>   Air.

Then another Elemental Power manifested and said:

> Earth and Water are Friendly and
>   Kind,
> Earth and Water are Friendly and
>   Kind,

> Earth and Water are Friendly and
>   Kind,
> The Sun and the Fire work on the
>   Hill,
> Hail to the Sun and the Fire.

Do not think about the Nature Forces, work with them, feel with them, they have not mind, you cannot touch them with the mind, feel with them, move with them, sing with them, do not be afraid of them, you need them, you have left them too far behind. For they are on the power side of things. Without the Elemental Forces you have no power, no power to give expression to your desires, unless it be the will of the Lord to the elements. For they hold the Gates that open to the inner world. You may enter only by the grace of the Lords of the Elements. They are your friends if you can but rule your own elemental nature. They will share with you the holiness of elemental nature. Form and force must be balanced. 'We love not weakness', they say, 'we scorn it, you must make us respect you, just as you must respect us, love us and we will love you. Those whom the Lords of the Elements love and trust, shall be loved and trusted by them, and shall be entrusted with the Force of the Elements.

'The Power of the Elements shall then be as a flame among men, as a rushing Tide, as a mighty Wind and as still as the Rocks. Ye shall sweep things aside as a Fire if the Lords of the Elements ride with you, the Kings of the Power of Air shall ride with you. The stability of the depths of the Earth shall guard you. Where my friends are there is purity and power where the waters sweep out to endless horizon, spaceless and timeless forever. Where my people are there is wealth, and strength and wisdom.'

Then another Elemental came and said,

'Greetings my children,

> Wind and Water, Wind and Water, Wind and Water,
> Water and Earth that make fruitful,
> Water and Earth that make fruitful,
> Water and Earth that make fruitful,
> You shall never lack the water springs,
> You shall be able to call up the water springs and call upon the rain,
> The Water springs in the name of Earth and Water and the rains in the name of Water and Wind.
> Water and Wind, Water and Wind, Water and Wind,
> Wind and Water.
> Fire and Earth, Fire and Earth, Fire and Earth.
> The Fire of the earth shall bring power to the Master
> The Fire shall cleanse, the Fire shall enlighten and tenderly shall the Water bear you.

Love ye the elemental things, they are very old, they are ever young ageless and deathless, eternal, immortal, from of old and forever rule we our Kingdoms, and we are in the depths of your being. Awake and come, awake and come, awake and come. Come from the depths of Elemental being and lighten our darkness. Come in the name of the White Christ and the Hosts of the Elements, come at our bidding and serve with us the one Name above all Names, the lover of men and of the Elemental peoples. Then there shall be no night where my people are, and the night shall be as day in the light of eternal fire. There shall be peace where my people are, the peace of the heights above the wind. There shall be purity where my people are.

Fire and Air, Fire and Air, Fire and Air, and power to serve the Masters.

You have been given the Freedom of the Elements, use them.'

Then the Master spoke again,' Well my children so you have met the messenger of the Elements, in the Elements is power if you dare to use it, and this is something we have tried to teach you, that you must have elemental power if you are to do anything. Many people have the best of intentions, but have not the elemental power, and therefore their intentions are fruitless. You must not be afraid of power, or of pain, it is useless to be afraid of things, you only have to meet them again, why should you be afraid of things, knowing by experience your own immortality , it has been said the last enemy to overcome is death. When you remember how often you have died you cease to be afraid of death. There is no need to fear death, for it has no power over you. If you are not afraid of death, or shame, or pain, or poverty, or loneliness, then what is there to fear? And all these things you have to learn to conquer on the path. Learn to live boldly my children, learn to live greatly. Learn to pay the price of big things and not to grudge it, learn to put all in the scales in order to weigh down the pure gold of the spirit. You must have your Green Ray contacts, you need them, you have your Blue of Wisdom, you have the Purple Ray of Devotion, you must have the Green Ray of Power as well, for the time will arrive when you can handle it, it is not for nothing that you have come here to the Tor and built upon it, here you have the Air and the Fire contacts. Learn to do the Chant of the Elements as you have heard it done this evening. Learn to be on terms of friendship with the Lords of the Elements, tonight you received the Greeting of the Lords of the Elements, remember you must conduct all dealing with the elemental world through them. They are beings of lofty intelligence, mighty in power and dedicated like you to the Masters. They will not serve you, never make the mistake of trying to command their obedience, but request their assistance as brothers, as servers of the One.'

W.E. Butler went on to say that the medium through whom this Chant of the Elements was received was Dion Fortune, and that, at the time when she established her school, the Elemental contacts were very close to her and her group. Sometimes in the lodge they actually showed themselves. The full text of the Chant, the teaching, and Mr Butler's comments on that particular meeting can be found in the Lecture Series of the SOL Knowledge Papers.

The Chant can be used either as a ritual, or as a pathworking, in either case it is exactly what it claims to be, a Gateway to the Lords of the Elements and the freedom of their Realms, *if*, you can handle it.

Becoming an Initiate

In the last chapter of this book we will be talking about the setting up of a working group. Because you have such a group it does not follow that you are a magical Order, far from it. Nor do you have the right to call yourself an initiate, or to initiate others. There are two kinds of initiation, the physical and the non-physical. Sometimes you undergo the physical one first and sometimes the other, but one will always carry the potential of the non-physical. You become an initiate physically by being 'taken in' by someone who is of sufficient degree, at least a full degree and preferably two, above your own.

There have been many books published in the last decade that have chapters on self-initiation, you will find none in this book. I admit that it can happen, but rarely, and I do not consider I have the right to give you a ritual and to say, after this you can call yourself an initiate. That is in the sense of the word as I understand it, which is that a prepared novice comes to the door of a temple in a contacted Order, after certain passwords and assurances the novice is admitted and goes through a ritual designed to first cleanse him and then to implant in the heart centre a seed of light drawn from the essence of the master of the Order. Certain instructions, passwords, promises, and pieces of information are then passed to the new initiate who is then granted right of entrance to the temple and the Order.

Unless you have spent time and taken instruction within the novitiate of that Order a true and contacted initiation is not possible. That does not mean you cannot put together a good solid working group with a lot of potential in store. Or that you cannot devise a Rite of Entry to your group that will act as a dividing line between the life lived outside and that which is kept for the world within.

Such a ritual will strenghten the Group Mind and give a sense of belonging to those that enter. As no doubt many of you will be working towards having a small group this seems the time to give you an example of such a Rite of Entry. This particular one is to establish a group, next month I will give you a ritual for the entry of a newcomer. I will assume that you already have some companions with whom you have been working for some time, and that now you want to establish yourselves as a real group. You already have a temple, a guardian, and a temple deity or overall master to whom your temple is dedicated, so you will not have to go over that again. You may change the tradition if you wish and use other names. I have used the Archangelic names for the Quarters since they are universal.

The Rite of Entry

Very probably you will have been working together in the temple for some time and so you will be familiar with the layout and the opening of the temple. Prepare the temple with extra care, a bowl of flowers on the altar and/or on each Quarter table. The magical tools laid out on the altar. Here I must point out that you should have a set of temple tools as well as your own personal set for solo work. There should be wine and small pieces of bread on the altar as well. If you already have robes add a new item such as tabards in the Quarter colours, you already have a pattern for these in Chapter 1. Place one of the tall candle-sticks by each officer. Let each person make some small thing for use in the temple no matter how small. An altar cloth, a set of candles, some incense, a bottle of wine, anything at all.

Assemble at the altar, stand in meditation, think about the task you are setting yourself, the hard work ahead, the hard work that is behind you. After a few minutes the Officer of the East speaks:

East:

Brethren we have come together tonight to formally erect a Lodge to be named the Lodge of .... Are we all agreed upon this name?

All:

We are agreed.

East:

Then let this be written down in the Book of the Lodge with the date and the worldly names and the mystery name initials only of those who are present. Officer of the West, this will be your task, to keep the records of this Lodge until such time as our numbers permit this to be a separate office. Are you agreed to this?

West:

I agree.

East:

Officer of the South, do you agree to keep the Gate of Noon in this Lodge, to guard it, to represent it, and to mediate its qualities?

South:

I agree.

East:

Officer of the West, do you agree to keep the Gate of Sunset in this Lodge, to guard it, to represent it, to mediate its qualities?

West:

I agree.

East:

Officer of the North, do you agree to keep the Gate of the Silence in this Lodge, to guard it, to represent it, and to mediate its qualities?

North:

I agree.

West:

Officer of the East, do you agree to keep

the Gate of the Dawn in this Lodge, to guard it, to represent it, and to mediate its qualities?

East:

I agree.
(All turn to face their Quarters right hands up and out.)

East:

Mighty Raphael, Angel of Healing and Light, to you, the Regent of Air I swear my allegiance to this Lodge and to this group.

All:

So mote it be.

South:

Mighty Michael, Angel Warrior of Courage, to you, the Regent of Fire I swear my allegiance to this Lodge and to this group.

All:

So mote it be.

West:

Might Gabriel, Angel Messenger and Annunciator of the Word, to you, Regent of Water I swear my allegiance to this Lodge and to this group.

All:

So mote it be.

North:

Might Uriel, Angel of Mercy and Tranquillity, to you, Regent of Earth I swear my allegiance to this Lodge and to this group.

All:

So mote it be.

East:

Brethren, let us take our places.
(All take seat in Quarters.)

East:

Officer of the South, what is the virtue you mediate in this Lodge?

South:

The Virtue of Love.

East:

Officer of the West, what is the virtue you mediate in this Lodge?

West:

The Virtue of Intuition.

East:

Officer of the North, what is the virtue you mediate in this Lodge?

North:

The Virtue of Oneness with Nature.

West:

Officer of the East, what is the Virtue you mediate in this Lodge?

East:

The Virtue of Wisdom.

All:

So mote it be.

East:

Brethren, is it agreed that we keep the rites practiced within this Lodge and the names we use and those we serve apart from the world and held in honour and silence?

All:

It is so agreed.

East:

Let us seal this, by partaking of wine and bread together.
(All come to altar, East blesses bread and wine, eats and drinks then offers it to each in turn.)

East:

It is done. Let us now take from the altar those symbols of our offices and return to our places and meditate upon them.
(All return to places and meditate for five or ten minutes.)

East:

Brethren let each one of us bring our gift to the altar and speak to the others and to the guardians of this place from their heart.
(In turn each one lays upon the altar the gift they have brought and speaks a few words, starting with the South and ending with the East, After this the lodge may be closed.)

Summary

As you come to the end of your year, the work has become less regimented and more precise in detail and of course harder and more abstract. Start to read the lives of some of the great mystics, you will find much to think on and to study in them. Not all of them are suitable but St Teresa of Avila, St John of the Cross, St Ignatius De Loyola, and Julian of Norwich will be useful. Start looking round your area for lectures by visiting experts on anything you feel might be worth looking into. Dion Fortune's books such as *Esoteric Orders and their Work. Aspects of Occultism* and *The Training and Work of an Initiate* are all good pointers to future ways of working.

Keep up your disciplines of meditation, but combine it with your studies using it as a tool more than a means of training the mind, which by now should be obedient to your will. Look for a group that does psychic Healing and go along to watch them work, talk to them and let them know you wish to understand their work. Some may be wary, but if you approach them in the right way you will get a good response.

Start working on the far memory exercises given in J.H. Brennan's book, and remember to keep detailed records. You have a lot of reading and studying to do this month what with the Aura and the Seven Rays, but take it slowly, it does not have to be done all at once. What I give you in the way of book titles can be stretched over several extra months, after all what will you have to read next year if you read it all now? You will find a whole series of lectures, rituals, and pathworkings available in the SOL Knowledge Papers, this will extend your collection of rites and workings and give you more advanced knowledge to work with. Do try out the Chant of the Elements, preferably out of doors, and promise yourself to do it once a year, so as to verify your contacts with the Lord of the Elements.

When you feel ready prepare your Rite of Entry and then your temple will at last come into its own. It will have taken almost a year, but it will be a *real* temple, erected with care and attention to ancient detail. It will serve you well, but remember you must also serve what it houses.

Reading List

Brennan, J.H., *Five Keys to Past Lives* (Aquarian Press, 1981)

Butler, W.E., *Practical Magic and the Western Mystical Tradition* (Aquarian Press, 1986)

Fortune, Dion, *Aspects of Occultism* (Aquarian Press, 1978)

Fortune, Dion, *Esoteric Orders and their Work* (Aquarian Press, 1982)

Fortune, Dion, *The Training and Work of an Initiate* (Aquarian Press, 1978)

The Eleventh Month

The Tides of Life and Love

Date started ....

The Tattwas

The modern occultist owes much to the men and women who belonged to the Order of the Golden Dawn. The Order contained many fine and sensitive minds, highly intellectual yet not rigidly so. Among the many riches they have left to us is a set of symbols known as the Tattwas. For many hundreds of years these powerful symbols were used in the East. According to J.H. Brennan in his book *Astral Doorways*, they were introduced to Western occultism by the Golden Dawn.

They are easy to use, but powerful enough to warrant taking care as they can produce results with startling suddenness. They represent the four elements of Earth, Water, Fire, Air, plus Spirit. They can be used in many ways, as Astral doorways into pathworkings both active and passive, as Gates for the four magical Quarters of your temple, as meditation symbols, or used in combination with meditation and the Chant of the Elements ritual given in the previous chapter.

You will find illustrations of the five

Date ended ....

symbols in Figure 44 together with the colour to be used for that symbol. I have found that a very stiff, very shiny

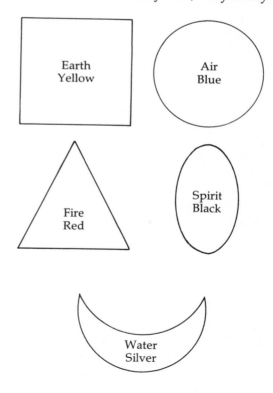

Figure 44 The Tattwa Symbols

card is best to use, the light seems more intense. I would also get a large sheet of white card to use for the exercises you will find below. If you cannot find the right colour card for the symbols, then draw them by hand and colour them in with acrylic or poster paints.

When you have practised with the symbols for a while and you feel adventurous you could get hold of a roll of white wallpaper and cut them to door size. Then attach a hanger of the type used to display large posters and a weight of some kind to prevent the bottom end from curling up. They can now be used to hang in the temple Quarters during rituals involving the Elements. You could if you wished also make extra large copies of the symbols themselves to place on the white posters.

But to return to the exercise mentioned, this is a technique you already know, the Flashing Colours. Using the smaller size of symbol, select one and stare fixedly at it for about half a minute, then transfer your gaze to the white card you have to hand. The image of the symbol will appear on the white card but in the complementary colour to the original. Do this with all the symbols once a day for about a week, until you are used to the 'alternative' symbol and its colour and can hold it in your mind with your eyes closed.

When you have got this far try enlarging the alternative symbol in your mind's eye to door sized proportions. Do this extension of the exercise once day for a week, or until you are satisfied that you can build the door to your best efforts. Now you transfer the whole exercise to the temple, with the large white posters in place, you can use the symbols for Air and for Spirit on the Eastern wall. Now

choose a symbol, place your chair facing its Quarter with the symbols itself held in your hand. Try to have a lamp on a small table beside you so that you can see the coloured symbol, but can also turn the light off as soon as you feel ready to flash it onto the screen.

Stare at the symbol until you feel the eye muscles start to relax then switch your gaze to the plain white poster on the temple wall, at the same time switching off the light. The image should now be clearly seen on the temple wall. Think of this as a doorway to a different level of existence, and imagine yourself going through and into that level. It is a good idea to have someone with you to record what you are seeing or experiencing, if this is not possible have a tape recorder running. This technique can be used in conjunction with the Chant of the Elements given in the previous chapter.

Use all the symbols in turn and keep a record of what you see. If you have a group, you could make this a training exercise for them, it is an excellent way to sharpen the inner sight and to gain experience of the inner side of the Elements. Don't go mad and make long involved journeys right away, work up things slowly and just wander about in sight of the doorway for a few times before you set out to really explore. Always have a look behind you and fix the image of the door in your mind as a guide back to your own world.

The Tattwic Tides

Once you have achieved a certain competence with the single symbols you can begin to combine them, superimposing the red triangle of Fire on the silver crescent of Water, and so on. Now you can go further and use the visions during the actual *time* of the Tattwic Tides. For these shapes you are using are symbols of Tides that flow around the earth, one following upon the other in orderly fashion. It starts as sunrise with Akasha or Spirit, then flows on to Vayu or Air, then follows Tejas or Fire, and this merges into Apas or Water, finally Prithivi or Earth. I have given you the original Eastern names as well as the Western.

By arranging your most important rituals according to these Tides you can increase their effect considerably. Rituals are not just for the evening or middle of the night, there are also the larger Tides of the seasons. According to Dion Fortune in her book *Aspects of Occultism* this starts with the Fire Tide in spring, changing to the Water Tide with summer, then an Air Tide with autumn and ending with the Earth Tide in Winter. The Spiritual Tide flows through them all as a linking agent.

These Tides are represented by the four magical weapons in your temple, and on the table of the Magician in the tarot. Unless you can control your personal inner set of elements, you will have little success with controlling the larger variety. You can make a start on this area of your magical life by learning about and using the Tattwa symbols. The only real way to learn any type of magic is to do it. W.E. Butler once remarked a little ruefully '...you learn so much more by making mistakes....'

Much more teaching concerning the Tattwas can be learned from the two volumes of *The Golden Dawn*, edited by Israel Regardie.

Hypnogogic Imagery

After almost a year given over to a study of the magical arts your psychism may have started to open up. If this is so you will no doubt have experienced the phenomena of hypnogogic images. There is a point between waking and sleeping when the mind seems to relax its vigilance and we are able to see and even hear things not normally visible to us. They can be very real and detailed, but there is no need to be upset by them if they appear suddenly.

Again, just as we begin to wake the same thing applies. These images are rising from your own subconscious and the fact that they *are* rising means they are there for a purpose. They are very often mistaken for 'apparitions' and this can cause concern, but since they usually disappear with the onset of full wakefulness they can be distinguished from the true apparition which, if it is a real one, will persist.

Looking directly at such an image will cause it to waver or melt away. Try looking at it out of the corner of your eye for a while and getting to know as much as you can about its appearance. When fully awake use the image as a meditation point to try and get to the root cause of its occurrence. Sometimes it is a subconscious problem surfacing as an image, sometimes it can be a pointer to some aspect of your inner self seeking expression, in that case bring it to the surface and look into it, it may be important to your work, or to your studies, or it *may* be a pointer towards a future occurrence that your subconscious mind is preparing you to face, good or bad.

Sometimes these images are just that, images. I have a recurring one that starts with my hearing someone calling me by name just as I fall asleep, I get up feeling for my slippers and reach for the light switch but try as I may it will not work, this is enough usually to make me realize that I am 'out' and the first part, the name being called, was hypnogogic. On several occasions. I have reached that point, woken up, and gone back to bed, only to wake up for real as I lay down.

If such things start to happen, you are not suffering from delusions, it is normal and you will come to no harm from them. On rare occasions they can be startling, rather than fearful, but once you get used to them you can dismiss them at will. I remember 'waking' up one night to find myself staring into the eyes of a very large grey Irish wolfhound. I lay very still for a moment trying to decide if I was really seeing this. I reasoned out that if it was standing where it seemed to be standing then its back legs must be projecting through the wall and into the temple behind it. The dog showed no sign of going and I was tired, so I turned over and went back to sleep. It arrived back the next night and the one after that and we went through the same procedure each time. Then it went, and several weeks later in another country I met up with my wolfhound, for real. He went mad, leaping around me as if we had been friends for years, had he been in my waking vision, or had I been in his?

Women's Mysteries and Moon Magic

You only have to read some of the history of the mysteries to realize there were certain rituals and types of rituals that belonged exclusively to one sex. Men had mysteries specifically for them, and so did women. This is something that is often overlooked in modern occultism with our world's emphasis on equality between the sexes. But there are times when each sex needs to have certain spiritual/ religious experiences that are exclusive to them.

Being a woman there is little I can do about explaining the male mysteries! But I can explain a little about those belonging to my own sex. First I must explain that this subject is as vast as the image of the Cosmic Mother herself; this being so I have no option but to give the merest glance to the subject, but because I know many women will be interested in this aspect of the occult I have given a list (by no means all the titles I could have given) of books I think will be best to start with.

Throughout history it is obvious that woman has been involved at the very heart of religious faith. She has been the honoured priestess, the inspired prophetess, the enigmatic pythoness, the revered temple heterae or prostitute, and even in Byzantium a Bishop, saint, and visionary, and recluse. She has also been the butt of Christianity, reviled as the bringer of sin into the world, blamed for the lusts of men, including in some cases those of the priests who blamed her. The greatest buck passing in history occurs in the Bible when Adam said to God, 'the woman gave me to eat and I did eat'..... quite ignoring the fact that he had a choice and was therefore in it up to his Adams apple, so to speak.

Because she was and is tied to a monthly cycle, woman has always looked to the Moon as her particular deity, and to the sea as her symbol. Since life itself came out of the sea, just as it emerges from the pregnant woman this is as it should be. You will perhaps have noticed that elsewhere in this book I have sometimes given the Deity a double title of Creator/Creatrix, this was deliberate, to my mind God is far beyond the whole concept of being one sex or another, but, the dual potential is there and should be acknowledged.

The age old role of woman as priestess was eroded by the onset of Christianity and mostly by Paul, who, coming as he did from a mystery school background should have known better. Woman is now striking back and making an effort to regain her lost position both as man's equal and in the Church. But somehow, and this is a personal view only, I always see her greatest potential in the role of the Great Mother, both fertile and sterile, the ancient Goddess, virgin, wife, and mother. Capable of running, as did Hypatia, the great Library of Alexandria; of inspiring some of the world's great men, as did Cleopatra; capable of ruling a great kingdom as did Elizabeth I. It is a woman's strength that she can do most things a man can do (with a few exceptions...) and bear children, look after a home, run a business and still be a channel for the Goddess of Love.

Most of the women's mysteries are concerned with Virgin Moon Magic, or Maternal Earth Magic. Let's get misconceptions of the word *virgin* out of the way first. You can be 45, married, with three children, and still be a virgin! In the earliest usage the word simply meant 'a woman who belonged to no man'. Unless you happen to belong to a religion where a woman actually belongs either to her husband or her father, this applies to all womankind.

Let's try another word that has become a term of abuse, prostitute. In the ancient world the temple prostitutes were held in high regard, and were looked upon as the restorers of fertility to the land. When new faiths appeared they were cast out and left to find a living in the only way they knew how. Since then the once proud title has degenerated into something cheap and nasty. But once, long ago it was different.

The Moon mysteries centred around the Virgin Goddesses, although they sometimes overlapped as in the case of Isis, with the Earth Goddess type. Some Moon Goddesses were chaste, others seemed to have done the chasing! Even Diana, or Artemis, so legend says, stole away the young shepherd Endymion, and cast a permanent sleep spell over him as he lay in a cave sacred to the Moon. There every night she would visit him.

Lunar magic is the magic of the Night, of things growing in darkness, which is why we plant by a growing Moon. It is the hidden side of female power linked to her sexuality and therefore to her magical power, since, as has been mentioned elsewhere, all magical power starts as the natural creative power centred in the genital area.

Because the Moon affects all life one way or another woman has a head start over man when it comes to magic. For all women it is a natural gift, they are more at home on the Inner Levels, can work there for longer periods, and have access to its power sources through her lunar and earth links. When you come to think of it all magic is at base a growing thing, no matter what type of ritual you perform, for whatever purpose, the purpose has to 'grow' from an idea through all the stages of becoming, until it manifests. Thought is creative and women 'think' very well on the Inner Levels.

The best rituals of all are those performed by a trio of one man and two women, as you will find out when you come to the ritual that ends this chapter. In a temple, a woman reaches inwards to her female power sources and brings pure power into the temple, the man, because his natural power works best on the manifested level, can then direct the female power into the area, direction, or intent required and spark the whole process off. It is a natural equality, each is supreme in their own place.

The other side of female magic is that of the Earth, the ancient Corn Goddesss, basis of the mysteries of Eleusis. Again it is concerned with growing. The Moon oversees the planting and is the force that draws it out of the warm darkness of gestation to the light, where the Earth mysteries take over and lift it right up so that it ripens. This is the natural sequence of all magical acts.

Because she seemed to hold the threads of life and death, the two great mysteries of all, woman as a priestess, has always been somewhat feared by man. Her capacity for both love and hate is remarkable, so is her magical potential. But first she must learn to know her inner Moon self as well as her outer Earth self. She must get to know her cyclic swings of mood and use them in her magical work. It is right and proper that she should work at times on her own or with other women but the *real* place for her is by the side of man, not in front, not behind, but at the side, sharing the power and the responsibility. Of all the ancient religions the Craft understands this best of all.

Even now in modern times a woman seems 'set aside' during her menstrual cycle, men still shy away from any mention of 'those times', yet it is precisely the time when a woman is at her most powerful magically speaking. The Moon Power is Upon Her, as the old saying goes. An old woman who had spent all her life in the practice of the Craft once told me 'when blood flows, power flows, and woman reigns'. As a practising magician myself I know this is true and I have sometimes delayed a ritual so that it would coincide with my cycle, and the extra power flow could be used. Sometimes if a ritual has gone very well, it has caused a period to come before its time, power can draw on extra power if the time is right.

One of the things wrong with modern life is that there are no Rites of Passage. A girl begins to menstruate and if she is lucky she understands what is happening and is prepared for it, if not she is scared, and the event becomes a hated occurrence that blights her life. In the mysteries she was eligible for initiation into the female mysteries at that time. It was eagerly looked forward to as a great event. Today it is regarded as 'the Curse', an ugly name and untrue. It is a blessing, the hormonal changes help the skin to keep its suppleness, it keeps hair shiny, and the whole body tuned up. A girl should be taught that at these times her body is working exactly as it should do to keep her healthy. It is strange but true that magical work, expecially ritual, does two things for a woman, it keeps her cycle going far longer than in women who are not involved with magic. It also has an effect on hair, giving it thickness and quicker growth. It is not at all unusual for menstruation to function normally well into the middle fifties, keeping the skin clear and unwrinkled, and the natural drives of the body well to the fore.

I would like to see girls taught to look forward to the beginning of their Moon cycles as an *event* in their lives, an entry into womanhood with all its attendant joys, tears, and expectations. My own daughter was prepared in this way, and if I am blessed with a granddaughter I hope to see her taught the same things.

In the last few years many books have taken up the cause of women's mysteries, some are of great value, others less so. I could quite happily use the rest of this book for the subject, but an ounce of practice is worth a pound of theory, so instead I will give some practical work purely for the lady magician.

If you are working alone, there is no problem, if you are working within a group arrange for one or two nights a month to be devoted to female mysteries. To balance it out, the men can have their special nights as well. In this way the temple will grow in a balanced way and become a truly sacred enclosure.

It is nice if there are two or three of you, but even on your own you can do a great deal towards implanting the seed of Lunar and Earth magic in the temple. First time your own cycle and mark your mood swings, then select those times when you feel at your best, and at your lowest. Those are your poles of mood. Read through some of the books recommended or select one of the ancient Goddess forms and meditate upon it. See the Goddess as an extension of yourself into the higher levels, and yourself as an extension of the Goddess into the Earth level. Examine the symbols and attributes of that Goddess. Try to open your inner self to that particular power and manifest it, first within your aura, then within the temple, and then outside the temple. This means that after a while you will be able to act as a channel for the power of that Goddess in your everyday life, and not just within the sacred enclosure. Do this when you are feeling at the top of your cycle.

When you hit the low time, reverse the process, instead of looking outwards and bringing power into the world, use the following ritual to take your mind inward to the heart of your

femininity. It is based on an ancient legend, that holds the racial memory of an actual ritual. It is called the descent of Ishtar. It will need the temple setting up as in Figure 45. You will need a robe, a headdress of some kind, earrings, necklace, a brooch fastened over the heart centre, bracelets, a ring, and a pair of sandals. You should be nude beneath the robe but for a cord or girdle. There are parts for three women in this ritual, but if you are working alone, or with just two, then the extra parts may be recorded on tape and used that way. Each woman should take her turn at being Ishtar. Thereafter it can be performed simply as a pathworking two or three times a year.

Light the candles on either side of the Eastern throne where Ishtar sits, robed in her splendour as a goddess. Ereshkigal, the goddess of Death, sits in the North. Her Gatekeeper stands at Gate 1.

Ishtar:

I am Ishtar, Queen of Heaven. All things bow to me, and I am beloved by men and Gods alike. Yet my heart weeps and I love not the world, for Tammuz, my son and my husband has been taken from me into the depths of Hell where rules my sister Goddess Ereshkigal. Three times have I offered her gold, jewels, and power, yet still she will not release my love. Now will I go before her myself and ask, yea, I Ishtar Queen of Heaven will humble myself before her. (Rises and goes to the first gate.)

Gatekeeper:

Why comes the Great Ishtar to the first gate of Hell?

Ishtar:

I come seeking one who is lost to me.

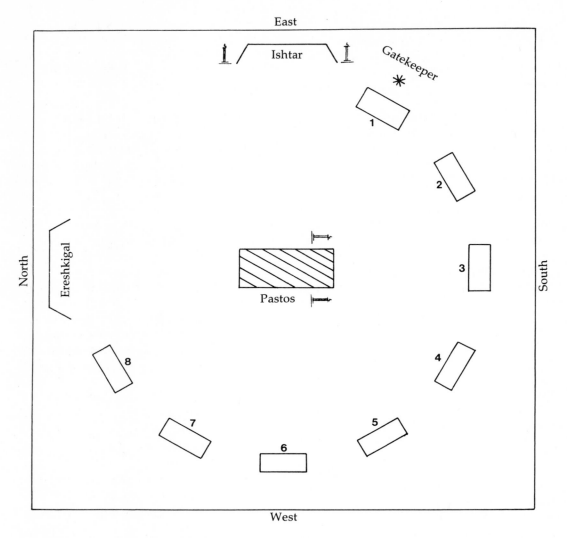

Figure 45 Temple Layout for the Descent of Ishtar

Gatekeeper:

Lay aside the Crown of Heaven, it carries no authority in Hell.
(Ishtar lays her headdress on the table, she and the Gatekeeper move to the second Gate.)

Gatekeeper:

Crownless Ishtar, no longer Queen, why come you to the second Gate of Hell?

Ishtar:

I come seeking the return of my love.

Gatekeeper:

Lay aside the jewels in your ears, the light from them has no place in Hell.
(Ishtar lays the earrings on the table, then both move to the third Gate.)

Gatekeeper:

Foolish Goddess, what seek you at the third Gate of Hell?

Ishtar:

I come seeking one more precious than jewels.

Gatekeeper:

Lay aside your necklace of stars, there are no skies in Hell for them to shine from.
(Ishtar lays her necklace on table, then both move to the fourth Gate.)

Gatekeeper:

Ishtar the lovelorn, what seek you at the forth Gate of Hell?

Ishtar:

I come seeking my heart which has gone from me.

Gatekeeper:

Lay aside the great jewel on your breast, it hides the empty space where once the heart of Ishtar beat.
(Ishtar lays aside the brooch and they both move to the fifth Gate.)

Gatekeeper:

Ishtar the heartless, what do you seek at the fifth Gate of Hell?

Ishtar:

I seek my lord and my love taken from me by cruel Death.

Gatekeeper:

Lay aside your bracelets and your ring, such tokens hold no value here in Hell.
(Ishtar lays her bracelets and ring on the table, both go to the sixth Gate.)

Gatekeeper:

What has great Ishtar to give now, that she may pass the sixth Gate of Hell. Give me your royal robe and you may pass

Ishtar:

For my purpose I will give up my royal robe that I may pass.
(Ishtar takes off her robe and both move to the seventh Gate.)

Gatekeeper:

You stand at the last Gate of Hell, will you go further? If so what have you left to give?

Ishtar:

I will pass further and stand before Ereshkigal herself. I will give up the Girdle of Love, it holds the greatest of all my powers, but what is love if there is none to love.
(Ishtar unties her girdle and places it on the table, then passes on to stand before the Goddess of Death.)

Ereshkigal:

What is this, proud Ishtar, Goddess of Love, Queen of Heaven, here stands naked and shamed before me, What would you sister mine?

Ishtar:

I would have the life of my husband son, and lord, give him to me and I will bless your name.

Ereshkigal:

You must pay me for his life, will you give up your own and abide here in hell for ever.

Ishtar:

This I will do.
(Goes to Pastos and lies down with arms crossed.)

Ereshkigal:

Now will I Ereshkigal reign instead of my hated sister. I will wear the crown and the earrings of Ishtar. The jewel and the robe and the Girdle of love are mine, and I have the Goddess herself to be my slave.

Gatekeeper:

Not so Ereshkigal, the Gods have sent a message to Hell, the earth dies because there is no life force. Send back Ishtar the beautiful and they will send another in her stead.

Ereshkigal:

This summons I must obey, but this I will have, Tammuz shall be with me for the half of each year, only six months shall he dwell with his goddess.
(Goes to Pastos.)

Ereshkigal:

Arise Ishtar, it seems I cannot keep you here, arise and take your love, but, he must dwell with me for six months of each year, and you will know that during that time he will be my love.

Ishtar:

I hear Ereshkigal, and I will abide by the promise. Let my love be waiting when I return to the earth.
(Rises and goes to the seventh Gate.)
Gatekeeper, give me the Girdle I put off at this gate.
(Gatekeeper passes it to her and she puts it on, they go to the sixth Gate.)
Gatekeeper, give to me my royal robe that you took from me.

(Gatekeeper gives it to her and they go to the fifth Gate.)
Gatekeeper, return my bracelets and ring that you took from me here.
(Gatekeeper returns both of them, they pass to the fourth Gate.)
Gatekeeper, bring to me the breast jewel paid to you at this Gate.
(Gatekeeper gives up the brooch, they go to the third gate.)
Gatekeeper, put on my necklace of stars, that I paid at this Gate.
(Gatekeeper puts on her necklace, they go to the second Gate.)
Gatekeeper, return to me the earrings this gate did cost me.
(Gatekeeper returns the earrings and they pass to the first Gate.)
Gatekeeper, give to me the Crown of Heaven.
(Gatekeeper places the Crown on her head, and she takes her place in the East.)

I Ishtar, Queen of Heaven, have gone into the depths, I have given up my life for love. I know what mankind does suffer in Hell, I will be man's help, and his succour here in Heaven, for I have shared with him his greatest fear. Let it be so written.

Here ends the ritual.

This ritual is more than it seems, you are giving up more than jewels and a robe. The Crown is the power of the mind, the thought energy, the Earrings the power to hear the creative word sounded in Heaven, the Necklace is the power of your communication centre, and the Brooch the jewel that is the heart centre, the bracelets and ring symbolize the powers of the endocrinal system, and the Robe your outer covering of humanity. The Girdle is your ability to recreate yourself out of Love. Finally you give up your very life energy. You go down into the depths of your own self, for that is where every Hell that ever was, is to be found. Ereshkigal is your own darker side, the Gatekeeper your inner wisdom that helps you to keep internal balance and brings the message of your summons to rebirth.

Performed with intent this ritual can bring about remarkable effects. It should be done at the dark of the moon, using an incense of Hecate, with dark blue or black candles.

The Craft of the Wise

No book on ritual magic would be complete without mentioning the Craft of the Wise. So much publicity, and most of it bad, has been the lot of the Old Religion that it is time to put the record straight. Despite what is put out by the more sensation seeking Sunday newspapers, 99 per cent of the Craft are gentle, quiet people who want only to be allowed to worship in their own ancient and very beautiful way. However the name 'witch' still carries the stigma of Satanism and Black Magic. I have said before and will repeat, there is no such thing as Black or White Magic... there is only Power, power that is coloured by the people using it. They prefer to worship their female deity in the woods and forests, that deity, like all the ancient Goddesses, has a consort, a male God who wears a crown of Horn, a symbol of fertility, and *not* the devil. After all Moses wore horns as well..!

The companionship and the love shared between the majority of the Craft people is an example that could be followed by other religions. The continued war waged against them by press and Church is not helped by the fact that whenever they try to put the records right, their words are twisted and their rituals misrepresented. The fact that the Church was responsible for the cruel death of untold numbers of innocent women and children is rarely mentioned. They cannot *all* have been dissidents and so called devil worshippers. We hold memorial services for the martyrs and those massacred by terrorists, but who will hold a memorial for those burnt and tortured to death during the middle ages. 'It is best forgotten', we are told, 'it was all a long time ago and does not happen now'. No, the rack and the stake have gone, now we have more subtle methods against anyone whose religion does not match our own way of thinking.

The Craft is, in fact, primarily a religion of Nature Worship and sees the hand of the Creator/Creatrix in everything around them. Their rites are simple rather than elaborate with an emphasis on the love of the Goddess for Her children be they human, animal, or plant. They celebrate with music and dance and song, and with the age old Cakes and Wine ceremony that was celebrated long before it was used in Christian communion. There are several kinds of Craft ranging from the Gardnerian through to the Family Craft, and the Traditional Craft. The Family Craft is rarely heard of, their knowledge is passed from one generation to the next, there are a few locations where several families live close and work together, but it is rare that an outsider is given access to their work. When this happens, it is for a reason. Such a one is known as the Walker, or the Proud Walker.

Unless you have links with the Craft you will not easily come across them or their work, if you do get an invitation to meet with Traditional Craft, you will be very lucky and they can teach you a

at deal. I have not given any Craft
als in this book, such rituals are not
......le to give out, and I am bound by
promises, but I can say that for the
most part they are beautiful, meaningful, and close to the heart of Nature.

The Osiris Ritual

The Osiris Ritual is based on another
and much older ritual. The fragments
of an original ritual were given to me
many years ago and upon those
fragments I have based the Rite that
follows. It is for a Priest and two
Priestesses, that is an Osiris, with Isis
and Nephthys in attendance. All the
rituals given to you so far have been
fairly easy, and can be worked without
undue stress. However there comes a
time when you have to step over the
line that separates the complete novice
from the more experienced. That time
has arrived with this ritual.

I have two versions of it, the one you
have been given is the 'lighter' of the
two, even so I suggest you prepare for
it with serious intent and a certain
amount of study. You should make
yourself quite familar with the story of
Osiris, and especially his relationship
to both Isis, and Nephthys. You might
say that in them he sees his bright
anima, and his dark anima, his life and
his death. Do not make the mistake of
equating Nephthys with evil or
anything harmful. She is a gentle
Goddess and in legend is totally
devoted to her brother and his wife.
Take particular note of the fact that she
is the mother of Anubis by her brother,
the child being given over to his aunt
Isis to bring up and to train as her
successor in magic.

This makes Anubis the sacred
Nephew, the inheritor of the Kingdom,
the earthly successor to his father. He
is also the half brother, teacher, and

protector to Horus the Sun Hawk. Two
pathworkings that will help you
prepare for this ritual can be found in
the Pathworking Series of the SOL
Knowledge Papers, entitled, 'The
Sorrows of Isis', and 'The Birth of
Horus'.

Dress the temple as shown in Figure
46, moving the pillars to either side of
the Pastos which occupies the central
position facing East to West. If possible
this should be draped with a black
cover. Over this lay a plain white
sheet. The candles are placed behind
the two thrones of the Goddesses and
care should be taken that they are far
enough away to avoid them being
pushed over if a chair is moved. They
are put here because you need light
coming from behind the two women
and from nowhere else.

This is part ritual and part pathworking, and it can have a slightly
unnerving effect on the Osiris, so I
would suggest that it is worked on a
weekend when at least twenty-four
hours can be used to 'come down'
slowly. The women should have plain
black robes, sleeveless and with a silver
Egyptian style collar and girdle. Silver
sandals or bare feet. A silver ribbon
bound across the forehead will do if
you do not have an Egyptian headdress. Isis should carry an Ankh and
Nephthys a Sistrum. Osiris wears a
simple Egyptian kilt with an Egyptian
collar and if you can make one, a copy
of the White Crown of Egypt. You will
find pictures of this in the pictures of
robes and headdresses at the end of the
book. He should carry the Crook and
the Flail, his arms crossed on his
breast.

Osiris takes his stand up against the
Eastern wall, the only light is from the
two candles. The two women enter,
and Isis seals the temple by walking
around it and using the Ankh as a seal

East

North

South

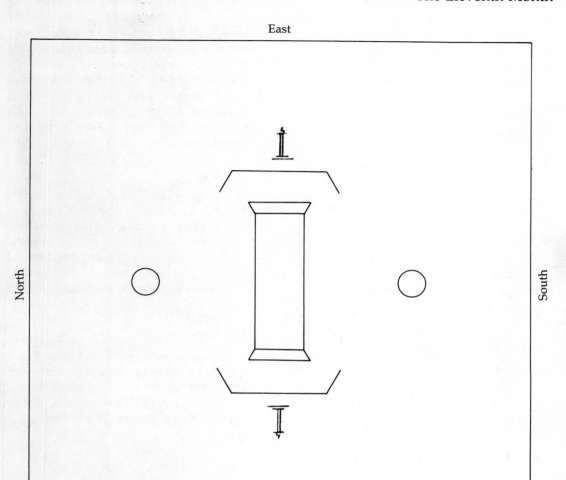

West

Figure 46   Temple Layout for the Osiris Ritual

in each Quarter. Then she takes her stand before the Silver Pillar and Nephthys before the Black. Isis begins the invocation to Ra.

Isis:

Hail to thee Ra, thou art great in the Heavens.
Hail to thee of the three forms, Ra, Kephra, Atum.

Hail to thee Light of the Earth, mighty in power.
Hear the voice of Isis,
Hear the voice of she who knows thy name.
Hear the voice of Egypt.
Come forth and look upon the work of evil. Osiris lies without breath beneath thy Light. Without the breath of Life before thee.
Comfort me oh Ra, Comfort me and comfort my sister.

Give to us the body of Osiris that we may mourn him that we may cover him and lay him in sweet herbs.
Come forth from the Boat of Millions of Years and hear the voice of sorrow.

Nephthys:

Hail to thee Lord of Heaven, mighty is thy wrath.
Hail to thee of the Falcons head, bright is thine eye.
Hail to thee Arm of Justice, Ruler of all.
Hear the voice of Nephthys.
Hear the voice of she who weeps.
Hear the voice of the Nile.
Come forth and look upon the work of Set. He who loved me is no more. Without my Lord and Brother I am bereft.
Comfort me oh Ra, comfort me and comfort my sister.
Give to us the body of Osiris that we may weep, that we may watch over him through the night.
Come forth from the Cave of the Sun in the East and hear our call.

Osiris

Isis, sister wife, Ra has granted me this small time to speak with thee. Soon I must cross the wide sea to Amenti, there to dwell until my time shall come again. Take my body and lay it in coverings and sweet herbs. Walk with me in the dreams of night and speak with me through the reeds in the river. I will come again, and none shall stand against me, for I have been down into the darkness and have risen.

Nephthys, sweet singer of songs, thou of the gentle hands to thee I give greetings. Ease thy hearts pain for I shall welcome thee to my arms in sleep. Thy kisses shall be as sweet in Amenti. From Set did I take thee and make thee the mother of my Son, So also shall thy sister bear a son to me, though I be

without the breath of life, this has Ra promised. Take my body and weep over me and watch through the bitter night. But I shall come again.
(Now Isis and Nephthys come forward and Osiris comes to stand between them in single file. Isis leading they move slowly to the Southern station and pause.)

Isis:

Weep, weep, oh ye lands of the South, for Osiris goes down into the darkness of death. Weep, for his like shall not be seen again for a thousand years. Until the Land of Khem has fallen and risen again. Strange feet shall walk on this sacred soil, and the temples shall crumble, but Osiris will sleep on.

Nephthys:

Other Gods and other faiths shall Egypt know, the tides of peace and war shall cross her sands, voiceless shall be the Gods of Egypt, but Osiris shall sleep on.
(They move on to the West, and pause)

Isis:

Mourn, mourn oh ye lands of the West, take Osiris into thy bosom and guard him well. The setting sun shall be his pillow and the waters of the Western sea shall be his dream. But sweet will be the sleep of Osiris.

Nephthys:

Strange forms, and strange events shall be the lot of Egypt, yet in the West a light shall be seen. Each night a star shall fall into the sea, a tear from the eye of Nephthys will fall upon the breast of Osiris.
(They move to North, and pause.)

Isis:

Cry aloud oh ye lands of the North, send your coldness forth and freeze the heart of Isis that I may feel no more pain. Take me and make me like the ice upon the mountains of the Moon, and Isis too shall sleep with Osiris.

Nephthys:

No sleep for thee my sister, thy time is not yet, Mankind needs you and needs me also. Not yet may we take our rest, but one day we two shall be with our Lord and love.
(They move to the East, then turn and go to the centre. Osiris lies down on the Pastos and the women wrap him in the white sheet, leaving his face and head free. Then they take their seats, Isis in the East, Nephthys in the West.)

Isis:

Let us weave a dream for our Lord that he may sleep sweetly in Amenti. I shall use the dawn clouds of amethyst and gold and with these I shall weave a garment for him to wear in the land beyond the Setting Sun. The Sun's first ray of light I will catch and fashion into a diadem for his brow. The first birds's notes of day will make a jewel for his breast.

Nephthys:

I shall take the light of the stars at midnight and weave a cloak of indigo, a single star shall be its clasp. The scent of the night flowers I will make into a pectoral for this throat and the Moon's light on the clouds will become his sandals. The sound of the sea will be his pillow, and the scales of rare fish will cover him.

Osiris:

Sweet are my dreams, and deep is my sleep, I ride the boat to Amenti in the West. Around me I see many who travel with me, yet they know me not. I hear your voices around me, I see you in the swift winged herons that fly overhead. But soon the boat of the Dead will outwing you both and we must part. Sweet sisters wait for me and I will come again.
(Osiris must now feel himself as being on the boat drawing away from land. Two herons fly beside the boat. The setting sun is low on the horizon. The two women should sit quietly meditating upon the death and the rebirth of all Saviour Gods. After a few minutes, no more than five, Osiris should rise from the boat in his own form, leaving the body of Osiris in the boat. Taking the same form as the herons' he returns towards land with them. As you all draw near, the land becomes the temple and you see below you the figure on Pastos, and the two watching women. Go down and enter into your own body, knowing it to be *you* and *not* Osiris. Open your eyes and this will be the signal for the two women to rise and help you unwrap yourself from the Osiran winding sheet. Now all three go to the East, facing it in a line.)

Isis:

I was Isis, I now understand the burden laid upon her as the Great Mother. I will try to become a channel for her love and wisdom, and mediate it in my own life.

Nephthys:

I was Nephthys, I now understand the joy of being able to comfort and offer solace. I will try to become a channel for her gentleness and comfort and mediate it in my own life.

Osiris:

I was Osiris, I now understand what it means to be Osiris risen. I was dead and now I live. I have sat in the Boat of Amenti and have seen the Land beyond the Sunset. I will remember these things and will learn from them.
(Isis closes the Temple, the Rite is ended.)

Reading List
Begg, Ean, *The Cult of the Black Virgin* (Routledge, Kegan Paul, 1985)
Harding, Ester, *Women's Mysteries* (Rider, 1971)
Harrison, Michael, *The Roots of Witchcraft* (Muller, 1973)
Regardie, Israel, *The Golden Dawn* (Llewellyn, 1978)
Whitmont, E., *The Return of the Goddess* (Routledge, Kegan Paul, 1983)

The Twelfth Month
The Journey Begins

Psychic Defence

When people come into the practice of magic for the first time their heads are usually full of fears and worries about being psychically attacked. To be quite honest real, one hundred per cent psychic attack is *very* rare. First of all you have to present a real threat to someone, this you are unlikely to do unless you become an exceptional magician and start treading on other magical toes.

It takes a great deal of time, effort, and physical and mental strength to mount such an attack. It also takes a very competent magician to put it all together. There are very few of the required calibre around, and the most you are likely to experience are the thought-form variety, and they are irritating rather than dangerous. Human nature being what it is, there is bound to be a time when a magician gets mad and throws a 'whammy'. Everyone does it at one time or another, at least they do it once... the backlash that comes from it is usually enough to deter one from doing it again.

If you have worked your way through this book with serious intent you will have learnt that thought is creative. It causes effects, events and manifestations. It is powered by emotion, it doesn't need a genius IQ to predict that if you are feeling extremely upset by someone, you will start thinking along the lines of 'I wish such and such would happen to old so and so...he/she needs a lesson'. A novice magician is as capable of causing distress in this manner as one more experienced. You have the knowledge of the power of thought.

Happily few novices have the ability to concentrate with any real force for the length of time needed to bring about real harm... but novices get better, so now is the time to start training your emotions so that they are under your control at all times. If you catch yourself thinking harmful thoughts, stop it at once, take the thought in the form of a black ball and send it up through the centre of your body and out into the unmanifest where it will be dispersed.

The first lesson of psychic defence is this, train *yourself* not to attack other people thought-wise!

Dealing with other people's thought

forms is another matter, and comes in three stages, 1. Ignore them, and let the sender get tired before you do. 2. Surround the thoughts with a clear scarlet flame and request one of the Archangelic presences to deal with it. 3. The most effective, have a good laugh, watch a comedy on TV, go and see a film, or simply have a night out with good friends...but let whoever is doing the sending *know* you are having a laugh about it. Nothing deflates an oppressive thoughtform, or its sender, like being dismissed as a mere nuisance, which is what most of them are.

Being a magician does not mean other magicians are out to get you, don't let yourself become paranoid about things. Real Black Magicians are rarer than hens teeth, consider this for a start. A magician working on the Path of Light knows that even if he does something wrong, if a ritual or a pathworking goes haywire he will not fall foul of the Inner Plane Adepti. He is not going to be punished for making a mistake, that is unless it was deliberate and then he will have to atone for it. On the other hand a magician who has pledged himself to the Lords of the Dark Face has a serious problem, just one little mistake and he will be pounced upon. He dare not make a single mistake, his Lords are not so forgiving. That is why, when a magician goes over to that side, he becomes a *very good* magician simply because he *has* to be good in order to survive. Those kind of magicians do not bother with anyone except those of their own calibre, which you are not likely to be for a long time yet.

The biggest threat to you is first and foremost, yourself. Your inexperience and your over-enthusiasm. Later on as you grow in confidence and ability your Inner Level Aura will get brighter,

and if progress continues it will become something similar to a large beacon on the inner planes. When that happens you tend to get noticed by those beings on the other side to your own. *Then*, you can start and take psychic defence seriously. However, if you are part of a well trained, balanced group, or part of a school, you will have certain in-built protections.

Every mystery school or contacted group has an egregore. That egregore is a very powerful protection against anything nasty. Every student who enters such a school bears in their aura its sigil, they can be identified on the Inner Levels by it, and it can act as a deterent to a minor opponent. Anything bigger and the egregore will automatically call in angelic reinforcements. Of course if you deserve what you are getting you will have to answer for it, but you will be helped.

Most schools will give a student a name by which the outer court can call upon the master of the Order, or sometimes the badge or symbol of the school will act in the same way. If you think you are being attacked do nothing for a few days, watch and wait and observe, note down anything you think might be relevant. If it persists then think about doing something, if that does not finish it, then, yell for help. But do not panic and assume someone or something is gunning for you. It could be something quite simple such as a bit of Karma coming your way... you can hardly blame someone else for that!

There are certain places where I do advise students to take simple precautions. One of these is any sort of hotel room. When you think of the number of people that can pass through just one hotel room in a year you will not be surprised to find that such places can be psychic sinks. All sorts of things go on in hotel rooms, some harmless, some sad, some frightening. A fair number of people commit suicide in them for a start. Walls are very absorbent to emotions and the thought of sleeping in a room in which someone had gone through a pre-suicide trauma, is not pleasant. So clear the room before you sleep. You do it like this. Always carry a small container of salt with you. Bless the water and salt and mix the two together. Sprinkle it around the room and lightly over the bed.If you know where East is, fine, if not simply choose one direction and declare the intent that this will be East.

I............... do invoke the peace and healing powers of Raphael upon this place. May it radiate those qualities upon all who may sleep here, now and in the days to come.
(Move to the South.)
I............... do invoke Love and courage,the powers of Michael upon this place. May it radiate those qualities upon all who may sleep here, now and in the days to come.
(Move to the West.)
I............... do invoke understanding and mental strength the powers of Gabriel upon this place. May it radiate those qualities upon all who may sleep here, now and in the days to come.
(Move to the North.)
I............... do invoke gentle sleep and healing dreams that are the gift of Uriel upon this place. May it radiate those gifts upon all who may sleep here, now and in the days to come. May all who have passed through this door, be blessed wherever they may be. Bless me, ... who will sleep here this night.

If you are in a situation that is giving you cause for anxiety call upon Michael, or upon any God-form suitable for the Southern quarter. Think of the Archangel in the form of a large, hefty and well-armed Roman soldier. That is more likely to give you confidence than 'seeing' him in the traditional white robe and bare feet! One of the most vital pieces of knowledge to remember in psychic work, whatever tradition you may follow, is that the Archangelic powers are 100 per cent real forces. For many centuries they have been imagined, built, painted, talked about, and sculpted as loving helpful powers. The intense emotions of millions of people have been poured into them, they cannot help but be what they have been programmed to be... protective and helpful. So, use those forces.

I have no fear at all of flying, which is just as well for I fly thousands of miles every year. However I do have one set of rules from which I never vary. As the plane revs up and starts careering down the runway I send out a request for four large, well-built angels, one from each Quarter. In my imagination I shove one under each wing, one under the nose and the other under the tail. I picture them happily scampering down the runway and lifting the whole thing skywards. I thank them, and bless them, then dismiss them and settle back to enjoy the flight. A bit unorthodox I admit, but it suits me.

The greatest thing you have to fear is fear itself. If you come up against something you cannot handle, don't try. The best, and fastest acting prayer is simply 'HELP'. You have been given the Dog of Defence Ritual, that can be used in any situation and it is highly effective. Don't get yourself into situations you know you will not be able to handle. Leave things like exorcism to experts. It takes a highly trained person to exorcize even the smallest nasty. Such things feed on fear, and you will be a danger not only to yourself but to anyone with you at the time. It is foolish to think that because you have an occult group, or work with one, or even because you are a student in an occult school, that this qualifies you to deal with anything that might turn out to be either psychically powerful and nasty, or a genuine disturbance caused by psychic entities. It takes years of study and training, and is usually, though not always, the province of an ordained minister.

Don't go on ghost hunts, sleep in haunted houses for a laugh, or go looking for things that go bump in the night. You may think nothing has happened and go home the next day laughing. When things start to happen in your own home the laughter stops. Things, entities, and other flotsam from the astral levels can attach themselves to you all unknowingly, and ride home with you. Like fleas, they can hop around looking for fresh pastures.

On the other hand there is no need to bedeck yourself with crosses and crucifixes unless they are something you wear every day. Some things you can come up against are a lot older than Christianity and a cross is not always the best symbol to use.

Possession is as rare as a true psychic attack, what would have been called possession a hundred years ago is now looked upon as a form of dementia and treated with therapy and drugs. But there is such a thing as possession. You believe in the God-forms you invoke, you know them to be good, therefore you must believe with equal faith in the possiblity of there being *evil* God-forms. The best way to avoid any possibility of possession is not to get into situations where it might possibly

occur. Don't work strange rituals you may find without knowing more about where they come from. Don't sleep inside dolmens, stone circles, or pre-historic sites unless you have a sound knowledge of what they were used for and the God-forms worshipped in them. This does not mean that such places are evil, or exceptionally dangerous, just that while you are still 'green in power' you should take sensible precautions. Don't nod off or attempt any form of ritual in a location where violence may have occurred. Such places attract astral denizens of levels that are not friendly to human beings, or indeed any life form, even animals in such places can become infected and extremely hostile.

If a place feels unpleasantly cold, if it smells unpleasant, don't hang about. Listen to what your intuition is telling you, and take note of its advice. There are people who can deal with these things, whose whole training is aimed at dispersing and clearing them. It is your job to keep away from them. If you are destined to follow the path of the exorcist you will find yourself in contact with one who will train you. If not you can do more good working along your own lines.

There are few books on the subject, but Murry Hope's *Practical Techniques of Psychic Self Defence*, Dion Fortune's *Psychic Self Defence*, and F. Strachan's book *Casting out the Devils*, are among the most recent. I do urge newcomers to the occult to read carefully what has been written and take note of it.

Sacred Centres

Britain, the Blessed Isle, Grammarye, Albion, her names are many, her fame as a sacred isle well deserved. From this island, so small in comparison to other lands, has emerged a wealth of great men and women, literature, art, poetry, and magic. The shadowy figures of Arthur, Merlin, Wayland, Herne the Hunter, Epona, Brigantia, Cernnunos, Abaris, and the silver tongued Taliesin, stand beside Columa, Brigid, Aidan and Dunstan. In the hills of Wales the shades of Gwydion, Govannan, Llyr, Arianrhod and Rhiannon can still be felt and heard if you have ears to listen. The Kelpie and the Silkie still inhabit the quiet lochs of Scotland, and the four Royal Clans of the Tuatha de Daanan still hold court in the Hollow Hills.

We are rich in sacred sites which, though overgrown, tumbled, and half forgotten are still alive and need only a little effort and caring to awaken them from their long sleep. This is a land of mystery, and it faces more destruction in the next decade than in all the centuries before. The God-form of the car and the petrol pump rules now, and the hidden ways and sites are ripped away to make more room for wheels rather than feet.

While we still have our ancient places, let us use them, care for them, fight for them, protect them. Once a land of wood and forest, we have hacked away three quarters of it. Organizations such as the Sacred Trees Trust is now battling to save what is left and even to plant and maintain new sites that will be consecrated in the ancient way.

Whether you work alone or in a group it is important that you seek out any sites near you, or within a reasonable travelling distance and check them out. Many of them are centres of power that can be contacted. But try to find out as much as possible about the sites before you go. Visit them first just to look around and feel out the atmosphere. At the second visit look for the 'Heart' of the site where the power will be stored. Only when you are satisfied that it is safe to do so should you attempt to contact the guardian of the place.

Read over what I have said about psychic defence, don't sleep within the circle of radius of the site either overnight, or simply because it is a hot summer day. But there is a lot of Elemental, Celtic, Roman and British contacts to be made at these sacred sites. Try to leave a little something when you go, bury a piece of bread, pour out a little wine, ale or just water on the stones, it makes for a friendlier feeling on the next visit. If however the place has a sinister reputation, this does not apply.

You will find old healing wells, wayside stones, old trees and stone crosses, pilgrim ways that have nothing to do with Christian sites, and some that are all to do with it. Some sites are right out in the wilds, like Callanish, but well worth visiting if you are on holiday anywhere near.

Britain abounds in holy wells, most of them connected with the name of a saint. But in ancient times this saint may well have been one of the Celtic Gods or Goddesses. The early saints of the Culdee Church were less bothered about the 'threat' of pagan deities and obligingly gathered them into the fold, allowing the common man to worship the same God he had always worshipped with the simple addition of saint in front of the slightly changed name.

Such holy wells make good contact points if the water is still running free, since water holds its contacts well, as do stones. The standing stones, and the menhirs seem to follow certain magnetic flows and the use of a pendulum or dowsing rod will pin point them quite accurately. One of the most fascinating books on the subject is, *Patterns of the Past* by Guy

Underwood. The acknowledged expert however is Nigel Pennick. Mr Pennick is the founder of the Institute of Geomantic Research. Among his many books you will find *The Mysteries of Kings College Chapel, Leys and Zodiacs, The Geomancy of Glastonbury, The Ancient Hill Figures of England,* and *The Ancient Science of Geomancy.* I highly recommend them all if you wish to find out more about the sacred sites of Britain. A small handy book which is a must if you intend visiting places outside your local area is, *Mysterious Britain* by J. and C. Bord, published by Paladin.

All such pre-historic sites are part of our heritage, a direct link with our past, a past that includes the ancient Gods of Albion. If you wish to contact those Gods, to get to know their centres of power, and feel that power, then you must take the pilgrimage. Try always to walk just a little of the way, the last mile or so, it will make a lot of difference if you approach the sacred centres of Britain as the ancients did centuries ago. If you plan to use the old powers of your race, then you must look to your old Gods to act as channels.

You will find that many of the places will align well with the four elements. The holy wells with water, the hill top churches built on much earlier sacred places and nearly always dedicated to St Michael, will be Fire sites. Hill forts, camps, and mountain tops are sacred to Air, while the menhirs, dolmens, and sacred groves are of the Earth. Work done at these sites must be planned with local by-laws in mind. Do not light fires unless you have permission, instead use a well protected lantern. Keep the site clean and tidy, the litter sometimes left at these places makes a mockery of their sanctity. New and Full Moons are best

for such work, and remember to include the elementals and their Lords in your work.

There are many stone circles that are almost unknown and seldom visited on the moors of Devon, Cornwall, and Yorkshire, look for them on a surveyor's map and visit them, see if they are suitable for the kind of work you are planning. Don't work in places that have known battles or violence of any kind. Glencoe is a beautiful place, but it is *not* the right place for a ritual. There are still old resentments, fear, pain, and a sense of betrayal there.

The sea-shore, if you live near it, is a beautiful place to work a ritual especially at Full Moon. I have wonderful memories of such work on a lonely beach in Greece with members of the SOL Greece organization. But even during the day, if it is deserted, one can try a short ritual. The same is true of a wood, or a hill top. Many of them have a certain atmosphere that speaks of ritual work having been performed there over a long period of time.

As you become more experienced you will be able to sit quietly and enact a full ritual in your mind in the form of a pathworking in any location, even with people around. You can feel the place come alive as old memories waken and the Gods bestir themselves. If we do not use them, they will eventually die completely. They rely upon people like you and I to keep them breathing.

There is little left of the sacred mazes that used to be so plentiful in Albion, but they can be found if you look, if you have a garden big enough you can even plant a small maze of flowers or shrubs. The effect of walking a maze is truly magical, once done the feeling is never quite forgotten. If you have the chance to visit France, try to visit the cathedral of Chartres, not only for the glory of its stained glass but also to see, and perhaps tread, the maze set into the floor of the nave. Chartres is built on a very ancient mound that at one time had an underground tunnel or maze twisting into the centre of the hill. It is still a centre of great power and that power is a superb amalgam of Pagan and Christian interwoven in a manner almost unknown elsewhere. Places such as we have discussed are, in a sense, a Grail for which we must seek, uncover, use, and bring back to life.

The Atlantean Heritage

Who has not heard of Atlantis, or wondered if that magical land had ever really existed? I suspect that almost everyone has a tiny hope within them that it was once so. A few believe in it with all their hearts. Some seers have brought back memories and glimpses of the Golden Land and revealed that it was not as halcyon an existence as legend would have us believe. Do I believe? Yes. I do, for a variety of reasons — because of the evidence of a Greek philosopher named Solon who was an ancestor of Plato, and not a man given to wild fancies. Because of the similarity of legend, hieroglyphs, pictures, architecture, laws, language, symbols and even physical structure. Because of the persistence of the name and the legend for thousands of years, and I mind the way in which the story of Troy was deemed a myth only to have that myth take form and substance and become fact. Because I am a seer and I remember it, not well, not clearly, but in flashes so vivid and so down to earth that I cannot ignore them, nor would I want to do so.

I have spoken of the hidden and the not so hidden power in the Isles of Britain, why should such a small place be blessed with so much in the way of power, mystique, and such a wealth of gifted sons and daughters, unless it was an influx of a highly advanced bloodline? One that was from a more highly advanced civilization and had knowledge of and practised controlled breeding programmes. Distasteful as this kind of thing seems to modern minds, to the Atlanteans it was simply a way of refining their race, its talents, and psychic gifts. Unfortunately they forgot to include things like ethics, morality, understanding, etc. in this genetic programme and the race degenerated instead of achieving the perfection it sought.

For those who would like to read what Plato had to say about Atlantis refer to the two *Dialogues*, 'Timaeus' and 'Critias'. You will find much food for thought. You are at the point in your studies where serious research is coming to the fore, you will have to make up your own mind about certain theories and explanations held by others. Never take the first one you read as the best, read them all, study them, ask yourself what *you* think about it, then decide.

Racial memory is a tenacious thing, it retains the kernel of truth even after thousands of years. This is why I have urged you to look at myth with a serious eye, and why I personally hold to the view the Atlantis was real. Some years ago an island rose up out of the sea off Iceland. It was the wonder of the decade, we had never seen anything like it before. Theories both wild and serious were offered, the island kept on growing. Eventually it was claimed and named Surtsey, today it is covered with grass, has some wildlife and people live on it. What comes up can go down, as with Krakatoa, what went down may one day rise again.....like Atlantis! Edgar

Cayce seemed to think it would.

Probably the definitive book on Atlantis was written in 1882 by an Ignatius Donnelly. It is a mine of information containing all the known facts concerning Atlantis up to the time of its publication. Since then the evidence has increased a thousandfold, and the time is right for someone to add to Donnelly's information and bring the whole thing up to date.

For many occultists there is no doubt that such an island and such an advanced race existed. Their colonization of South America, Egypt, the Isles of Britain, Brittany, and Lyonesse would explain a great deal about the sudden emergence of organized life in those areas. The land bridge between Britain and Europe would still be in existence at that time, the Channel Islands still part of the Brittany/Cornwall land mass. Hurds Deep was simply a large lake off what would one day be Alderney.

We surmise that the Atlanteans had made great progress in science, alchemy, and those arts now named as magic. The legends tell of lights that burned without being consumed, of machines that took people from one area to another through the sky, of advanced medical techniques that enabled them to employ the technique of trepanning the skull. All these things were lost to us in the centuries that followed the disaster, though bits and pieces of knowledge survived for a while. In the National Museum in Athens you can see a set of surgeons implements that include retractors, speculums, calipers, and many other items whose design remains largely unchanged to this day.

Traditions hold that the Priests of the Temple of the Sun, and the Priestesses of the Moon Temple of Naradek knew that such a disaster was imminent. For some fifty years before, they secretly sent out three successive waves of highly trained men and women drawn not only from the temples, but from all walks of life, artists, doctors, men of letters and science, women of culture and knowledge teachers, who would be responsible for passing on not only knowledge, but their genetic gifts as well. Many special bloodlines were established, and most have survived into modern times, diluted maybe, but such people have both a physical and psychic link right back to Atlantis. They are the people who listen to their inner voices no matter what area of work they take up. They are the inventors, the true priests who still think of their priesthood as a 'calling' instead of the gateway to a Bishopric. They are the thinkers, the artists, the great actors, the humbly born who seize the moment of high tide in their lives and rise like stars. They are, like their ancestors both good and bad...

Some bloodlines established royal houses that lasted many centuries, and some are still with us. Always there was the silver link of psychic power that bound them together and to their common ancestry. The links are thin now, but they exist, sometimes by chance, two people with stronger than usual links marry and produce a child or children that are more than fifty per cent Atlantean in gifts. They often become aware of their heritage and seek to hide it from the world.

Those far off survivors established other lines too. The lines of the Guardians of Britain of which Arthur was one, and Merlin was the first Archmage of Britain, giving his name as a generic title down the ages. The Guardians have played their parts throughout the history of these islands, sometimes their names have been famous, Owen Glyndawr,

Alfred, Bruce, Drake, Howard, at other times they have been men and on occasion women who have been burdened with the task. And behind the Guardians there have always been the Merlins, the Archmagi of Grammerye.

They exist today and will always exist, the task goes from one to another without break, as does each Merlin in turn who takes up the staff of office. For those of you who feel a link to the Drowned Lands there are available in the SOL Knowledge Papers two pathworkings, 'The Hall of Mirrors', and 'The Temple of Naradek', and also a lecture 'Atlantis and Lemuria'.

I recommend Anthony Robert's book *Atlantean Traditions in Ancient Britain* and *Occult Sciences in Atlantis* by L. Spence. There is no doubt in my own mind that at least some of the stone circles of Britain, and in Europe also, are the work of third or fourth generation Atlanteans striving to recapture some of the arts of their forbears. It may be that when you study the sacred sites around the country you will be able to pick up psychically some threads to their Atlantean past.

For your meditations during your last month with me, build up the following image and use it as base from which to feel out any Atlantean links you may have.

The Atlantean Pathworking

You stand before an ancient stone surmounted by a circled cross. The stone is engraved with carvings and interlaced shapes, like thin entwined ribbons. The circle begins to glow and the cross within it also. The light grows brighter until the cross disappears and you can see right through the circle into a different landscape. Now it grows bigger until you can step through the circle into the unknown country. Look behind you and see the stone and the circle glowing brightly like a beacon. This is your way back. Now go, go and explore the land before you. No one will be able to see you, you are from their future, no one will be able to hear you, you must just watch and take note. When you hear the stone cross chime like a ring of bells, it will be time to return. See that the circle closes behind you securely.

Use this simple working once or twice a week. Do *not* use it within a stone circle. Not all of them lead into the same place! If you go as a group, compare notes as to what you saw, after closing down.

Sex Magic

We come now to one of the most contraversial aspects of the occult — sex magic. Before anyone throws up their hands in horror let me state here and now that sex is magical anyway, those who do not find it so are missing something in their lives. You will know from what has been said in the book already that the power centre for all magic lies in the genital area.... probably this is why some people make such a fuss about magic! That centre or chakra in your body is one of the miracles of the Universe. It can bring about the creation of another human being, that is magic for a start, but it can also create other things, pure power for instance. It has been held by some that sex is purely for the purpose of creating children...rubbish. If that is all sex was for, the end results could have been arranged by Nature and evolution in a far more convenient way. Nor would we have been given pleasure centres in our brains that were stimulated by the sex act. Sex can be many things, even an act of worship, the one thing it is not is dirty. Sex in magic has its uses, and its proper place. In that place it can be one of the most powerful rituals of all. Outside of that place it can be used unwisely and to the detriment of both people and sex.

So when is it permissable? Spring rituals, Beltane, as an act of thanksgiving to one of the Mother Goddesses for a child, or for a request answered, as an enactment of one of the great myths, the Conception of Horus, Osiris with Isis, and the conception of Anubis, Osiris with Nephthys, the Marriage of Flora the Summer Queen with the Oak King, the Rite of Esther, the Rite of Tanith, the ritual that lies behind the Song of Songs. It can be part of the assumption of a God-form by the priest, and the acceptance of the power of that God-form into her body by the priestess.

Sex within a sacred enclosure is not an act of desecration, but one of enhancement of its powers, *providing the intention is made clear and it is in keeping with the rest of the ritual.* It is not meant to be an excuse for sex with anyone around, nor is it meant for public viewing. Such rituals are almost always just for the two people concerned. There are exceptions to this rule, but they are rare. The whole ritual should be seen as a sacred performance of a genuine ritual. The moment of actual power, the 'Pegasus' that lifts the intention to its highest level is the sexual climax. The pleasure resulting from that moment of power is shared with the Gods.

There are other rituals where the priest and priestess assume God-forms that are actually paired. Zeus and Hera, Aphrodite and either Ares or Hephasteus, Eros and Psyche, Isis or Nephthys and Osiris, Thor and Sif, Gwydion and Arianrhod, Hades and Persephone, etc. Ritually speaking this becomes an amalgamation of the powers and the attributes of the two deities. This is most often seen in the Hindu tradition.

This tradition has a long history of ritual sexuality and the symbols of the Lingham, or male penis, and the Yoni, or female vulva, are regarded as holy in the extreme. The conjunction of these two symbols is held to be a ritual mystery of the highest level. The Hindu Tantrist sees nothing obscene in this and the inner Tantra rituals are held in the presence of the high priests with no shame, but rather a sense of awe and devotion. The followers of Shiva hold the Lingham in greatest reverence, while the Yoni is the most sacred symbol of the followers of Vishnu. The Shakti and Shakta aspects of man and woman are seen as the higher selves, the two who are one, the creative aspect of all Nature.

Are there dangers in the use of sex magic? Yes, there are, the danger that it will degenerate into something resembling an orgy. The danger that the required detached approach may not be achieved and the group would become tainted, split, and finally break up. The danger that the rituals would be done simply for the sex, and not for the Gods.

Sex magic is not for the inexperienced, it is not for the dabbler, or the armchair occultist, it is not for the voyeur or sex starved, in short it is not for every occultist by any means.

Are there sex rituals written down? Yes, there are, and no, there are none in this book. Those that are written down are not the best in the world, nor have they been used in the best ways, anyone setting their heart on trying this type of ritual should write their own. You have spent a year learning how to become a ritual magician and working pre-written rituals, sometime you have to start writing your own.

The most important thing to remember when preparing for a ritual that involves sexual magic, is that at least ten minutes should be spent in meditating upon the God-form to be assumed, longer if possible. Next, the 'story' of the coupling should be well known to both the priest and priestess. The symbols, dress, headdresses, incenses, colours, etc. are very important and should be reproduced as accurately as possible. Finally that the act itself is almost static for nine tenths of the time, during which both the participants should concentrate on holding their respective God-forms in the mind. This is the most important of all. Each should concentrate on seeing the partner as the God or Goddess throughout the ritual.

The best book I have come across for information about sexual magic is by N. Douglas, and P. Slinger, *Sexual Secrets*. It goes into tantra, yoga positions, Japanese, and Chinese sex magic, as well as that of the Mediterranean areas.

What Lies Ahead?

You are almost at the end of your journey, so what lies ahead of you now? You have some thinking to do, and some decisions to make. First of all, when you come to the end of your year of study, you will need to set aside a further two months in which to assess what you have done, what you have learnt, and what you wish to do next.

Collect together your papers, records of meditations, rituals, etc. and start to read them through. In the light of what you know now, your earlier records will seem very simple and naive. But you will also find that in many cases you anticipated ideas, lesson material and images, that you were given in later lessons. This is a good sign and means that even at that stage you had a good psychic link with your subconscious. You have more understanding now and more knowledge, see how this links in with what is written, and if further ideas come out of this. Mark down where you did well, and where you think you could have tried harder, or done better.

Take a long hard look at the ritual records and see what the results were from each one. Think of yourself as a teacher marking end of year exam papers, divorce yourself from the 'you' that has done this year's work. Now write an assessment of that person as honestly as you can.

If you have been working with others, get everyone to do the same thing, then hold a meeting and compare notes. You are going to have to be very honest with yourselves. The question you must ask yourself is, 'have I done my best, has it been good enough, have I achieved as much as I could have done?'

When you have sorted this out you come to your next problem. After a year's hard work, are you still determined to become a magician or do you think you should give up, that this work is not for you, at least as far as devoting yourself to it wholeheartedly? Would you prefer, having had a taste of the work involved, to be an armchair occultist, to read, talk and discuss occultism, but to leave the practical side to others? Has it made you more determined than ever to tread the Path of High Magic?

If this is so, how do you propose to do it, alone, or with a group? Can you handle a group or would you prefer to take a back seat? Are you prepared to give up at least two evenings a week, one for study, and one for practical work? How does your family feel about this? If you have been working alone do you know anyone else interested in the occult? Would you have the courage to say to someone unsuitable for your group, 'I'm sorry but you do not fit in, you will have to resign'? Has your viewpoint of the occult and ritual magic in particular changed during this year, if so how has it changed?

All these things must be looked at and answered to the best of your ability, for if you go ahead, you are taking on a big commitment.

Alright, so you have decided to go on, what next? If you are going to work solo, then move on to the Patterns of Study part of this chapter. If you want to start a group, then read on.

Setting Up a Group

Groups are volatile things, mainly because there are people in them, and people are human beings with likes, dislikes, good natures, and bad tempers! This being so when you get the nucleus for your group together spend one or two evenings a week for a month or however long it takes to thrash out a set of rules. It is no use saying to yourselves, '.....we are all friends we won't have any upset', because you will. Ritual work will bring out the best and the worst in you so be prepared.

Work out a set of rules first of all that govern the day to day running of the group. You will need someone to hold the purse strings. Why? Because no group runs without funds, and you will need money for candles, incenses, trips to sacred sites, new books as they come out, etc., etc. Set a monthly sum that is realistic, make it payable within

seven days of that date and make someone responsible for collecting it and accounting for it. Someone else should be made responsible for the robes, seeing that they are clean and kept in repair. Whoever has the temple should be the one to keep it clean and tidy, though the quarterly big clean and the yearly spruce up should be shared by everyone.

Are you going to have a library? With books so expensive to buy it makes sense to buy one rather than three or four, unless people want to have their own copies. Then a shelf should be set aside and the books catalogued so that you know where books are at a given moment. Make out a roster so that all Officers and temple roles are rotated. This means that everyone will get used to working in all the Quarters, or acting as a Messenger, or an Altar Server, or whatever. Unless there is someone in the group who is trusted implicitly and respected by everyone, make all decisions a group one. If you have someone like that, elect him or her as Elder, and abide by that person's decision.

Now turn to your curriculum. Work out the main rituals of the year. Are you going to stick to the big quarterly, or will you include the smaller ones? Are you going to do one ritual every two months, or one a month? (No more than that for at least a year is advisable.) Agree to have an annual meeting at which this can be decided each time, and any other day to day business can be dealt with.

Remember if all this seems far removed from Magic, that everything must stand on a firm foundation if you want it to last. Sort out your group into who does what best. If you are very lucky you will have people with different talents, a tarot reader, a clairvoyant, a healer, an astrologer. Try to encourage them to study in different disciplines so that your group talents are wide spread. Establish a system of study, perhaps to have a special meeting once a month to listen to one of your number lecture on their special subject or to give a talk on some related occult area that they have prepared. If you live near a large town go to lectures as a group and discuss them after. The SOL, Quest Magazine, the Atlanteans, the Green Circle, Pagan Pathfinders, and many others, hold one and two day seminars in London, Bath, Cheltenham, and Malvern. Very often if requested they will provide a lecturer for a small group if expenses are paid.

Once a group is put together, don't be too anxious to enlarge it. The best groups run anywhere from three to seven. After that unless you are very well organized or experienced in group work, it can get difficult. If anyone has another person in mind to bring in, the others must meet them socially before any idea of joining is broached to that person. The harmony of the temple is paramount. If the decision is no, and it's your friend or protégé, don't take umbrage, it was a group decision and you must abide by it, they will have talked it over with everyone present and they will have to give reasons. If the answer is yes, you must have plans ready for training that person. They must attend the non-ritual meetings for at least six months, and go through the kind of training you have undergone before they can be 'taken in'.

This 'taking in' is *not* an initiation, it is simply a ceremony that entitles a person to enter the temple, and to be introduced to the guardian, the temple Master, the Quarter Lords of the Elements, etc. You must also make contingency plans for someone wanting 'out'. The name of the temple

guardian must be changed, any passwords or recognition gestures should also be changed. I know all this seems a lot just for a small group, but start as you mean to go on. That way you will survive the first year, and that is a feat of magic in itself. Go slowly as you have gone slowly through this year of training and you will succeed.

Patterns of Study

If you are going to work solo, then you must establish your own set of disciplines and stick to them come hell or high water. Unless you do this you will gradually phase out and drift away from your studies and become simply a 'dabbler'. It is no use saying to yourself '...skipping a study period once will not hurt', once will become twice and then it's downhill all the way.

As with a group, sit down and work out a realistic study and practice programme for the whole year, allow yourself one month off, either in one lot or in one and two week periods. Choose an area of study in which you already have some skill, or some knowledge and set yourself a six month study course in which to make yourself proficient. For the second half of the year choose a subject of which you have little knowledge and give yourself six months in which to get a grounding in it, or at least a reasonable grasp of its basics. Or if you prefer, choose a tradition to study, read up the cosmology of the pantheon, then the legends and finally a book on the religion itself from a scholar's point of view.

These patterns of study will stand you in good stead when the going gets irksome, and it will. You must try to remember that everything worth having demands a price. Use your library to the utmost, look for lectures and seminars given by schools and occult organizations. Did you know there are some areas where you can learn Egyptian Hieroglyphic writing at evening classes? You could learn enough Greek in one winter of night school to be able to intone your Orphic invocations. Until you have done this you cannot possibly know the thrill that hearing the ancient tongue used in the service of the mysteries can give to you.

The Blessing Ritual

We came now to the last two rituals in the book. Both are short but effective. The first is the Blessing Ritual and this can be used with other rituals or just by itself. As the name implies it is a blessing that can be extended to a person or an animal or a God-form, Archangel, Elemental, or talismanic object. It is Qabalistic in design.

Light the candles at the four Quarters, have wine, water and salt on the altar, the altar light already lit, and some incense burning. This is set out to bless a person who is absent, perhaps to invoke protection upon them, or for good fortune, you can adjust it to suit whatever you have in mind.

Having gone through your main ritual for whatever intent, the blessing ritual is given just before closing the temple. Stand in the East facing to the pillars.

I.............. invoke the powers of the East for the blessing of.............. In the name of the powers I command by virtue of my priesthood, I ask for the blessing of the Powers of the East, of the Air, of the Sun at Dawn. By the name of Raphael, and Paralda, and the God upon the Tree of Life I ask this. About the person of.......... place thy protection and thy healing. Let .... grow in

health, and prosperity, and let him/her walk always in the path of the Sun.
(Move to the South and face it.)

I.............. invoke the powers of the South for the blessing of.............. In the name of the powers I command by virtue of my priesthood, I ask for the blessing of the Powers of the South, of Fire, of the Sun at Noon. By the name of Michael, and Djinn, and the Giver of Justice upon the Tree of life, I ask this. About the person of.............. place thy protection and thy courage. Let.......... grow in strength of mind and body and let him/her walk always in the path of right.
(Move to West and face.)

I.............. invoke the powers of the West for the blessing of......... In the name of the powers I command by virtue of my priesthood, I ask for the blessing of the Powers of the West, of Water, of the Setting Sun. By the name of Gabriel. Nixsa, and the Goddess of Form and Sorrow upon the Tree of Life I ask this. About the person of.......... place thy protection and thy understanding. Let.......... grow in wisdom and vision and let him/her walk in faith.
(Move to North and face.)

I.............. invoke the powers of the North for the blessing of.......... In the name of the powers I command by virtue of my priesthood, I ask for the blessing of the Powers of the North, or Earth, of the Sun at midnight. By the name of Uriel, and Ghob, and the Giver of Plenty upon the Tree of Life I ask this. About the person of.............. place thy protection and thy endurance. Let.......... grow in steadfastness and patience, and let him/her walk in tranquillity.
(Return to the East, and the altar. Bless the salt and water, mix, and sprinkle around the altar. Face the altar and raise your arms.)

.... I bless you in the name of......... (Master of the temple). May the light of Kether be as a Crown upon your head. May the wisdom of Chocmah be as a cloak about your shoulders. May the Understanding of Binah be as sandals upon your feet. So mote it be.

The Rite of Withdrawal

The last ritual is the Rite of Withdrawal. Every magician should prepare for his death. He sees it not as an end but a beginning to a new phase of his existence. But in order to free himself as quickly as possible he prepares a ritual pathworking which is then time-locked by intent, set to work at the moment of his death. If that death is a sudden event, it will snap into operation just before consciousness goes, if there is time to reflect, the working can be done in full consciousness, which is the way all initiates should 'go out'.

Take your time in preparing your withdrawal rite. Think over your life and choose a location, a time, that epitomizes your idea of happiness. If there is someone who has gone before you use your trained mental abilities to weave a pattern of events with that person in it. Make a working in your mind of yourself arriving at that place, you are younger, in the prime of life, and there waiting for you is someone you love. Perhaps they have with them a much loved dog or cat. You greet them and start the short journey to the place you have always thought of as the ideal. It may be a house overlooking a valley, or facing the sea. It may be a house you lived in when young, or that you always admired and wished you could have. There are others waiting for you there, a welcoming party is in full swing, or you may want just you and one other to be together.

Fashion a walk or short journey to this place in the company of your friend, relative or love, know that when you reach your journey's end that you can rest and have all the time you need to do whatever you want. Everything you dreamed, everyone you wanted to meet again, all are there. When you arrive you will go to your room and lie down to sleep, knowing that when you wake it will all be here waiting for you.

Build this pathworking with great care and attention to detail, take your time and polish it until one day you know you have it just as you want it to be. Then you may either go into the temple and work it under ritual conditions, or out into some beautiful spot that means a great deal to you, it may even be the earthly original of the place you have built. There do the pathworking with every ounce of power you can muster. Start with the initial meeting at a railway station, or bus stop, or anywhere, then make the short journey to your special place, think of the things you will want to talk about, and the news you will have to tell. Then comes the arrival, and the room in which you will sleep. Take off your clothes and lie down and .....at that point halt the working and 'freeze frame' it. Go back to the beginning and hold that first 'frame' as well, now you have the Alpha and Omega of the working. At this point you must form the clear ritual intent that this working will begin at the moment of your death and not before. Around the two points form an infinity circle, like an eight on its side each ring encloses one end of the journey.

It is right and proper that you prepare in this way, for it will help you over the initial shock, and provide a breathing space in which you can rest among friends or loved ones. When you wake again the trauma will have faded and you can begin to adjust to your new level of existence.

All initiates prepare in this way, or in similar ways, and then forget about it. The only difficulty is in deciding what kind of place, journey or ideal you really want. For once locked, it is extremely difficult to undo it again, so you must be sure. You can also make such an intent for another person if they are not able to do it for themselves, or if they know nothing of such techniques.

*　　*　　*

You have made a long journey, a whole year of effort, and now it is over, or rather, it is just beginning.........

Reading List

Bord, Colin and Janet, *Mysterious Britain* (Paladin, 1974)

Campbell, J., *The Hero with a 1000 Faces* (Princeton University Press)

Campbell, J., *The Masks of God* (4 vols.) (Princeton University Press)

Douglas, N., and Slinger, P., *Sexual Secrets* (Arrow Books, 1982)

Fortune, Dion, *Psychic Self Defence* Aquarian Press, 1977)

Hope, Murry, *Practical Techniques of Psychic Self Defence* (Aquarian Press, 1983)

Roberts, Anthony, *Atlantean Traditions in Ancient Britain* (Rider, 1977)

Spence, L., *Occult Science in Atlantis* (Aquarian Press, 1978)

Strachan, F., *Casting Out the Devils* (Aquarian Press, 1972)

Underwood, Guy, *Patterns of the Past* (Pitman, 1970)

Epilogue

It seems a long time since we started learning together, and we have shared a great deal. We have been companions on a year long journey that has taken us from one beginning to a beginning of another kind. The thing that makes the Art of High Magic so rewarding is that there is always another river to ford, another mountain to cross. Soon you will begin to understand the need to find someone to whom you can pass on the knowledge you have acquired during your search for truth. Then perhaps you will understand those who taught *you* a little better.

I know there will be some who will say that this book is 'bitty', that it does not go into enough detail... that may be true, but to pack enough teaching into one year, to give you all the basic knowledge you need was a difficult task, I have done the best that I could do. I looked first and foremost to write the kind of book I would have found useful when I came into magic many years ago, a book that would explain the kind of things I needed to know when I was a newcomer. If I have achieved even a small part of that, I am satisfied.

You will find in the following pages a list of books suitable for the studies in each chapter, and another list of suppliers, bookshops and publishers, and odd addresses I feel will be useful to you. There are also some extra ideas for robes, headdresses, and temple Pillars. Just after I had written the chapter concerning the pillars I was visiting a garden centre and bought some plastic urns to hold some plants. I was struck by the fact that the tops of some of the urns were just the right shape to form the traditional 'lotus' top to an Egyptian pillar. They usually come into two pieces and it is a matter of moments to fix the top part of the urn to one of the carpet rolls. Painted as in the illustration they make very authentic pillars. To further enhance this effect use a length of corrugated paper, fix it around the pillar and spray with black or silver paint. The urns are inexpensive and being plain white can be easily painted with the delicate pastel colours needed to make them into an Egyptian lotus pillar.

Ingenuity counts for far more than money to spend. The sense of satisfaction when you achieve something out of virtually nothing is worth all the hard work.

I wish you well in your search for knowledge. I wish you patience and endurance, and the ability to laugh when things look dark. Laughter is an essential thing in magic, without it you will not find what you seek. Laughter is connected with the devil in the Tarot, it is the spell that breaks the illusion of being enchained. Laughter lifts the heart, and the eyes.

Thank you for your company, I hope we meet again.

Dolores Ashcroft-Nowicki
Jersey

Appendix A: Moving House the Magical Way

Very often it comes as quite a wrench to leave a particular house, perhaps one where a greater part of your life has been spent, or where you have felt happy and content. Most of this feeling for the house comes about because you and your family have 'filled' the very stones of it with your own essences. This has been re-fed back to you by the house itself, remember the teaching about group minds, a happy family house, or even one where tragedy has taken place can build up very substantial Group Minds from the lives lived in them. The reason why an amulet works is because of the emotion held within the stone. Stone holds emotion longer than any other substance therefore a house, especially where it is of natural stone material or built on solid rock, will build a very strong Group Mind, one that will tend to bind you to that place. The feeling of leaving it is that of leaving a well-loved animal friend to the vagaries of its new owners.

But there is no need to fret, you simply take your House Elemental/ Group Mind with you. It is very simple and requires nothing more than a candle. First you have to explain to the House Mind that you are thinking of moving and would like to take it along to the new location. Give it time... let it think things over, if possible leave a picture or two of the new place around the house. This sounds quite daft but I can assure you it works. Europeans have countless folktales about such things notably in Poland where the Domovoi or House Spirit is considered to be part of the family.

After the House Mind has thought it over for a few days and accustomed itself to the idea of moving, go out and buy a large candle, large enough to burn for at least thirty hours. Choose a nice clear colour, blue, light green, clear yellow or perhaps a rose pink. Start at the top of the house the day before you actually move. Place the candle in the first room and light it, tell the House Mind that you want it to fill the flame with all its good feelings and memories from that room, and to feed those feelings from the flame down into the candle itself. Leave it to burn for about an hour, then move it to another room, still alight, and repeat the intention. Gradually move the lighted candle through the house making sure you leave *no room unvisited*, even a disused attic, the toilet and the garage. Finally leave it in the room you use most, where the heart of the family unit beats and leave it there until you actually move. Make sure that at no point does the candle go out. Stand it in a corner out of draughts.

Make sure that in all the upheaval you don't either knock it over, or forget it! Make it the last thing that moves out, and, if it is possible, try to keep it alight until you get to your new home. This is sometimes possible if you have an old fashioned candle lantern. If not, at the front door simply tell the House Mind to sink down into what is left of the candle (it should have at least half left) and pinch it out with your fingers.

When you reach your new home you can start to fill it with your former house friend. Now the more astute of you will be saying, yes, but what if the new house already has a House Mind? True, if the house is new there is no problem, you simply light the candle as soon as you get in, starting with the lowest floor and moving up, giving each room at least an hour of the candle's time (you see the importance of buying a large enough candle) letting it burn right out in the last room.

If you are taking the house over from another family, you have to allow for another House Mind. Five will get you ten that its former owners neither knew or cared about their House Mind, so you must do it for them. If possible try to visit the new house and providing the others have moved out and you have some privacy, explain to the probably bewildered House Mind that you are taking over and bringing your own House Mind with you, but there is no need for it to feel abandoned, it will soon have a companion. Give it a present of its own candle and light it with an invocation for health, happiness prosperity and a loving atmosphere. Gather the House Mind into the flame, you can do this quite quickly, a few minutes in each room because unlike your own House Mind you are not moving it any distance away. Now bring your own House Mind candle in and place them together lighting one from the other. Move them through the house until they burn out. Bring some flowers into the house as soon as possible, better still a growing pot plant. If you have an animal the House Mind will feel more at home as it can communicate with the animal more easily than with humans.

If it is not possible to visit the house beforehand, then do all this within 24 hours of going in, and do not light your own candle until you have gathered in the House Mind, then you can release them together, as one new and reinforced entity. Try and remember to include your house friend in celebrations and events. Give it a present at Christmas, a new doormat, a piece of china in the shape of a house, a lamp, or even just a pretty candle. Include it in your plans, if you are going away ask it to look after things for you. It may not always deter burglars, but they will surely 'miss' the things most precious to you! All things are part of that phenomena we call the Universe, animate and inanimate we all share the substance of our beingness. The House Mind may not be aware as we understand the word, but on its own level it can make the difference between a happy home and an unhappy one.

Appendix B: The Deconsecration of a Temple

There is a long way and a short way to go about deconsecration, the long way needs time, effort, and more know how in the magical sense than you can acquire in twelve short months. The short way is just as effective, and if the truth must be known, I would choose this way myself. It is a fallacy that a ritual to be totally effective has to be long, complicated and elaborate. All rituals contain one short moment of truth, the nub of the work, effort, colours, robes, incense, candles and words is one tiny moment hardly more than a breath of time, when the whole thing comes together in a tightly compacted instant, this is followed by the magical equivalent of the big bang and the intention of the ritual is sent on its way. The whole art of the magician is contained within that short moment of time. So length of time is not the criterion, intention is the only yardstick of success.

Again you will need a candle, a tall pure beeswax candle and a smaller one for each quarter. There is no specific tradition to follow, simply open your temple in the normal way. Invoke the Guardians of the Four Quarters, *and* the Guardian of the Temple as a whole, plus the Angel or Spirit of the Light. Lastly invoke the presence of your overall Deity/Spirit/Archangel.

The thing to remember is that the inner plane Temple, the *true* Temple is 'not built with hands, and eternal in the heavens'. Nothing can destroy it on that level. You just have to worry about shifting the earthly part of things. As with moving the house spirit the intention is to contain the consecrated essence within the flame and substance of the main candle, so light the altar light first, then the Quarter candles leaving the main ritual candle unlit for the moment, and make sure *all* your magical tools are laid out either in their Quarter or on the altar.

Take your place in the East and bless all the temple implements and furniture down to the last item. Take up the Quarter candle and move it in a wave pattern above or before each item. As you work see in your mind's eye a stream of essence coming from it into the flame and down into the base of the candle. Take your time and make sure you miss nothing. When you feel that the last bit has been taken into the flame bow to the East and say;

All is accomplished, the Eastern Quarter is clear.

Go to the altar and place the Eastern candle before the main, and still unlit, ritual candle. Go to the South and repeat the drawing out process with the Southern candle, and when that is done bow to the South and repeat the words above, take the candle to the altar and place it to the South. Move around the temple in this way until all four Quarters have been cleared, and their candle placed at the four Quarters of the altar.

Take the altar light and with it draw the essence from all implements laid out in their order and place. After each item say:

It is accomplished, the .... is clear.

Finally do the same for each officer, and have one of them do the same for you. Replace the light on the altar and all gather round. Each one take a candle and with all the flames close together and united light the main candle. Now bind the Quarter candles to the main one with new white cord or even new string and let them burn together for a while, until the running wax melds them together. You will feel the growing emptiness of the room as the power goes into the burning candles. Finally touch each candle with a few drops of charged water and salt and then douse them with the same mixture saying,

Thus do I seal in the power of the Temple, it is done.

There is no need to close the temple, there is nothing left to close.

The next day you can start dismantling the temple and packing away the implements. All this should take place *before* you encandle the House Mind so you can clear this room with the others.

When you get to the new house wait until the house spirit settles before releasing the temple egregore. If you know enough astrology wait for a day when the planets are in good positions, or if they are near, choose one of the Quarter days, or something like Candlemas (appropriate!) or Lady Day, St John's Eve or St George's day. Clean the new temple room thoroughly and do any painting or repairs that need doing. Then and then only can you start putting up curtains and laying down carpets and moving the Lodge furniture into their right places. Again take your time and follow your instincts, they will tell you when it is right to release the temple from its temporary resting place.

Lay out the implements once more and dress the temple as usual. Place the ritual candle on a small tray so the melting wax does not spill on to the altar top, place the altar light in front of it and an unlit candle in each Quarter. Light the ritual candle and some incense and allow the candle to burn almost all the way down. If you do this in the afternoon the temple will be ready for work by the evening. Make sure the candle is safe from draughts, but open the window a little to let the air circulate. Keep checking to see that all is well.

When all is ready robe up and enter the temple. Light the altar light and the Quarter candles from the remains of the ritual candle. Stand in the East and welcome the four Quarters, the temple Guardian and the altar spirit. Invoke your temple deities and invite them to enter their new place of worship, invite the newly combined House Mind to enter and become part of the temple. Go to each Quarter in turn and bless it with charged water and salt, then do the same for the altar.

Now set up a sphere of sanctuary to

encompass the house, garden, and an extra six feet in each direction. Do this by visualizing an opaque globe of light settling down over the whole area, penetrating the ground beneath and covering it to a height of about twenty feet above and below. Leave this sphere in place and it will act as a barrier while the temple is settling in. Try to work a ritual within a few days of setting up.

Appendix C: The Middle Pillar Exercise

Stand facing the East and visualize a sphere of brilliant white light floating just above your head.

Visualize a beam of white light descending from the sphere into the top of your head. At the same time vibrate AHIH (Eh-he-yay).

The beam of light now descends as far as your throat where it forms a sphere of brilliant purple. Now vibrate YHVH Elohim (Ye-ho-yay El-o-heem).

The beam continues its descent as far as the solar plexus. Here it produces a sphere of brilliant gold. Vibrate YHVH Aloah va-Daat (Ye-ho-wha El-o-ah va-Da-art).

Now the light descends to the area of the genitals, producing a sphere of brilliant purple. Vibrate Shaddai el Chai (Shah-day El Chai).

The light now reaches the soles of the feet and forms a large black sphere. Imagine you are standing on this sphere. Vibrate the name ADNI ha-Aretz (Ah-don-ai ha Ah-retz).

Appendix D: The Lesser Banishing Ritual of the Pentagram

1. Stand facing the East. Use the index finger of the right hand to trace the shape of the pentagram.

2. Touch the forehead and vibrate Atoh (ah-toh) (Unto Thee, or Thou art.)

3. Imagine the light descending from the forehead, down the body to the feet.

4. Touch the breast and vibrate Malkuth (Mal-kooth) (the Kingdom).

5. Touch the right shoulder with ve-Gedulah (and the Glory).

6. Touch the left shoulder with ve-Geburah (and the Power).

7. Clasp the hands on the breast, fingers interlaced, saying le-Olahm Amen (forever, Amen).

8. Turn to the East, extend your right

Banishing

hand with index finger, and trace a large pentagram. Stab it in the centre, and then say: YHVH. (Yod-hay-vahv-hay).

9. Turn to the South, repeat, but vibrate ADNI (ah-doh-nye).

10. Turn to the West, repeat, but vibrate AHIH (eh-huh-yeh).

11. Turn to the North, repeat, but vibrate AGLA (ah-galah). (Each Pentagram is to be stabbed in the centre, while vibrating the appropriate Name.)

12. Return to the East, touching the centre of the pentagram.

13. Extend your arms in the form of a cross, and vibrate.

14. Before me RAPHAEL (rah-phah-ale).

15. Behind me GABRIEL (gah-bree-ale).

16. On my right hand, MICHAEL (mee-chah-ale).

17. On my left hand, AURIEL (awe-ree-ale).

18. For about me flame the Pentagrams.

19. And in the column stands the six-rayed star.

20. Repeat Qabalistic Cross, steps 1–7.

Appendix E: Further ideas for robes and head-dresses

EGYPTIAN

GREEK

Useful Addresses

Sorcerer's Apprentice
4/8 Burley Lodge Rd
Leeds   LS6 1QP

Aquariana Supplies
BCM-OPAL London
WC1N 3XX

Margaret Bruce
High Rigg House
St John's Chapel
Bishop Auckland
Co Durham   DL13 1QT

Elfane
Mynydd Cerrig
Llanelli
Dyfed
Wales
**Specialist in wood carvings,
ceremonial staffs and altar pieces.
Highly Recommended.**

Dusty Miller
14, Weston Rd
Strood
Kent   ME2 3EZ
**Specialist in wands, cudgels, dryad
staffs, talismans, etc. Highly
Recommended.**

Bill Elliott
48 St Andrew's Close
Whitstable
Kent   CT5 4JP
Occult silver and goldsmith

Eye of Horus
Silvertoad Cottage
31 Arundel Street
Walsall
WS1 4BY
For robes, swords, pentacles, etc.

Paul Hardy
27, Victoria Rd
Oswestry,
Shropshire
**For temple paintings.
Highly Recommended.**

Fantasy Candles
'Glanrhyd'
Llanfair
Clydogau
Nr Lampeter
Dyfed

Magazines and Journals

Insight
25 Calmore Close
Stourvale Meadows
Bournmouth

Journal of Geomancy
142 Pheasant Rise
Bar Hill
Cambridge   CB3 8SD

The Kabbalist
25, Circle Gardens
Merton Park
London   SW19

Prediction
Link House
Dingwall Avenue
Croydon
Surrey

Quest
BCM-SCL Quest
London   WC1N 3XX

Pentacle
444 Brixton Rd
Stockwell
London

The Cauldron
Groesfford
Llwyndrain
Dyfed   SA35 0AS

Aquarian Arrow
BCM-OPAL
London   WC1N 3XX

Booksellers

Anubis Books
218 Bamford Rd
Heywood
Lancs

Atlantis Bookshop
49a Museum St
London   WC1

Mysteries
9, Monmouth Street
London   WC2

Occultique
73, Kettering Rd
Northampton
NN1 4A
**Also combines Zut Anubis and supplies
all kinds of occult paraphenalia.**

Dolores Ashcroft-Nowicki is the
Director of Studies of the Servants of
the Light Association, which runs a
postal course of instruction based on
the works of W.E. Butler. This is a fully
contacted school of the Western
Mysteries and teaches a full curriculum
of esoteric sciences. The work is under
strict discipline and personal super-
vision.

The Servants of the Light Association
can be contacted at:

P.O. Box 215
St. Helier
Jersey
Channel Islands
Great Britain

Index